Fifth Edition

Interdisciplinary Instruction

Fifth Edition

Interdisciplinary Instruction

Unit and Lesson Planning Strategies K–8

Karlyn E. Wood

State University of New York College at Old Westbury

Long Grove, Illinois

For information about this book, contact:
Waveland Press, Inc.
4180 IL Route 83, Suite 101
Long Grove, IL 60047-9580
(847) 634-0081
info@waveland.com
www.waveland.com

10-digit ISBN 1-4786-2712-3
13-digit ISBN 978-1-4786-2712-8

Printed in the United States of America

7 6 5 4

To my wife, Louise, our children, and our grandchildren

To my colleagues and students in the School of Education, State University of New York/College at Old Westbury

About the Author

Karlyn Wood received his EdD degree from Hofstra University. He is a Professor Emeritus of the School of Education at the State University of New York/College at Old Westbury on Long Island, where he has taught courses in foundations of education, child development, and interdisciplinary instructional strategies. He supervised and conducted seminars for student teachers and was the Chair of the Childhood Education and Literacy Department. Karlyn also taught at the elementary level, where he taught third and fourth grades, served as district reading consultant, and coordinated an experimental elementary program. His publications include articles in *Language Arts, Childhood Education, The Journal of Child Development,* and *The Journal of Teacher Education.* His papers have been included in *Education Digest, Sociological Abstracts,* and *ERIC.* He is a member of ASCD and the Kappa Delta Pi International Honor Society in Education and is a former member of the American Educational Research Association and the Association Montessori Internationale.

Brief Contents

Contents

Preface

Traditionally, instruction in our schools has tended to isolate the academic disciplines—or subject areas—from one another. In contrast, *interdisciplinary* instruction always *begins with a central topic, theme, or problem;* the topic is then investigated using those disciplines that can assist in the inquiry. The topics students study can vary greatly; some are typical of those usually included in state social studies or science curriculums; however, topics from other disciplines, such as literature, mathematics, and the visual and performing arts can also become the basis of an interdisciplinary study.

Although mandates from the federal and state governments have made teachers fearful of making changes in their teaching, there continues to be interest among many educators in the interdisciplinary method. Interest has been stimulated by legislative steps taken by state departments of education as well as the need to focus more on thinking and reasoning skills that are now required by *Common Core State Standards* (CCSS). At the same time, federal mandates, including *Race to the Top* and *No Child Left Behind*, have produced circumstances that make teachers wary about experimenting with new approaches in their classrooms, fearing that their schools will lose some federal funding if students' mandated test scores should fall.

Since the first edition of this book, all states had developed lists of their individual content learning standards prior to the CCSS; many of those lists strongly suggest the need for interdisciplinary studies. Some curriculum mandates also stress some use of the interdisciplinary approach. For example, the New York State Education Department has required teachers in grades three through six to develop at least one interdisciplinary project with students in their classes each year. As a result, some teachers and administrators in New York have indicated greater interest in interdisciplinary program designs and practical ways to plan for their implementation. Many teachers are anxious to learn exactly what interdisciplinary *projects* and *units* should involve as well as how they differ from other instructional activities.

The interdisciplinary approach has been followed by early childhood teachers as a standard method of instruction for many years. Preschool and kindergarten teachers have routinely planned their instructional programs around central themes, which are then used as much as possible in teaching daily lessons and activities. Most primary grade teachers feel that they understand the method and that they have been equipped for it by their college preparatory programs. Although there may be interest in interdisciplinary instruction in the intermediate grades and middle school, teachers at those levels may feel they have had less preparation and experience with the interdisciplinary approach than their early childhood colleagues.

The purposes of this book are: (1) to provide pre-service and in-service elementary and middle school teachers and administrators with a handbook that introduces the interdisciplinary method and offers practical suggestions on how to plan interdisciplinary or multidisciplinary units for and implement the method in classrooms; (2) to offer step-by-step explanations and examples of how to design both interdisciplinary and multidisciplinary unit plans; and (3) to review practical lesson-planning protocols with example plans for elementary and middle school teachers. I have based this book partly on the materials that I have developed for students in my courses in teacher education.

I have purposefully kept the two theoretical chapters as brief as possible so that the emphasis in the book can be on the *thinking processes* involved in designing *interdisciplinary* and *multidisciplinary* units—two unit types suitable for students at differing levels—and the critical lesson planning process for the design of lessons and activities that follow both interdisciplinary and more conventional methods.

This book is intended for use in methods courses at both the undergraduate and graduate levels; it is also appropriate for in-service courses taught in schools and teacher centers. The practical explanations and examples should prove especially helpful for teachers who have not previously studied interdisciplinary instruction and those looking for ideas to improve their planning technique.

College instructors who emphasize a constructivist approach to teaching and who advocate aspects of the interdisciplinary approach in their social studies, science, and generic methods courses should find this book helpful to students' understanding of the theoretical and practical aspects of using the interdisciplinary approach. Instructors of other methods courses, including literacy and mathematics methods, should find it valuable in helping students to bridge relationships between those disciplines and others they teach.

To emphasize the planning processes and illustrate the essentials of those processes as clearly as possible, I have included examples for each component in the planning processes explored in chapters 3, 4, and 5. The models for designing interdisciplinary units and the protocols for planning lessons in this book illustrate specific strategies for the planning processes in which all teachers engage continuously. They represent *some* ways to design units and lessons—although surely not the *only* ways. While the processes pay special attention to the *backward design* point of view expressed throughout this book, I stress the belief that there is no single planning method that will necessarily work satisfactorily for every teacher.

Organization of the Book

The first and second chapters provide the theoretical framework for the interdisciplinary approach. The first chapter discusses the theory supporting interdisciplinary instruction; it includes an outline of distinguishing features of the approach and provides the rationale for its use in elementary and middle schools. The subtle differences among interdisciplinary, multidisciplinary, and integrated instruction are explained.

The second chapter reviews several important requirements of teachers who plan to use the approach with their students. The chapter concludes with current challenges to the implementation of interdisciplinary instruction in today's schools.

Chapters 3 and 4 are specifically designed to teach the *processes* involved in planning interdisciplinary and multidisciplinary units. Chapter 3 details the steps involved in planning interdisciplinary units while chapter 4 provides information about the multidisciplinary unit, an alternative type of unit that is particularly suitable for students in the intermediate grades and departmentalized middle schools. Both chapters include detailed explanations of each planning component followed by examples. Complete examples of the unit plans are provided at the end of those chapters. Both chapters can serve students as references during in-class practicum sessions so that instructors can use valuable class time to interact directly with students as they study the components of each unit planning process and design their own units.

Chapter 5 provides information about the lesson-planning process. In addition to specific steps in planning a lesson, the chapter also reviews several important preliminary considerations, such as students' learning and development, teachers' questioning techniques, and applications of Bloom's Taxonomy. Specific protocols to follow for several different types of lessons are explained and illustrated with example lesson plans. The chapter also includes suggestions for organizing field trips and for designing classroom research centers for student exploration and practice in connection with units of study.

Chapter 6 provides information on assessment. It includes discussions of authentic assessment as well as traditional examinations. Rubrics are explained and illustrated.

Each chapter concludes with a summary and a suggested activity. A comprehensive bibliography appears at the end of the text. It includes early theoretical works for those who would like additional background material or who plan to undertake their own research on topics included in the chapters, as well as literature that reflects current thinking and trends on those topics. Suggested readings by the various topics addressed in the book are added for additional related information.

The appendix includes ten sample web designs from previous editions; others are included as examples in chapters 3 and 4.

New to the Fifth Edition

The references and bibliography have been updated and augmented. The chapters have been revised and updated to provide the most current information on the interdisciplinary approach, unit planning, and lesson planning. Each chapter begins with a set of questions to guide readers as they study the text.

Throughout the book, the learning standards in the unit plan examples refer to:

- *Common Core State Standards* (CCSS), cited under public policy provisions: Copyright © 2010, National Governors Association Center for Best Practices and Council of Chief State School Officers. All rights reserved.
- *New York State Learning Standards*, cited under terms of the New York State Education Department for learning standards in mathematics and English/language arts, copyright 2005; arts, social studies, and physical education, copyright 1996.

They are representative of similar standards in other states.

The lesson- and unit-planning components and processes follow the order suggested by *backward design.* (See chapter 1.) Lesson plan examples for each of the lesson-planning protocols discussed in chapter 5 follow explanations of those protocols. The various steps in each of the sample lesson-plan procedures are annotated to explain their purpose in the procedure design. Rubric examples are included in chapter 6 on assessment.

To the Reader

When I started teaching, I had little understanding of the interdisciplinary method, and I was certainly unaware of all I would need to learn over the next few years to use it in my own classroom. As a young, inexperienced teacher, I began my career in an elementary school district that was proud of its *multidisciplinary* philosophy, where teachers were expected to use a multidisciplinary approach at every level—from kindergarten through the sixth grade. I began studying the method from the outset, but it was not until I observed the enthusiasm of the other teachers who had been using it for some time that I became committed to developing the skills I would need to carry it out myself.

Throughout the first two years, I found multidisciplinary—or interdisciplinary—teaching far more challenging than I had ever anticipated, and it is likely that I would have given it up altogether if I had not been given a great deal of counseling and moral support from other teachers and administrators in my school. I learned from my colleagues how important it was to reserve extra time to plan for this kind of instruction and soon found myself spending countless hours after school on a task I found nearly overwhelming—trying to write plans for the interdisciplinary units I was teaching. In those early experimental years, I paid little attention to the important planning *process* and instead, spent—or misspent—most of my energy searching for the best way to write unit and lesson plans. Eventually, I realized that I needed to learn more about the planning process itself, so in time, my concentration shifted from the *writing* of plans to the *thinking* involved in designing them. I had discovered that the planning process was far more important than the format of the written plan. However, my attempts to locate information on the interdisciplinary approach or the unit planning process at that time revealed that little useful material was available. Even the most popular instructional methods textbooks in use at our local universities had little to offer on the subject.

Seventeen years later, when I began teaching in a teacher education department, I found that there was still little written about interdisciplinary instruction that I could use with my students, so, out of necessity, I began preparing my own textbook. To develop those materials, I drew on my 17 years of experience with the method in elementary schools and focused on the sequential thought processes involved in unit and lesson planning. The first edition of the text was based largely on those materials.

After using the first four editions of the text with students, I have found them to be helpful for students who are preparing for their initial teaching experiences. The text has been published under two previous titles: *Interdisciplinary Instruction: A Practical Guide for Elementary and Middle School Teachers* (1997, 2001, and 2005) and *Interdisciplinary Instruction for All Learners K–8* (2010). The title of the fifth edition reflects its greater emphasis on the unit- and lesson-planning processes because those skills are well known to be critical to success in teaching. It is my hope that the fifth edition of this book will help both pre-service and in-service teachers to further explore the interdisciplinary approach and be of help to them as they design interdisciplinary and multidisciplinary units and use practical lesson planning protocols.

Acknowledgments

The quest for knowledge is a lifelong pursuit in which we learn from our experiences and from one another. Teachers often play an important role in facilitating this process. For most of us, some teachers will be especially well remembered for their positive contributions. To begin, I would especially like to thank my wife, Louise, for her patience and support as I have prepared the manuscripts for each edition of the book. I consider myself fortunate to have been taught by the late Myrtle Cope, an exemplary master teacher. I thank her for the early influence she had on my decision to become an elementary teacher and for the example she provided me with her constructivist approach to education, a philosophy that continues to influence my teaching practice.

I would also like to acknowledge the late Roland Chatterton, a forward-thinking educator and pioneer in multidisciplinary education. Dr. Chatterton introduced me to interdisciplinary methodology; it was he and teachers with whom I taught in the Merrick (New York) Public Schools who facilitated my own development as an interdisciplinary teacher.

My colleagues in the School of Education at the State University of New York/College at Old Westbury have provided much support, and I thank them for their interest and encouragement throughout the project. I am especially indebted to Amy Hsu, Gretchen L. Johnson, Jossie O'Neill, Margaret Renner, Stephanie Schneider, Basilio Serrano, and my colleague, Gareth B. Wilmott of the Merrick Schools, who have provided me with valuable feedback on my plans and manuscript revision drafts. I want to thank them for their time and their many helpful suggestions. I also want to express my appreciation to my students in the School of Education at the SUNY/College at Old Westbury. With their permission, several of their lesson plans and unit-plan web designs are included in my book.

I wish to thank my reviewers of the first four editions for their input and suggestions: JoAnne Buggey, University of Minnesota; Patricia Calderwood, Fairfield University; Cynthia G. Kruger, University of Massachusetts, Dartmouth; Joyce Frazier, University of North Carolina-Charlotte; Stephen Hancock, University of North Carolina-Charlotte; Belinda Hill, Saint Martin's University; Barbara Kacer, Western Kentucky University; Stephen Lafer, University of Nevada-Reno; Cynthia E. Ledbetter, University of Texas at Dallas; Linda S. Levstick, University of Kentucky; David Locascio, Longwood University; Donna Merkley, Iowa State University, Rhonda Truitt, Catawba College; Kathleen Velsor, State University of New York at Old Westbury; and Bruce Young, Covenant College.

I would like to acknowledge artist Nina Wood for the drawings she prepared for me that have been adopted for cover illustrations for several editions of the book. Thanks also to the editors, copy editors, and final production editors for all previous editions of this book: Colleen Brosnan, Mary Harlan, Annette Jacobs, Kathleen Riley King, Sheryl Langner, Yasmeen Neelofar, Kris Roach, Rebecca Robb, Kathleen Sleys, Ben Stephen, Debbie Stollenwerk, and Swapnil K. Vaidya, for their expertise, patience, interest, and counsel.

Finally, I would especially like to thank Gayle Zawilla, my editor at Waveland Press. This edition would not have been possible without her interest and considerable help throughout the publication process.

Introduction to Interdisciplinary Instruction

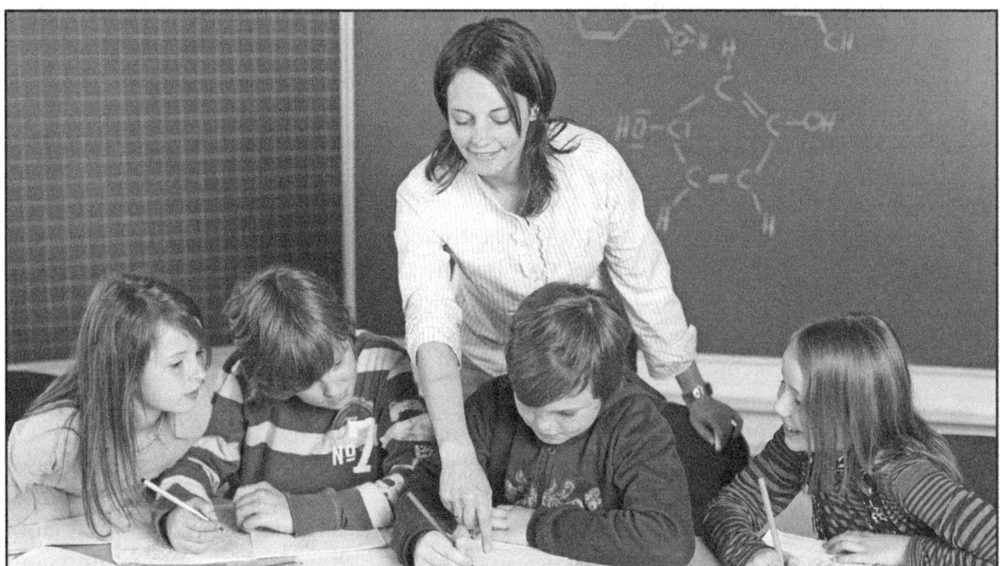

Overview

This chapter provides an introduction to the interdisciplinary approach and its theoretical foundations. The essential concepts reviewed in this chapter present a framework for the planning strategies offered in subsequent chapters of the book. The explanations are designed to answer the following questions:

- How is the interdisciplinary approach distinguished from other teaching methods?
- Are interdisciplinary, multidisciplinary, and integrated instruction the same, or do they differ is specific ways?
- How are interdisciplinary and multidisciplinary studies designed and taught?
- Why use interdisciplinary instruction with the diversity of learners we have in our elementary and middle schools?

Distinguishing Features

In 1933, a method of teaching that was strongly advocated by John Dewey involved students in "projects," investigations requiring the use of more than a single academic discipline. Dewey (1916) believed that to be educative, it was necessary that such projects "present problems that awaken new curiosity and create a demand for information" (p. 218). While not identical to Dewey's *project method*, interdisciplinary instruction is a problem-centered approach to the study of topics, themes, major questions, or activities that is based largely on Dewey's ideology.

Although the interdisciplinary approach is not new, it has not been widely practiced in American schools. In recent years, however, there has been renewed interest in this approach because of the need to find alternative ways to address new standards that have been prepared over the past several years by each state in the country. The recent Common Core State Standards (CCSS), as well as individual state and federal mandates for testing and improvements in student achievement and the quality of instruction, have fostered the need for even more changes in instructional methods. The interdisciplinary approach can address some of the major changes required by the CCSS because it involves students in the kinds of critical thinking mandated in those standards. Because interdisciplinary instructional methods address the core standards so well, it may also be helpful in raising students' achievement levels without resorting to the "teach-to-the-test" approach. As a result, teachers may be encouraged to incorporate at least some aspects of the interdisciplinary approach in their teaching.

A central purpose of this introductory chapter is to examine the features of the interdisciplinary approach and the rationale for its use in elementary and middle schools. It has been suggested that the interdisciplinary approach may help improve the quality of education in our schools, enhance personal meaning, and better meet the needs of our diverse student population.

The initial discussion describes several distinctive features of interdisciplinary studies. These studies are organized as comprehensive instructional units that are planned using either an interdisciplinary or multidisciplinary format. An interdisciplinary study has at least four unique characteristics:

- Interdisciplinary studies are organized in comprehensive interdisciplinary or multidisciplinary unit plans that focus on a specific topic, theme, or problem.
- Interdisciplinary studies are explored by using the skills and techniques—the ways of knowing—associated with any academic disciplines that can inform the topic, theme, or problem under investigation. They provide for coherence because they are not bounded by subject divisions, but reflect the natural relationship between different disciplines of knowledge (Beane, n.d.).
- Interdisciplinary studies place equal emphasis on the mastery of the processes involved in learning about a topic, theme, or problem and the mastery of content—concepts, facts, generalizations, and principles.
- Interdisciplinary studies accommodate student diversity by providing for the differentiation of student investigating and reporting techniques.

Comparing Interdisciplinary, Multidisciplinary, and Integrated Approaches

Although some educators may consider *interdisciplinary, multidisciplinary* and *integrated* instruction to be identical or nearly the same, others suggest that they differ in specific ways. Interdisciplinary and multidisciplinary instruction both involve the use of "two or more academic subjects or fields of study" during the exploration of a topic or theme (Agnes, 2008, pp. 744, 946). Integrated instruction is similarly defined as "learning experiences organized around developmentally appropriate topics, themes, or concepts which provide opportunities for students to draw on standards from more than one subject" (Early Elementary Resources Guide, 1996, p. 23). It should be noted that the terms *interdisciplinary approach, interdisciplinary method,* and *interdisciplinary instruction* are used throughout this text; the three terms refer to the overall method involved in teaching both interdisciplinary and multidisciplinary units. Variations in the two unit types are explained in detail in chapters 3 and 4.

Parker (2012) suggests that the three approaches have distinct characteristics. For example, although *multidisciplinary* instruction makes use of two or more disciplines when exploring a specific topic or theme, it maintains a somewhat greater focus on the individual disciplines involved in the study. Information from the different disciplines is then combined and reported only at the conclusion of the study (Chatterton, 1968). There is an even clearer distinction between the interdisciplinary and multidisciplinary approaches in fields other than education. For example, in the medical field, "Multidisciplinary research teams work in parallel or sequentially from their specific disciplinary base to address a common problem. Interdisciplinary research teams work jointly but still from a discipline-specific base to address a common problem" (Slatin, Galizzi, Devereaux Melillo, & Mawn, 2004, p. 62).

Integrated instruction suggests the incorporation of one subject within others. It is similar to the interdisciplinary approach and organization of curriculum. An example of this is found in programs that emphasize reading and writing—taught as literacy—across all disciplinary areas in the curriculum of a school; literacy skills are taught as integral and essential to each discipline. Another view of integrated instruction is found in social studies, within which several disciplines—history, geography, economics, and other social sciences—are *integrated* to form a new subject in which its several disciplines become integral parts.

Another feature of the integrated approach is that it may provide clear connections with students' lives apart from the school environment because it involves "learning constructed in an innovative and purposeful way that shows relationships between what happens within and outside of school" (Williams-Boyd, 2003, p. 179). Beane (1997) also emphasizes the social aspects of an integrated approach in his definition of it as a curriculum that "is concerned with enhancing the possibilities for personal and social integration" (p. 19). A report to the Minnesota State Legislature by the Minnesota Board of Teaching (2006) also attempts to clarify the differences between interdisciplinary and integrated instruction:

> Interdisciplinary curriculum, which draws content from particular disciplines that are ordinarily taught separately, is different from integrated curriculum, which involves investigation of topics without regard to where, or even whether, they appear in the typical school curriculum at all. (p. 2)

Perhaps the most important feature the three approaches discussed above have in common is that they all involve attention to more than a single academic discipline. Therefore, they are all *interdisciplinary*. In chapters 3 and 4, the design and planning of interdisciplinary units (which can be used at all grade levels) and multidisciplinary units (which are especially well-suited for departmentalized middle schools) are explained and illustrated with examples. The comparison of some of the main differences between these two unit types is shown in Exhibit 1.1.

Exhibit 1.1 A Comparison of Interdisciplinary and Multidisciplinary Units.

Description	Interdisciplinary Unit Design	Multidisciplinary Unit Design
The unit focuses on the study of a topic, theme, or problem.	X	X
The unit is appropriate for elementary grades K–3.	X	
The unit is appropriate for elementary grades 4–6.	X	X
The unit is appropriate for departmentalized middle school grades 5–8.		X
The unit is planned by a classroom teacher.	X	
The unit is planned by a departmentalized team of teachers.		X
The research process guides the development of the unit and its procedures.	X	X
Procedures of the unit parallel interdisciplinary research in fields other than education.	X	
Procedures of the unit parallel multidisciplinary research in fields other than education.		X
Students are actively involved in developing questions and suggesting areas to be researched.	X	X
The topic, theme, or problem can be subdivided for research either by discipline or subtopic.	X	X
The unit design provides for a series of lessons and activities related to the unit topic, theme, or problem.	X	
The unit design can make provisions for student committee research.	X	X
The unit design provides for disciplinary instruction by a team of teachers.		X
Instruction in all or most disciplines is provided mainly by the classroom teacher.	X	
Instruction in each discipline is taught separately by members of a departmentalized teaching team.		X

The interdisciplinary approach involves students in the exploration of comprehensive interdisciplinary or multidisciplinary studies of topics, themes, and problems. Those studies have commonly been organized as activity-centered units for elementary and middle school students. Planning activity-centered units typically begins by first determining the specific lessons and activities that will make up the unit study. Unit objectives and assessments follow.

Interdisciplinary and Multidisciplinary Studies: Organization and Design

A more appropriate alternative to activity-centered planning is *backward design,* a planning process developed by Wiggins and McTighe (2012). Whereas activity-centered planning usually begins with considering the various lessons and activities the teachers will include in a study, backward design first determines the unit goals (or objectives) and assessments and only then makes decisions about the specific lessons and activities. The lessons and activities are aligned with the unit goals and the assessments. According to Wiggins and McTighe, backward design involves a three-step—or three-part—process (pp. 17–28).

Before engaging in the process, a topic, theme, or problem on which the unit of study will rest is selected, and it is usually based on curriculum requirements of the state and local school district. Once a selection has been made, the unit-planning process involves the following three-part process:

- Part 1: Identifying the learning standards, goals, and essential questions of the unit
- Part 2: Determining unit assessment strategies
- Part 3: Planning the unit learning experiences, the lessons and activities to be included

Backward design emphasizes long-term development of *enduring understandings* and *big ideas.* "A big idea is a concept, theme, or issue that gives meaning and connection to discrete facts and skills" (Wiggins & McTighe, 2012, p. 5). Scientific concepts like *adaptation* and *natural selection* are examples of big ideas. Backward-designed units engage students in the exploration of the essential questions to which a specific topic, theme, or problem is related. This is particularly appropriate for interdisciplinary and multidisciplinary unit planning because of the important ideas and concepts these units help to develop.

Both backward-designed and activity-centered planning have positive attributes and some potential drawbacks. Activity-centered planning is familiar to most elementary teachers, and students usually enjoy the activities that are planned for them. However, unit assessments may tend to be limited to the development of the isolated knowledge that the individual lessons and activities of the unit develop. Assessments may not be adequately related to major unit goals, especially to important, enduring understandings. It is possible that activity-centered plans may focus so much on the separate lessons and hands-on activities that the unifying, interdisciplinary concepts of the unit do not become clear to students.

Backward design is a logical and intellectually sound planning process. Employing this technique helps to ensure that all components of the unit plan are aligned with one another, including the learning standards, goals, essential questions, and assessments. However, backward design may not be as familiar as activity-centered planning to elementary teachers, and at first some teachers may find determining the big ideas and enduring understandings for their units difficult and evasive. Wiggins and McTighe (2012) warn us about this:

> We predict that you will be somewhat disturbed by how hard it is to specify the understandings and what they look like in assessment, and how easy it is to lose sight of goals related to understanding in the midst of planning, teaching, and evaluating student work. (p. 9)

The unit-planning strategies described in chapters 3 and 4 for interdisciplinary and multidisciplinary units combine features of both activity-centered and backward-design planning processes. The planning process explained in those chapters involves the following components:

1. Determining the unit topic, theme, or problem
2. Identifying the unit standards and goals:
   a. Learning standards
   b. Goals: the understandings, knowledge, skills, and dispositions the unit of study aims to develop
   c. Essential questions: the thought-provoking, often divergent questions that address the unit goals
3. Determining the unit assessment plan by preparing a summary of the strategies that will:
   a. Address the unit learning standards
   b. Assess development of the unit goals and essential questions
4. Developing the unit learning plan:
   a. Indicating the overall picture of the of possible lessons and activities for the unit by preparing a web design for an interdisciplinary unit or a unit chart for a multidisciplinary unit
   b. Writing descriptions of the lessons, activities, and strategies included in the web design or unit chart in the projected sequence in which they will be taught during the study, which will later be planned in detail and aligned with the unit goals and essential questions

Examples of topics, themes, enduring understandings, and essential questions are listed in Exhibit 1.2.

Regardless of the approach, all unit plans need to address the *Common Core State Standards*, the learning standards recommended by national professional organizations, and/or those that are required by individual state departments of education and local school districts. The organizational structure of the unit needs to encourage students to use the disciplines—subjects or domains—that can help them to gain a better understanding of the topic, theme, or problem to be investigated.

Exhibit 1.2 Examples of Topics,* Themes, Enduring Understandings, and Essential Questions.

	Examples	
Focus of Interdisciplinary Studies	**Lower and Middle Elementary Grades**	**Upper Elementary Grades and Middle School**
Topics	-Myself and Others -My Family and Other Families -Now and Long Ago -My Community and Other United States Communities -Communities around the World -Local History and Government	-History and Government of the United States -History and Government of Canada -Latin America -Eastern Hemisphere Nation -Exploration and Colonization of the Americas
Themes	-Changes-Technology–Human Systems -Human Needs and Wants–Places and Regions -Economic Systems–Interdependence–Culture *Note that themes can span all grade levels.*	
Enduring Understandings	People make choices due to unlimited needs and wants and limited resources.	Constitutions, rules, and laws are developed in a democratic society to protect its citizens.
Essential Questions	-Why do people recycle or not recycle? -Why do people live in communities? -Who is a friend?	-Is global warming real? -What were the major causes and effects of European exploration? -How can we cope with diminishing natural resources?

*The topics listed above are examples of those that appear in many state curriculums.

While many interdisciplinary and multidisciplinary studies are organized and planned to explore topics, themes, or problems associated with social studies, units can be planned that are centered in any discipline, subject, or domain. An interesting and exceptionally well-developed example of an interdisciplinary study that begins with the arts and evolves to include history, literature, science, and other areas of the curriculum is *Spaces and Places* (Pappas, Kiefer, & Levstik, 2006). This is a unit for students in an upper elementary grade or middle school.

Much earlier, Elwyn Richardson (1969), an elementary teacher in New Zealand, also used the arts as the basis for his unusual interdisciplinary, crafts-oriented program. Richardson's students explored their natural rural environment and completed art projects made from raw materials found in that environment. Richardson also involved his students in interdisciplinary literacy, science, and mathematics activities related to their explorations and findings.

Using the Skills, Techniques, and Ways of Knowing in the Disciplines

Students who are involved in studying holistic topics or themes addressed by interdisciplinary or multidisciplinary units are exposed to additional skills and ways of knowing inherent in the different disciplines that are explored as they investigate those topics. Although we need to determine the goals and essential questions of a study in advance, we also need to encourage students to become participants in the planning process. Students should be encouraged to raise questions they would like to include about the new study; their questions can be added to the essential questions the teacher has prepared. Guided by the essential questions and the topical questions that students suggest, they will need to think critically about the issues involved and learn to apply the skills and techniques from the various disciplines involved in the study to help them in their inquiry.

The interdisciplinary approach provides students with many natural opportunities to observe the connections and to note relationships among the disciplines. Jacobs (1989) emphasized the importance of this characteristic for teachers as well as students, suggesting that teachers need to intentionally "apply methodology and language from more than one discipline to examine a central theme, issue, problem, topic, or experience" (p. 8).

Emphasis on Process and Content

For many years, educators have debated the relative importance of *process* versus *content*. Disciplinary, subject-centered instruction tends to focus on helping students acquire *content*—facts and general information. One of the more important distinguishing features of the interdisciplinary approach is that equal importance is given to content, *learning processes, skills,* and *ways of knowing* that are unique to the different disciplines, subjects, or domains.

Although no consensus exists among educators about which focus is more important, the processes involved in inquiry and scientific investigation play a significant role in interdisciplinary and multidisciplinary studies. Teachers who use this approach tend to agree with Dewey's (1916) advice that *equal* importance be attributed to content and to process in student investigations. It is assumed that students need to amass facts and develop concepts while they become proficient in the application of important academic learning processes that then "become the models they will use for later exploratory behaviors" (Gardner, 1993a, p. 31). In this way, students gain insights about and practice the different ways of knowing in the disciplines.

At upper elementary and middle school grade levels, students undertake more complex forms of inquiry, using processes that naturally stimulate their higher-level thinking and reasoning skills. In addition to gaining knowledge and practicing the learning processes, all students have numerous and meaningful opportunities through authentic investigations to practice their reading, writing, and computational skills in their unit investigations.

Differentiation of Student Investigating and Reporting Alternatives

The interdisciplinary approach accommodates students' diverse strengths and learning preferences and offers many opportunities for the differentiation of instruction. Tomlinson (2001) describes four elements to be considered in the differentiation of instruction: (1) the *content* that is taught and the ways students are given to develop it; (2) the different opportunities students are given to *process* information; (3) the various ways students are encouraged to complete their culminating *products*; and (4) the way the *learning environment* is constructed to facilitate students' differing ways of working to gain information. We know that all students do not learn, nor are they able to demonstrate what they have learned, in the same ways.

"Designing and facilitating multiple paths to reach defined learning goals is one of the hallmarks of successful differentiation" (Carolan & Guinn, 2007, p. 45). When we plan for interdisciplinary studies, students are afforded many natural opportunities to follow *multiple paths* and use a variety of materials and equipment. For example, some students are capable of reading to gain information on a topic; others may need to view visual materials or listen to oral presentations to process the same knowledge effectively. Some students may profit more from other activities, such as conducting interviews, performing Internet searches, or using WebQuests. (A WebQuest is a carefully planned set of steps to be followed by students when they investigate a specific topic using the Internet.)

Differentiation in the interdisciplinary approach permits the students alternatives and opportunities to prepare their culminating reports in a variety of ways, including writing reports, organizing panel discussions or debates, presenting dramatizations, designing PowerPoint presentations, and/or preparing art projects.

In early grades, some students may be able to report their findings by planning a puppet show, performing a dance, and so on. In brief, below are features of interdisciplinary instruction that distinguish it from other educational approaches:

- Units of instruction are organized to investigate topics, themes, or problems. Students gain insights about enduring understandings, knowledge, and skills associated with their studies.
- Essential questions aligned with the unit goals and learning standards assist students as they investigate important issues and develop related concepts.
- The skills, techniques, and ways of knowing in applicable academic disciplines are all employed in unit studies.
- Equal emphasis is placed on the value of the processes involved in learning, content understandings, and knowledge.
- The interdisciplinary approach provides for differentiation of investigating and reporting methods that address students' diverse abilities and interests.

The Rationale for Using an Interdisciplinary Approach

Why should an interdisciplinary approach be used for students in elementary and middle schools today? Before answering this question, consider how a group of children are likely to receive instruction—for example, about a specific social studies topic—in a school with a conventional approach to its curriculum. Observe how one group was taught about the island nation of Japan during an eight-year period.

In the first grade, children usually study about families. Stories about families from several cultures around the world are read to them; one story might be about a Japanese family. The children may have learned a Japanese folk song in the second grade and a traditional Japanese dance in the third grade. In the fourth grade, an art teacher may have had the children experiment with origami. The children also study geographic regions of the world in fourth grade, including some discussion on islands and island nations. Finally, in middle school, the students study aspects of Asian cultures, including the Japanese culture.

The sequence in the description is characteristic of a traditional, or subject-centered, approach to a social studies topic. Instead of being provided with an interdisciplinary inquiry of Japan and Japanese culture holistically at a specific grade level, the students are offered isolated bits of information in a fragmented study that is spread across eight years. Most lessons and activities are taught to the entire class at the same time, and typically, all students are mandated to meet the same requirements; there is little differentiation of instruction or assessment strategies.

At first, it may appear logical to approach a topic this way. We know that adults can internalize related information received over a period of time. However, we also know that it is more difficult for most children to do so, particularly because of the differences in their cognitive development and aspects of diversity.

The general assumption of the approach described in the Japan example above is that students are all able to learn in the same ways and to show what they have learned through identical assessments. There is little consideration in this fragmented approach for what is known about cognition in young children. In 1969, Piaget and Inhelder strongly suggested that thought in young children is often *centered*; in the child's mind, isolated concepts and bits of information remain unrelated. Later, Gardner (1991) suggested that the mind of a young child—5 to 7 or even 10 years old—is intuitive, resourceful, highly imaginative, and creative. He also posited that the same mind is limited by a "tendency to stereotype and simplify. . . . It contains a swirl of symbols, scripts, theories, and incipient notions and concepts, which can be involved in appropriate ways but which also remain to be sorted out in a more secure manner" (pp. 110–111).

In view of these cognitive limitations, an important reason for using an interdisciplinary method is that students investigate topics *holistically*, and there are more opportunities for students to differentiate in the ways they gain information and show what they have learned. The contrast with the traditional method described in the Japan scenario is evident. As a result of interdisciplinary studies, young students may be less likely to misinterpret and more likely to make better sense of their world.

Learner Diversity and Multiple Intelligences: Theories of Sternberg and Gardner

An especially strong argument for differentiation of instruction is evident in Sternberg's (1985) theory. Sternberg proposed that we all possess three kinds of intelligence—*analytical*, *creative*, and *practical*; these are accommodated particularly well in interdisciplinary instruction. Sternberg (2006) also explained the importance of recognizing the diversity that exists among the ways learners process information. Sternberg found that this is particularly important to recognize in non-mainstream cultural groups, and he supported his theory by citing examples of several cognitive and practical differences he found among students in Alaskan Eskimo and Kenyan cultures.

Gardner's *multiple intelligences* (MI) theory (1983, 1993b) expanded upon Sternberg's three kinds of intelligence. Gardner initially proposed that there are at least seven areas of intelligence. Later, he added an eighth intelligence, *naturalist intelligence,* and a ninth, *existential intelligence,* both of which have since been analyzed (Kane, 1999). At first, Gardner was reluctant about including existential intelligence, which he considered a *half-intelligence,* mainly because the part of the brain that deals with existential questions was unclear (Gardner, 1999; Smith, 2002). Even so, Gardner (1999) seemed to suggest that existential intelligence meets the criteria he established for an intelligence area: "Perhaps surprisingly, existential intelligence scores reasonably well on the eight criteria. . . . Although empirical psychological evidence is sparse, what exists certainly does not invalidate the construct" (p. 64). He concludes that "existential intelligence . . . may well be admissible" (p. 64).

Both Gardner and Sternberg have maintained that students process information in multiple ways. An interdisciplinary approach can facilitate these ways because students routinely use multiple sources of information to investigate topics, and they are encouraged to choose from a variety of media and methods to report their findings. In Gardner's MI theory, human beings operate in the nine—and possibly more—intelligence areas listed in Exhibit 1.3.

Exhibit 1.3 Gardner's Multiple Intelligences.

Intelligence	Strength
Linguistic, or verbal, intelligence	The ability to use language well and to learn through verbal methods such as reading, note taking, listening, writing summaries and reports, and conducting interviews
Logical-mathematical intelligence	Using mathematics and logic, forming hypotheses, and conducting scientific inquiries
Spatial intelligence	Detecting spatial relationships, noticing likenesses and differences visually, creating art and design, and thinking by visualizing in pictures
Musical intelligence	Using music as a tool for thinking, demonstrating feelings and attitudes with music, and associating thought with music
Bodily-kinesthetic intelligence	Using the entire body to help master or to explain ideas and concepts
Interpersonal intelligence	Understanding others, working effectively and cooperatively with other people, and sharing tasks and responsibilities
Intrapersonal intelligence	Understanding oneself and being able to analyze one's personal performance in order to grow and change
Naturalist intelligence	Recognizing flora and fauna, discriminating among them, and having a sensitivity to phenomena in the natural environment
Existential intelligence	Having interest in and raising questions about the meaning of life, death, and why things are the way they are

Gardner suggests that his "theory gives educators a way of thinking about individual gifts and how to accommodate teaching to them" (Brandt, 1988, p. 34). Thus, if students are developing in any or all of these intelligence areas, they will still need opportunities to grow in the others. Clearly, such opportunities will occur naturally when educators link "the multiple intelligences with a curriculum focused on understanding" (Checkley, 1997, p. 11). This understanding is a primary focus of the interdisciplinary approach. Thus, replacing isolated, subject-centered, disciplinary instruction with interdisciplinary methods in elementary and middle schools may help to facilitate optimal development for our students who have diverse abilities and ways of learning.

Although Gardner's theory is widely accepted among educators, some learning theorists, sociologists, and psychologists insist that there is still a need for research to provide empirical support. For example, Allis (1999) cites a number of social scientists who hold more traditional views of intelligence and who disagree with multiple intelligences theory. However, even though there are concerns about MI theory, it continues to have considerable backing from other educators and learning theorists—including Sylwester (1995, pp. 108–116), who prepared a comprehensive overview of MI theory, indicating that it is supported by research on the human brain. Also, many teachers find MI theory useful, as it is comparatively easy to relate to and apply practically in their classrooms.

Campbell, Campbell, and Dickinson (2004) have suggested that MI theory supports the interdisciplinary approach: "With MI-based teaching, discrete subject matter distinctions begin to dissolve, enabling teachers to plan interdisciplinary units" (p. 289). Interdisciplinary lessons "cross subject-area lines" and accommodate students' multiple intelligences (Moran, Kornhaber, & Gardner, 2006, p. 25).

Social Interaction: Theories of Piaget and Vygotsky

Students also need opportunities for the kind of social interaction and guidance that teachers and capable peers can provide naturally in interdisciplinary studies. Piaget (1970) believed that social interaction between students and teachers was necessary to develop arbitrary social concepts, but he also cautioned about the use of too much direct verbal instruction or reliance on demonstrations in teaching, especially with very young children. Piaget believed that these approaches might inhibit the development of operational (generalizable, useful) knowledge. In particular, Piaget expressed concern about the use of excessive direct instruction in developing scientific and mathematical knowledge.

It is possible that Piaget may have attributed less importance to the value of the kind of social collaboration that is typical with interdisciplinary methods in fostering the development of some concepts. The value of social interaction in promoting optimal learning is clearer in Vygotsky's (1978, 1986) premise of a *zone of proximal development* (ZPD). According to Vygotsky, the ZPD is "the distance between the actual developmental level as determined by independent problem solving and the level of potential development as determined through problem solving under adult guidance or in collaboration with more capable peers" (1978, p. 86). In the ZPD, Vygotsky is plainly suggesting the importance of instructional methods that promote learning through social interaction among students, teachers, and peers.

Learning theorists agree with Vygotsky about the value of both culture and social interaction in the process of knowledge acquisition. A comprehensive discussion of Vygotsky's theory and the significance of social interaction for student learning is provided by Wertsch (1985), and Case's (1985) Canadian studies of early development also support Vygotsky's theory about the impact of social interaction and instruction in early childhood on children's cognitive development. Case also suggests that interdisciplinary instruction promotes children's problem-solving skills.

In *Acts of Meaning*, Bruner (1990) also discusses the importance of social interaction and the value of adult instruction and *scaffolding*—providing a temporary support system for students until they are able to work independently. In their review of Vygotsky's theory and its implications for classroom practice, Forman, Minick, and Stone (1993) provide a compelling argument for interdisciplinary studies by suggesting that such studies provide natural opportunities for students to interact with one another as well as with their teachers. The authors also stress that this kind of social interaction is essential for optimal learning.

Support from Research on the Human Brain

The interdisciplinary approach is also supported by findings from research on the human brain. In recent years, educators have been examining those findings to determine the need for changes in curriculum and instructional practice. As a result, several educators have prepared research-based materials that can be helpful for teachers.

Robert Sylwester's (1995) straightforward overview of the brain and its functions is a succinct yet comprehensive discussion of this important topic. In his book, Sylwester explains the value of helping students make connections and detect relationships between what they are taught and their personal experiences. In addition, he mentions teaching techniques that help to foster these links and which are often used by interdisciplinary teachers, including "debates, role playing, simulations, songs, games, films, and novels" (p. 103). Sylwester also recommends activities, such as "student projects, cooperative learning, and portfolio assessments" (p. 132), all of which address diversity in learners and are activities routinely found in interdisciplinary instruction.

We also know that learning is more likely to occur when the brain is not threatened (Bronson & Merryman, 2013). Students need to be willing to risk making mistakes in a classroom environment where they feel that they will not be ridiculed when wrong. Such a safe learning environment can also encourage students to be more honest about what they know and do not know. Honesty and willingness to admit error are fostered in an atmosphere where the brain is not constantly defending itself from ridicule, either from peers or teachers. Willingness to admit one's errors is one of several *dispositions* or *habits of mind* that also include openness to new ideas, having a questioning attitude, being persistent at tasks, and so on (Heck & Roose, 2005; Wiggins, 1993). These ways of thinking are all critical to students' success and can be fostered through interdisciplinary instruction.

Another implication for the interdisciplinary approach from human brain research indicates the need for holistic studies. It has been found that information learned in isolation tends to remain in isolation and appears to be more difficult for young students to process, recall, and use (Hardiman, 2001; Lowery, 1998; Westwater & Wolfe, 2000).

Although research on the human brain continues to be the topic of a number of conferences for educators and has stimulated the production of new curriculums and instructional materials, it is important to realize that there is yet no consensus about its educational implications. For example, Jorgenson (2003) has voiced concern about developing curriculum and materials based on human brain research. He recommends that "educators must recognize the limitations of the fledgling cognitive-neuroscience movement as it currently can contribute to our profession" (p. 364). Willingham (2006) has voiced similar concerns about endorsing changes in teaching based on brain research until there is evidence that such changes will make a difference.

Even though the debate over the educational applications of brain research is likely to continue, Eric Jensen (2005, 2001) reminds us of findings from brain research suggesting that the brain makes associations and constructs meaning better when it finds patterns like those that interdisciplinary, holistic methods provide. Jensen feels that, in general, interdisciplinary instruction is more meaningful at all age levels because it helps students to note relationships among the various disciplines for the topics they study. He also suggests that interdisciplinary studies may be especially meaningful to older students because they may be more capable of detecting patterns due to their greater knowledge base.

Benefits to Diverse Learners and Students with Special Needs

Another important reason for using the interdisciplinary approach is its effectiveness as an alternative to traditional approaches for students with special needs. In 1975, Public Law 94-142, the Education of All Handicapped Children Act (now known in its latest iteration as the Individuals with Disabilities Education Act of 1990), was enacted, mandating that children with handicapping conditions be placed in the least restrictive instructional environment possible, preferably in regular classrooms. To comply with this regulation, classroom teachers began working with children who were previously taught in special classes apart from other students. At that time, most teachers had little or no preparation for their new role, so they had to experiment on their own, trying creative approaches and methods in order to include—not just accommodate—their "new" students.

Many students with special needs must still spend part of the school day in special-assistance settings outside their regular classrooms. Their frequent absence from the classroom can make their inclusion in the regular program of activities difficult for teachers. The flexibility afforded by the interdisciplinary approach can help teachers overcome this problem to some extent. Because interdisciplinary units are usually completed over a period of time, not all children need to be present in the classroom at the same time, especially during periods of individual and group research and project development. Those who leave the room for special help can rejoin their classmates and work on unit assignments when they return as well as at other times during the day.

Differentiation of research and reporting techniques is also fostered during an interdisciplinary study. Students are encouraged to use a variety of resources to locate information, so those who have difficulty reading to obtain information can use alternative methods. Such methods include interviewing, studying pictures, listening to recorded audio materials, and viewing videos and teacher-prepared presentations. Students can also interact with computer software programs and websites on the Internet. Materials can be selected carefully to ensure that minimal reading is required.

Reports need not be limited to writing papers or answering questions from a textbook selection. Students can be given alternatives that interest them, such as performing demonstrations, painting pictures and murals, and preparing dioramas and other constructions to show the concepts they have gained.

The Use of Multiple Sources of Information

In contrast to conventional approaches, no single textbook is used exclusively in an interdisciplinary program. Classrooms are equipped with textbooks from many publishers on topics and themes in social studies, science, English/language arts, and other disciplines. In each classroom, the available materials are written at, below, and above grade level to accommodate as many ability levels as possible. Instead of relying on one or two sources, students consult multiple sources, helping to ensure that they will gain a more inclusive view of history and historical events.

An adequate supply of textbooks is needed for students; in fact it is often helpful to have texts in social studies and other disciplines from several different publishers available in sufficient quantity for students to use. However, textbooks alone are not sufficient for interdisciplinary studies because they "belong in the reference category, along with encyclopedias, dictionaries, and thesauruses" (Daniels & Zemelman, 2004, p. 36). Students need access to other materials, such as trade books, single-topic nonfiction books, and other literature related to unit topics. Multimedia technology and access to the Internet can provide up-to-date information for students. Some items not normally found in the classroom can usually be borrowed and brought into the classroom from public and school libraries and media centers.

A variety of materials also helps to ensure that students have access to information about the contributions of all segments of our population. Most topics require that we have resource materials in the classroom to adequately address the diversity of our people as well as historical issues, such as slavery, the Holocaust, and the Armenian genocide, as well as human-rights issues and world problems that might be given minimal treatment or neglected in a single textbook.

The significance of this kind of exposure for students is effectively dramatized in a statement by Milagros Henriquez (1995) as she accepted an award at her graduation for outstanding work related to multicultural education: "Multicultural education is *basic* education for students in the twenty-first century." In our multicultural society, the interdisciplinary approach offers students access to information that only a rich variety of materials can provide.

Meaningful Applications of Ways of Knowing and Skills in the Academic Disciplines

Most real problems in life are investigated or solved by using more than one discipline. For example, when we purchase a new home, economics is a major factor but not the only one. Location (geography), architectural style (art), nearby educational facilities, and other community resources also need to be considered before a final decision can be made. Interdisciplinary instruction routinely and realistically follows this example by encouraging students to use the ways of knowing associated with any disciplines that can be applied logically to the topics they investigate.

We are all concerned about students' academic skills and with providing sufficient practice in those skills. In many schools, workbook and duplicated exercises may have little or no relationship to the unit studies students are pursuing at a given time. If so, those exercises are simply "practice for the sake of practice." We know that skills practice as well as the investigation of "almost any subject . . . is best taught when it is needed to accomplish something else" (Wakefield, 1993, p. 137).

The interdisciplinary approach responds to Wakefield's suggestion because it always provides for the application of skills in meaningful contexts. As topics, themes, and problems are explored, students find that they *need* to use their inquiry skills; *need* to read for information; *need* to compose e-mail, letters, and reports; and often *need* to give oral presentations to their class. Students use mathematical skills as they prepare charts, graphs, and maps; they make use of technology to search for information or invent new designs for their projects; they follow the scientific method while working on related science experiments and activities; and they explore drama, music, and dance and gain experience with various art media. In fact, the interdisciplinary approach can provide so many spontaneous, purposeful opportunities for students to practice their academic skills, prepare projects, and work with construction materials that teachers who have previously used artificial duplicated materials and other conventional practice items may no longer feel the need to use them as often. Even so, it will be necessary to provide skills instruction apart from unit studies to ensure that students will be prepared for the practical applications afforded by those studies.

Other studies have found that the interdisciplinary approach results in greater enthusiasm on the part of teachers, students, and their parents; higher attendance rates among students; and improvement in standardized test scores (Bolak, Bialach, & Dunphy, 2005). Teaching teams using the interdisciplinary approach in middle schools have expressed greater job satisfaction and have found that their students achieve at higher levels (Flowers, Mertens, & Mulhall, 1999).

In brief, the rationale and support for interdisciplinary instruction involves:

- Gardner's theory of multiple intelligences and the importance of social interaction in the learning process;
- The studies of Piaget and Inhelder on knowledge acquisition in young children;
- The emphasis of Vygotsky, Case, and Bruner on the value of social interaction in the learning process;

- Support from research on the human brain;
- Benefits to diverse learners and students with special needs;
- Benefits derived from the use of multiple sources of information;
- Meaningful applications of the ways of knowing and skills in the academic disciplines; and
- Increased enthusiasm of teachers, students, and parents and increases in scores on standardized examinations.

Summary

The discussion in this chapter has attempted to clarify the underlying theoretical base and rationale for the interdisciplinary approach to instruction and to establish the framework for designing interdisciplinary and multidisciplinary units of instruction. Chapter 2 focuses on the requirements of teachers who use this approach and the challenges to interdisciplinary programs in the schools today.

Activity

Read the following description of how two fifth-grade teachers introduce a new unit on Westward Expansion to their classes. Consider the distinguishing features of the interdisciplinary approach that have been outlined in this chapter and the main differences between the ways the two teachers approach the same unit study.

> Ryan Jackson teaches fifth grade in an urban elementary school. His students are ready to begin studying a new unit on an important topic in American history for the next several weeks. During the usual time for social studies, Mr. J. began his introduction to the topic with several questions. First, he asked the students to relate anything they know about how our country grew from the original thirteen states to its present size. One student, Emily, said that she thought that new land was bought by the United States after the Revolutionary War. Another student, Bryan, said he believed that wars were fought to take over new land. Other students offered several additional ideas. While the students were contributing their thoughts, Mr. J. made a list of what the students said they knew or thought they knew on the board at the front of the room. He recorded what the students said without editing their responses or commenting about the ideas they expressed.
>
> After the students had no additional contributions, Mr. J. stated that the new study the students would be pursuing was one that would explore what is known historically as the period of Westward Expansion, an important topic in American history. Then, he asked the students what they would first need to do to prepare for the study. One student, Jimmy, said that they would need to search the Internet for information. Aisha, another student, said that they would need to know what they wanted to find out before they could do that. Then another student, Katherine, said she agreed with Aisha and that they would need to make a list of some questions before they would be able to begin their study. At that point, Mr. J. expressed his agreement that the class would need to prepare questions for the study and that making such a list would be the first task. (He had decided to save the essential questions he had prepared in advance until the students had an opportunity to suggest the questions that most interested them. He would then determine if the essential questions were included among students' questions; if any were missing, he would then add them to the final list.)

Mr. J. then gave the students an assignment in preparation for the next social studies period. Everyone was asked to make a list of three questions that he or she thought would be helpful in exploring the topic of Westward Expansion. During the next research period, their questions would be listed on the board, missing essential questions would be added, and discussion would be held to determine the most important questions the class would research. Mr. J. also explained that, at that time, a decision would also have to be made about how to approach the research, and he suggested two possible ways to proceed for students to consider: (1) The questions could be divided among several student committees, or (2) everyone could undertake researching all the questions. He told his students that a decision would be made at the next session. To end the lesson, Mr. J. asked students if they had any questions about what they needed to do before the next class session.

In another fifth-grade class, Grace McAllister was also beginning a new study of Westward Expansion. She started the first lesson during her regular time for social studies by asking the students to take out their social studies textbooks. When the students appeared to be ready, Ms. M. told the students to turn to page 168 in their books, and then she asked one of the students, Michael, to read the title of the chapter on that page. Michael read, "Westward Expansion: The Growth of the Union." Ms. M. then asked the students if they had any ideas about what the title meant. One student, Allison, said that it probably meant that people were going west. Another student, Shannon, said that it could mean that our country is growing in some way. Several other students offered ideas that were similar.

Next, Ms. M. told Anthony, another student, to begin reading the chapter aloud. After he had read one paragraph, another student was asked to continue. The entire chapter was read in this manner—each student reading a paragraph at a time. At the end of the reading, the students were told to take out a sheet of paper and to answer a set of 10 questions about Westward Expansion at the end of the chapter for homework. Ms. M. also explained that answers to the questions would be collected the next day.

- How does each teacher involve students in the study of the topic?
- Which of the two classes do you think will engender the greatest interest in the topic? Why?
- Consider each of the distinguishing features of the interdisciplinary approach that are reviewed in this chapter. Which teacher has planned an interdisciplinary study? Cite evidence from the descriptions to support your answer.

Challenges of the Interdisciplinary Approach

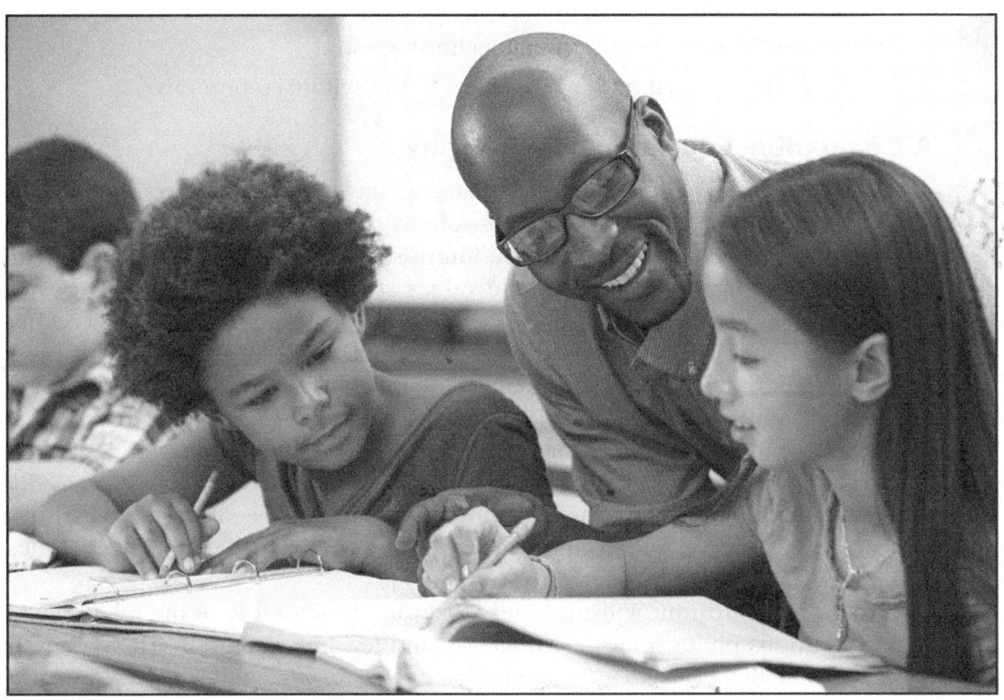

Overview

This chapter responds to two questions often asked by teachers and school districts regarding the use of the interdisciplinary approach:

- What are the special requirements of teachers who are considering the interdisciplinary approach in their classes?
- Why haven't interdisciplinary programs been developed and implemented in more American schools?

Requirements of Teachers

What does interdisciplinary instruction require of teachers? While interdisciplinary instruction can offer an appropriate alternative to more traditional methods, to be comfortable with it the teacher must possess the following attributes, each of which will be discussed in the following sections:

- A compatible philosophy of education;
- A considerable store of knowledge;
- Excellent skills in classroom management;
- Skill in planning lessons, interdisciplinary units, and multidisciplinary units;
- Skills in the use of instructional technology; and
- The ability to collaborate with others in the school community.

A Compatible Educational Philosophy

A primary factor to consider when using the interdisciplinary approach is determining if one's educational philosophy is compatible with it. One philosophy that is clearly compatible with the interdisciplinary approach is *constructivism*. This point of view recognizes and values student diversity, and it advocates instruction that places students at the center of the learning process. It is a democratic philosophy that fosters the idea that students need to process and *construct* knowledge for themselves. The primary role of the teacher is to provide pathways for students and resources for them to use as they strive to gain new knowledge. Rather than being responsible for *transmitting* knowledge to their students, the teacher assumes the role of *master learner*. A constructivist teacher works to differentiate instruction in order to accommodate the many needs of individual students. Such a teacher understands and applies a variety of learning techniques and processes and shares them with students.

Long ago, Kimpston, Williams, and Stockton (1992) wrote of the relationship between various philosophies of education and teaching methods. Their analysis indicates that the *experimentalist* and *reconstructionist* philosophies are also compatible with the interdisciplinary approach. This is true mainly because those philosophies also emphasize respect for student diversity and the importance of promoting the processes involved in learning. Experimentalism—often called *progressivism*—stresses the importance of considering the *whole child* as well as the need for active participation and experimentation by learners. Reconstructionism focuses on the study of social topics that often form the basis of interdisciplinary studies. Teachers who subscribe to these philosophies are therefore more likely to feel comfortable with interdisciplinary instruction than those who do not.

General and Child Development Knowledge

We are aware of the need to develop sufficient background knowledge for the content areas we teach. In addition to a good fund of general knowledge, we also need to be skilled researchers in order to guide our students through the research processes involved in their interdisciplinary studies. It is also important to remember that our knowledge and skills can help to ensure that we are able to provide what Vygotsky (1978) referred to as *scaffolding*—supporting students temporarily while encouraging them to become independent and to accept responsibility for their own learning as soon as they are able to do so. In a related discussion, Montessori (1964/1912) refers to the tendency of teachers and other adults to assume the role of *servants* when working with students. She makes her point dramatically: "In reality, he who is served is limited in his independence" (p. 97). Independence can only be achieved by students when we avoid giving more help than they need by supplying answers to problems they can solve on their own.

Equally important, we need to have a thorough background in theories of learning and be able to apply our understandings of cognitive and affective development when planning for instruction. An awareness of diversity in students' thinking and reasoning abilities can help us tailor instruction more effectively for students who work at different levels. Lillard (1972) has suggested that developing observation skills is the key to such awareness; others, including Armstrong (2009) and Kornhaber, Fierros, and Veenema (2004), show practical ways to design lessons and activities that address the diverse ways students learn. Brooks and Brooks (1999) relate contemporary developmental theory with classroom practice and offer alternatives to traditional textbook learning activities that are especially useful for interdisciplinary teachers. Clearly, by making use of our knowledge of students' diverse abilities and their individual ways of learning, we can design more effective interdisciplinary studies.

Classroom Management Skills

Planning, scheduling, assessment, record keeping, and behavioral management skills are all directly related to success in managing a well-organized classroom. Several suggestions for managing student behavior are described below; discussions of unit- and lesson-planning strategies as well as assessment techniques are included in discussions in chapters 3–6.

An especially important part of classroom management is that of recognizing the need to maintain appropriate student behavior. The ability to use the interdisciplinary approach and behavior management have a close relationship (Johnson, Rice, Edgington, & Williams, 2005). Management of students' behavior is critical for success in teaching; it is especially critical for interdisciplinary and multidisciplinary studies because a great deal of activity usually occurs in the classroom during unit work. At those times, it is necessary to manage several different student activities simultaneously. Both formal and informal work periods are needed, so we need to be flexible and willing to adapt to the unique types and levels of activity that arise. At the same time, we need to be sensitive to the often-subtle difference between student actions that are productive and those that are potentially distracting—and sometimes chaotic. There is usually a constant hum during busy work periods, but if the level of noise begins and continues to rise, it is usually a sign that students have completed tasks, lost their focus, and need redirection.

Johnson, Rice, Edgington, and Williams (2005) suggest that "behavior management must involve a *proactive* rather than a *reactive* approach; teachers find that many potential problems or challenges can be prevented" (p. 32). Experienced teachers have found that the following suggestions can help improve student behavior and maintain a healthy emotional climate while using any approach, including interdisciplinary instruction. The suggestions are useful general guidelines for behavior management.

Maintain a Professional Approach to Discipline. During the course of an interdisciplinary study, students frequently work together on research and projects. Certainly, it is important that they show respect for their peers during times when they are working closely together. We can set an example for students by being polite to them. To avoid embarrassing them, we should always discipline students privately. We need to keep from demonstrating anger and be brief, but firm, when administering corrective measures.

Encourage Student Participation. Students need to be active participants as they pursue the study of interdisciplinary topics. It is important from the first day of a school year that we invite their participation. When students find a classroom that is already decorated with displays, pictures, and charts on the first day of school, they may feel that the classroom belongs only to the teacher and that their participation will not be invited.

Interdisciplinary studies offer opportunities for students to become involved in decision making. It is not always possible for students to determine all of the topics they will need to study due to state regulations and standards; however, it is possible "to open up a discussion in which members of the class try to figure out together why someone apparently thought the subject was important enough to be required" (Kohn, 2006, p. 257). Students can be involved meaningfully in deciding the questions that will be pursued, and determining the titles of their interdisciplinary studies; they can participate in preparing bulletin boards, creating murals, and deciding how to display their reports, art, and construction projects. Students who share ownership of their classroom and the activities that go on in it are likely to assume more responsibility for how it is used (Pappas et al., 2006).

Develop Standards for Appropriate Behavior. "In the first month or two in a classroom, the children and the teacher go through a period of mutual exploration and of growing trust" (Channon, 1970, p. 50). Students usually have a good general idea about what is and what is not appropriate behavior. Asking them to participate in composing a set of classroom rules at the beginning of a school year is a fairly standard practice. While this can help to ensure that they at least know what the rules are, students often simply suggest the rules we already have in mind. Kohn (2006) gives us three reasons why generating rules at the beginning of a year may not be as productive as we may think:

> . . . rules turn children into lawyers, scanning for loopholes and caveats, narrowing the discussion to technicalities when a problem occurs . . . [turning] teachers into police officers, a role utterly at odds with being facilitators of learning . . . rules usually enfold within them a punitive consequence for breaking them. (pp. 72–73)

Whether or not we invite students to outline the rules, it will be especially important to establish our expectations for students' behavior during the frequent research periods and group activities that interdisciplinary studies require. Instead of creating lengthy lists of rules to post, it may be more useful to hold community discussions periodically to think about ways to foster positive behavior in the classroom.

Be Consistent with Behavior Expectations. Students expect their teachers to be fair. Fairness means maintaining the class rules that have been established, avoiding favoritism, and sharing one's attention among students as equitably as possible.

Remain Alert. Students look to their teachers for guidance. They expect us to exercise our natural authority as adults, provide clear directions, and have reasonable expectations, both for their behavior and for their academic work during the course of an interdisciplinary study. We must constantly be aware of everything that is happening in the room, something Paul Chance (2008) calls "teaching on your feet." This can be particularly difficult in interdisciplinary instruction, because students often work on different projects and research activities both individually and in small groups during lengthy work periods.

Maintain Physical Proximity with Students. During the work periods associated with interdisciplinary instruction, simply walking closer to students who are not behaving well lets them know that we are aware of what they are doing. Proximity alone can often correct minor problems, such as occasional off-task behavior or failure to share responsibilities in a committee or cooperative group activity.

Avoid Overreacting. Try not to overreact. This is especially important when rules are broken or when students who usually behave well suddenly present a problem. At such times, we should analyze the situation before reacting.

Expect the Unexpected. We cannot prevent surprises from ever arising when teaching. It is therefore important to be prepared for them and not be discouraged when they occur. Planning carefully will usually help us to be better prepared when something goes awry during a lesson or an activity period. Although unexpected events can be disconcerting at times, they can also be informative, even refreshing.

Try Different Approaches to Problem Behavior. In an emotionally healthy classroom environment, it is usually only a few students who will need frequent reminding about their behavior. Although the goal should always be to help students learn to control their own behavior, we may need, at least temporarily, to accept responsibility for students who are not able or willing to do so. Although it may be necessary to intervene and take responsibility for a student's behavior for a time, our ultimate aim must be what Maria Montessori maintained was essential in student/teacher relationships: a gradual process of transferring responsibility during which the student is helped to become "the ever more active partner and the teacher the more passive" (Standing, 1957, p. 303).

Be Creative When Handling Annoying Behaviors. Students can become argumentive while working in committees during their interdisciplinary studies.

We can ask students who complain about one another to put their complaints in writing before we attempt to make judgments. Sometimes complaints seem less important to students after they take the time to write about them. Ellis (2010) recommends that teachers have students solve classroom management problems by applying the same inquiry skills they would use to investigate other problems. Doing so keeps the focus on ways to solve problems instead of focusing on who to blame.

Lesson- and Unit-Planning Skills

Learning how to design units and lessons that interest students, involve them, address their diverse styles of learning, and provide adequate guidance are as vital for interdisciplinary instruction as for other instructional methods. A number of useful lesson-planning *protocols* can help to make the lesson-planning task somewhat easier. A protocol is a useful, step-by-step method, a template that can be used to design a lesson for a specific type of instruction. For example, different protocols for lesson planning have been developed for instruction in various disciplines, including the areas of literacy; reading, listening, and viewing lessons; experiments in science; as well as for teaching skills in mathematics and other areas. Other planning procedures can help in structuring research projects and organizing field trips. Several especially useful lesson-planning protocols are explained and examples provided in chapter 5.

Teachers who use the interdisciplinary approach also need to be skillful in designing comprehensive interdisciplinary and multidisciplinary units of study. In the early grades, interdisciplinary unit planning requires ingenuity and creativity to develop lessons related to a unit topic or theme and its objectives. Students in intermediate grades and middle school are able to undertake more sophisticated forms of research; this requires that we have a thorough understanding of research processes. Interdisciplinary and multidisciplinary unit planning are explained and illustrated with examples in chapters 3 and 4.

Skills in the Application of Technology

Today, it is essential that all teachers become skilled in the uses of technology and its many applications. Real-time online communication and interactive computer applications available for devices such as smart phones and tablets have become essential tools for students and teachers alike. Technology is cited as a discipline in most state curriculum guides, and it is addressed in state curriculums and common core learning standards. Instead of teaching technology as a separate subject in elementary and middle schools, it should be integrated across the curriculum. The emphasis in schools and colleges of education is primarily on this kind of integration. The following paragraphs illustrate several ways in which this is evident.

Many elementary and middle schools are now connected to one another via the Internet and through networking services to colleges and universities. Videoconferencing and distance learning are available in some schools to promote interaction among students and teachers in many parts of the United States and other nations.

Elementary and middle school students can design their own websites, where they publish and share their ideas, writing, and projects with others. Most word-processing programs can convert documents prepared by students to the hypertext markup language (HTML) format required for web pages. Special software programs, such as *Web Workshop* from Sunburst Communications, are available in versions appropriate for students from Grade 2 to Grade 12. The software enables students to easily prepare their materials for posting on the Internet. Older students can learn to use more advanced software, such as Microsoft Publisher.

Using the Internet, "Learners can go anywhere in the world on virtual field trips; they can perform scientific experiments; and they can engage in real-time research" (Recesso & Orrill, 2008, p. 4). Students can learn to conduct conventional searches and elaborate WebQuests for information on the topics they are investigating. A WebQuest involves more than a simple search for information on a topic because it involves a carefully planned set of steps that are followed during the search process. March (2003) explains that "a real WebQuest is a scaffolded learning structure . . ." and that "the best WebQuests inspire students to see richer thematic relationships, to contribute to the real world of learning, and to reflect on their own metacognitive processes" (p. 42).

As an important part of the search process, students learn how to locate the most reliable sources by using websites with Uniform Resource Locators (URLs)—or Internet addresses—with suffixes such as *.org* (professional organizations), *.gov* (government sources), and *.edu* (educational institutions). In addition to suffix identification, we can teach students to apply a number of other criteria, such as contacting a webmaster about a document or a site they are considering for a report. Kathy Schrock (2015a) has prepared a helpful set of criteria that elementary and middle school students can use when they are attempting to determine the validity of sources they locate on the Internet—what Donald Leu and his colleagues (2014) refer to as *media literacy*. In addition, Schrock suggests careful perusal of other information on a website, such as the author and the author's credentials, the purpose of the site, documentation of sources, links to other related sites, and the date of posting.

Wikis and blogs provide students with opportunities to collaborate with others on projects and to voice their opinions on the interdisciplinary topics they are studying. Students can sign up for a wiki website that allows them to contribute or modify information, raise questions, and offer suggestions to others who visit the site. A *wiki* (a web application that allows collaborative modification, extension, or deletion of its content and structure) is simple to use; it has only three menu items. The *edit* menu permits users to construct new web pages or modify existing pages using simple word-processing techniques; they click on *save* to save any changes; and *links* allows students to link new pages to others.

A *blog* (or web log) can be created using a number of applications available on the Internet. Students can include ideas, comment on events, or contribute other material such as stories, poetry, and various reports. The blog differs from a wiki in that it is the sole property of the person who creates it. Thus, a wiki is useful for cooperative group efforts while the blog is an opportunity for individual students to post their work.

Students can access articles online from many newspapers, journals, and periodicals to use in their research. They can also access electronic copies of original documents for their research of historical topics (e.g., the Declaration of Independence) on the Internet from the Library of Congress, museums, and other sites. Some museum and institute websites include works of art and video demonstrations.

As students gather information for their interdisciplinary studies, conventional technological resources are also useful, including interactive DVD programs and comprehensive electronic versions of dictionaries, thesauruses, atlases, and encyclopedias that are readily available on the Internet as well as CDs. They can utilize multimedia program resources, including the latest versions of such early, well-known programs as *Rainforest, Oregon Trail,* and the *Carmen Sandiego* series. Students can develop their own timelines—in either English or Spanish—with TimeLiner (distributed by Tom Snyder Productions).

To prepare reports of their interdisciplinary investigations, students can learn to use word processing, spreadsheets, and database software; accrue data from multiple sources; take notes, write papers, and write letters; and make use of e-mail. They can also learn to use desktop publishing as well as Microsoft's *PowerPoint* presentation software and graphic organizers such as *Inspiration* or *Kidspiration*.

Resources for Teachers. Technology offers us new interactive tools for instruction that we can use to address the diversity of students we find in our classes today. Through the Internet and other forms of technology mentioned above, we can offer students extra help and practice not always available in texts and other conventional materials.

Online services afford opportunities to exchange lesson and unit plans throughout the United States and to interact with groups of teachers with similar interests in interdisciplinary instruction. One of the most popular and helpful sources is the *Kathy Schrock's Guide to Everything* website (http://www.schrockguide.net/), which was mentioned earlier for its helpful list of criteria for evaluating websites. Share My Lesson (www.sharemylesson.com) offers opportunities for teachers to contribute and find lessons on many topics. This website also includes other resources for teachers, such as lesson-planning tools and examples, and other materials on curriculum, homework, clip art, and so on.

Teachers can use presentation software and digital photography to prepare slide shows to use along with other teaching techniques. Even in the primary grades, students and their teachers can learn to use digital cameras effectively (Pastor & Kerns, 1997). The latest generations of smart phones have dramatically improved their image capabilities, making the digital camera a tool that is available to a large portion of the student population (Udell, 2013). Photos and videos may be created to record students' projects and to develop multimedia records of oral reports, field trips, and other investigations. Local organizations, such as community library systems and the United Federation of Teachers' New York City Teacher Centers Consortium, give teachers access to technical and instructional assistance to help them integrate the computer and other technology in their teaching. Among others, the benefits of using photography in classrooms to prepare slide shows are many, including their visual appeal to students, the ability to record information and places visited on field trips for research, and to foster sharing of experiences and research activities among students. A slide show designed by Stacey Werder offers many other thoughts about the uses of slide shows in the classroom, including the increasingly popular PowerPoint presentation (http://www.slideshare.net/SJW01/benefits-of-images-and-slideshows-in-education-presentation).

Several commercial companies produce interdisciplinary units. The plans vary in quality, so if they are used, they will need to be examined carefully and adapted for different student groups. For example, Good Apple offers instructional materials designed specifically for young children. The New York Times Company Learning Network (http://learning.blogs.nytimes.com/) publishes numerous instructional plans on topics suited to older groups in middle schools and secondary schools. Sunburst Communications has produced numerous programs in nearly every discipline for students at all age levels. This company is also responsible for well-known interdisciplinary units called *Voyage of the Mimi I and II*—plans that include guidebooks for teachers, a CD collection, and accompanying materials for students. These examples are just a few of the many options available.

Educational television has continued to play a role in some areas of the United States. For example, Public Broadcasting Service (PBS) offers videos on historical and other topics (http://www.pbslearningmedia.org/). Some PBS stations also air educational programs designed for instruction at various grade levels. Program guides include topical references and complete descriptions of each program that are prepared in advance. The PBS STEM Education Resource Center (http://www.pbs.org/teachers/stem/), an online service for teachers of students in kindergarten through grade 12, includes predesigned interdisciplinary problems that are offered at three general levels: grades K–2, grades 3–5, and middle school.

Online services devoted to educational purposes allow teachers to help students investigate topics individually, in cooperative learning groups within their classrooms, and with students in other schools. Excellent examples of such services include National Geographic's website (nationalgeographic.com), Smithsonian Kids (si.edu/kids), and the International Education and Resource Network (iEARN) (iearn.org).

The Internet (including online applications such as YouTube that feature educational videos), educational television, computer software, and digital cameras will supplement—not replace—other ways of teaching and learning. In some schools with limited budgets, teachers who plan to use interdisciplinary instruction will continue to use conventional audiovisual technology such as CDs and DVDs, and in rare cases even older film projectors and/or overhead projectors. PowerPoint presentations, smart boards and liquid crystal display (LCD) projectors are rapidly becoming standard in elementary and middle school classrooms as well.

Several excellent books are useful sources of information for teachers excited to learn more about the uses of technology in their classrooms. The bibliography section of this book lists several that should be helpful.

Collaboration with Others in the School Community

Opportunities are always possible for collaboration among teachers who use the interdisciplinary approach. Cooperation between the classroom teacher and specialists is a form of *team teaching* that can contribute significantly to the interdisciplinarity and quality of instructional units. We often work cooperatively with others in specialty areas such as art, music, physical education, special education, and with the school nurse, custodians, or others in the school environment. If specialty-area teachers are notified when classroom teachers are planning new unit studies, they may be able to include lessons or activities that add significantly to the study.

For example, an art teacher may reserve a class period for instructing students on a papier-mâché project that relates to their current unit work. It is possible that after observing the process followed by the specialist, we may be able to use it ourselves in the future, without assistance, to generate more creative activities during another unit.

In some elementary and middle schools, interdepartmental teams are organized. For example, a four-teacher interdepartmental teaching team may include a social studies teacher, literacy or English/language arts teacher, a science teacher, and a mathematics teacher. The team may be assigned either a block of time or separate periods in which to work with a group of students. The teachers have a scheduled time for planning in which they design interdisciplinary or multidisciplinary units, decide how to allocate the time in their block, develop the unit objectives, plan for assessment, and determine how they will each relate lessons in their classes to the unit topic or theme.

Teachers of art, music, health, and physical education may also work with the team as consultants for these special aspects of a study. It has long been known that ideally, students are included in the planning sessions; this kind of student participation in the planning process has been found to have considerable value in interdisciplinary instruction (Stevenson & Carr, 1993). Inviting student participation in the planning process presents students with a working model of democratic organization. A way to organize a multidisciplinary unit by a middle school team of teachers in a departmental structure is explained in greater detail in chapter 4.

In schools with self-contained classes, another team-teaching structure can be arranged. This structure usually involves two or more teachers who combine their classes and work cooperatively with the same students. This plan requires that teachers designate the specific areas of expertise they will offer students. The teachers can rotate serving as the main instructor while the others assist; however, all teachers are involved in teaching academic skills and processes. As in the case of departmentalized plans, teachers in self-contained teams must have time reserved in their regular teaching schedule to plan together. This time is also used to share knowledge of individual students' progress, interests, strengths, needs, and limitations in the different skill areas as well as to review the teaming process itself.

Both departmental and self-contained team-teaching arrangements are compatible with the interdisciplinary approach. Because team members work as a unit, instruction can be consistently and genuinely interdisciplinary or multidisciplinary rather than divided into unrelated disciplinary studies. Both structures can be designed so that they afford teachers scheduled time to plan together and to exchange information on the progress of individual students. When a teaching team lacks administrative support or common planning time, it is difficult for a team to work efficiently to ensure that the teachers involved are working toward the same unit goals.

Finally, sharing of plans can benefit all teachers. Units "should be shared with all faculty, administration, and community members so that they can have the opportunity to contribute their knowledge and skills" (Coffey, n.d.)

Challenges to the Development of Interdisciplinary Programs

Many challenges confront teachers today, so planning for and launching any new teaching method, including interdisciplinary instruction, may not seem urgent, especially when compared with the focus on new standards and the drive to continuously raise test scores to meet federal and state requirements. Accommodating an increasing diversity of learners and planning for differentiation of instruction are also noteworthy concerns facing teachers today. Demands requiring change are indeed not new in our profession. Twenty years ago, Miller (1995) wrote:

> Teachers are told that they have to set higher standards for all students, eliminate tracking, tailor lessons to kids' individual needs (including those with various disabilities), adopt small-group and cooperative learning techniques, design interdisciplinary and multicultural curricula, work in teams with other teachers, promote "critical" and "creative" thinking instead of rote learning, attend to children's social and emotional needs, rely on "performance assessment" instead of multiple-choice tests, get with the latest technology, encourage active learning in "real-life" contexts, use fewer textbooks, and, on top of everything else, become "agents of change" in their schools. (p. 2)

Some of the factors—both positive and negative—that tend to affect the ability to make changes, especially those that might result in movement toward the interdisciplinary approach, include the reluctance to change; mandates of the Common Core State Standards; and legislation affecting school funding, such as Race to the Top and the earlier No Child Left Behind (NCLB) regulations. There is also considerable need for support from state and local school systems when making any educational changes. Parents and the community must be involved in the decision-making process for major changes in an instructional program to be successful. Finally, lack of adequate empirical research on the interdisciplinary approach continues to be a major factor.

Today, many teachers are incorporating some, if not all, aspects of interdisciplinary instruction in their teaching. It isn't difficult and often is quite natural to include other relevant disciplines when planning lessons in reading, mathematics, science, and art; it is evident that the content of social studies makes it particularly well suited to combining several disciplines when preparing lessons or units of study. Comprehensive interdisciplinary units are much easier to develop and teach when elementary teachers are provided with adequate materials and encouragement from their school districts. In middle schools, teaching teams that have opportunities to plan together cooperatively can design and teach multidisciplinary units; each teacher on the team can then assume responsibility for exploring the unit topic and teaching lessons related to his/her disciplinary specialty.

Each year, new voices add their criticisms of and recommend modifications to U.S. educational programs. The rapid introduction of the Common Core State Standards is a primary example of such recommendations that have been introduced and adopted by many states, local school districts, and teachers with little time to prepare for them. Historically, most changes evolve slowly. This observation is not new; almost 50 years ago, Leonard (1968) talked of the slow pace of change in education and cited several major reasons for the reluctance of some teachers to act rapidly on any changes that are recommended. Leonard's thinking is logical, and it still applies today:

> A certain caution in educational matters is quite understandable. A school child is far more complex, embodying far more variables, than NASA's entire satellite communications network. Baffled by this complexity and inhibited by a reluctance to "experiment" with children's lives, educators feel justified in clinging to methods that have been developed, hit or miss, over the centuries—even when they are shown to be inefficient. (p. 214)

Leonard's reasoning makes the cautious acceptance of changes in teaching understandable, especially if the changes suggested are extensive or if evidence from research supporting their effectiveness is insufficient. As suggested earlier, one of the principal reasons for reluctance to try the interdisciplinary approach can be attributed to a lack of adequate research by teachers and schools where it has been implemented. Therefore, we have little information regarding how it compares to other approaches, particularly regarding differences in the ways it addresses diversity and facilitates differential instruction. Insufficient research may well be the main reason why interdisciplinary instruction has not been considered more often by those who make decisions about curriculum matters in our schools.

The slow pace of change toward interdisciplinary instruction is especially disturbing when its potential values for students are considered, particularly those discussed earlier. It is possible that, as state departments of education continue to add their support and recommend the approach, more school systems will encourage their teachers to try this approach to instruction. In the future, schools that do so must undertake studies of its value and issue formal reports of their experiences.

Common Core State Standards, Race to the Top, and No Child Left Behind

There has been considerable public concern for underachieving students in the United States. Responding to that concern, Race to the Top, part of the American Recovery and Reinvestment Act of 2009 (Public Law 111-5); and Public Law 107-110, the No Child Left Behind Act of 2001 (NCLB), were signed into law.

Each of these initiatives was designed as an attempt to improve education for all children and particularly to address the needs of the disadvantaged school population. The first of these initiatives, No Child Left Behind, was dramatic in its scope and included provisions that established a new and central role for the federal government in education. The focus for funding for NCLB was intended to target school districts with high concentrations of poor children and was designed to give greater flexibility to states in their spending of federal allotments. The main provisions of NCLB beginning in 2002 are outlined in Exhibit 2.1.

Exhibit 2.1 Provisions of No Child Left Behind.

Academic Year	Provision
2002–2003	Schools must submit must submit annual report cards showing achievement and other data.
2004	"Reading First" was established to fund research-based reading programs for students in grades 1–3, with a priority for high-poverty areas and an early-reading program targeted to 3–5-year-olds in disadvantaged areas.
2005–2006	Teachers in core content areas must be "highly qualified." Generally, this suggests being certified in their field. Annual testing is required in reading and mathematics.
2007–2008	Annual testing aligned with state standards is required in science once in elementary, middle and high school.
2013–2014	Targeted proficiency levels must be reached for all schools.

A significant provision in 2005 regarding the requirement for "highly qualified" teachers was aimed at uncertified teachers in some of the nation's schools. By the year 2006, "teachers of core academic subjects [were] expected to have a bachelor's degree, full state certification, and proven competency in the subject areas they teach" (Darling-Hammond & Berry, 2006, p. 14). This was a first-of-a-kind federal legislation. Although most teachers involved in NCLB have been certified at the elementary, middle school, or secondary level, there is currently no special "license" to use any particular instructional approach.

No special certificate is currently required in interdisciplinary instruction, yet there appears to be some movement in that direction. For example, one state has considered the addition of a certificate in interdisciplinary instruction for middle school and K–12 special-area teachers (Minnesota Board of Teaching, 2006). It is possible that other states and school districts will gradually follow to include such certification; if so, this could be the very kind of support that many teachers need in order to encourage them to explore the interdisciplinary approach.

Legislation tends to focus primarily on reading and mathematics test scores to determine if schools are successful. However, educators are voicing their concern about the narrow focus of this reasoning, especially since the introduction of testing related to the Common Core State Standards. Schools that do not perform well become subjected to punitive actions that most often affect the most vulnerable schools and students.

Teachers say they do not have time to teach lessons and units in social studies because of the considerable demands for testing required by the new core standards regulations. According to Checkley (2006), "teachers, particularly in elementary school, would love to teach social studies, but they must adhere to schedules that allot time for math and reading instruction and little else" (p. 1). Teachers and students

> . . . are under excruciating pressure to improve test results, often at the expense of meaningful learning, and more low-income and minority students are dropping out. . . . You can see practice tests replacing student-designed projects, children appearing alternately anxious and bored, terrific teachers quitting in disgust. (Kohn, 2003, p. 20)

"Any balanced curriculum, regardless of its approach, should highlight the interconnectedness of various fields of knowledge. . . . Restoring curriculum balance to the schools will require vigorous and committed leadership" (Cowelti, 2006, p. 67). Teachers who become committed to using the interdisciplinary approach will contribute to that restoration of balance because during the course of an interdisciplinary unit, students have ample opportunities to practice all academic skills in meaningful contexts.

Is there a solution? Margaret Renner (2007, p. 15), in a paper delivered at the Oxford University Round Table on Literacy, suggests five conditions that could help correct the serious deficiencies in the accountability system.

- If educators write the policy, implement the models, and determine the levels of accountability;
- If the political agenda can be deleted from policy making;
- If the *haves* view their responsibility in terms of preserving a generation;
- If action research drives policy and informs instruction; [and]
- If children believe that education is about growth and development (a process) and not just scores (a product).

Renner stresses the need for action research and accountability: "Teachers know that data must inform curriculum . . . , that accountability, like research, should never result in punitive action . . . , that accountability involves differentiated instruction and the inclusion of learning styles," and "that interdisciplinary practices result in integrated knowledge" (p. 14). Yet, we can only achieve these goals with adequate support.

Race to the Top also aims at educational reform. It provides for awards as incentives for states that comply with its regulations. According to the U.S. Department of Education (n.d.), awards in Race to the Top would go to states that are leading the way with ambitious yet achievable plans for implementing coherent, compelling, and comprehensive education reform. The current emphasis on teacher evaluation systems and testing may not stimulate teachers' willingness to attempt changes in their teaching; they may fear that any changes, including movement toward interdisciplinary instruction, could have negative effects on test scores of the students and their evaluations.

System Support

A number of important factors are involved in making any systemwide changes in curriculum and instructional approaches. Initially, an orderly process for instituting any change must be outlined. Models already exist for instituting such changes. For example, Fullan (2011) and Wiles and Bondi (2015) provide insights and suggestions for educators contemplating curricular revisions. These writers include valuable outlines of the tasks involved and leadership requirements for a successful change process.

Oliva (2013) describes several alternative models useful in making curricular changes. He also proposed his own model, which appears to be well suited for the shift from traditional to interdisciplinary programs. The Oliva model begins with an outline of program aims and the philosophical and psychological principles on which the new curriculum is to be based. Other steps involve an analysis of community and student needs and stating goals and objectives. Listing steps toward implementation of the new program and evaluation procedures completes the process. Oliva's model is flexible, and his suggestion that interdisciplinary programs extend across the curriculum indicates that the model is applicable not only for elementary programs, but also for introducing interdisciplinary instruction in departmentalized middle schools.

Adequate planning, staff preparation, and systemwide support are the primary keys to success in the movement toward any change in our schools. Any methodological change can place heavy demands on teachers and an entire school system; this is especially true of the interdisciplinary approach because both in-service preparation and new instructional materials will usually be needed.

If further progress toward interdisciplinary instruction is to be made, more teachers will need preparation for their new role, and also the necessary support to make the transition from more conventional methods. The teachers who are not currently using aspects of the interdisciplinary approach must be consulted and involved in the change process from the outset. Whenever teachers are not included in the initial decision-making steps or when administrative support is weak, the movement toward any instructional change is unlikely to succeed.

The teaching staff should also be involved in selecting the topics for their interdisciplinary or multidisciplinary units to ensure that the topics studied align with their state curriculum mandates and learning standards. Teachers must be given more autonomy and trust in their classrooms to select methods that work best for them and their students; they also need time to share their unit and lesson plan designs with one another during the regular school day.

Several other nations are known for the respect and freedom they provide for their teachers. For example, according to Hancock (2011), "Teachers in Finland spend fewer hours at school each day and spend less time in classrooms than American teachers. Teachers use the extra time to build curriculums and assess their students." The author indicates other striking differences:

- teachers are provided time during the school day to work on curriculum and to meet and design instructional plans;
- only minimal amounts of homework are assigned; teachers are free to create and use any method that works for them;
- cooperation is fostered among students;
- professional educators make all decisions about education;

- schools provide many social services;
- students spend 30 percent less time in school; and
- there is only one examination given, and it is given at the end of the senior high school year.

If the Finnish model is producing so much better results than we have been able to achieve in American schools, we need to look more closely to determine if there may be ways for our schools to incorporate some of the same provisions (Hancock, 2011). It is clear that what is typical in Finland will not occur in the U.S. without the backing of those involved in making educational policy decisions.

To become more supportive, some administrators are experimenting with different ways to promote greater collaboration among teachers (McKibben, 2013). These are principals in schools having an "open-door" policy in which they are out of their offices much of the day, in classrooms and often working with students. According to one principal in a St. Louis elementary school, "Part of it is the ability to go out and stand and just be approachable" (p. 4).

Materials and Equipment

The staff may also need additional materials. Both the kinds and the quantity of instructional materials will change with the introduction of interdisciplinary instruction in a school. For example, instead of having a textbook from one publisher for each child in a class, a teacher will need a collection of five or six copies of social studies and science textbooks from each of several publishers. This approach gives students access to more than one viewpoint as they research their unit topics. Purchasing the new materials will initially involve additional funding, which may be difficult for school systems to find today.

Teachers must have an adequate supply of trade books—single-topic books—on the unit topics studied in their classes. In elementary schools, some of these books should be kept in individual classrooms; others can be centrally located in the school library or media center. In addition to books, the school media center should house enough periodicals, videos, and other multimedia resources to enable students from different classrooms who are studying similar topics at the same time to have an adequate, up-to-date supply to efficiently conduct their research. School librarians are especially well prepared to assist both teachers and students in selecting materials that are relevant to the topics of the units being researched.

All classrooms should be equipped with computers, have Internet access, and have an adequate supply of software. Teachers should have access to software catalogs from various suppliers so that they can study the many new programs that are continually being developed. Computer networking opportunities with college and university libraries and other community resources should be carefully explored and added when found to be valuable and feasible. Many school districts have developed "acceptable use" policies for technology. While there are some differences in their acceptable use agreements, the one by the Davis School District in Utah is an excellent example to study (http://www.davis.k12.ut.us/domain/2416).

The Need for Parent and Community Involvement

Any commitment to major changes in a school curriculum must also involve parents and the community. Parents are usually included in some aspects of school life, but often their participation has been limited to routine matters, such as field trip supervision, fund-raising, and involvement in parent–teacher organization activities. A somewhat more important role for parents is one that is "best interpreted to mean being consulted, having one's opinion taken seriously, and becoming part of the equation when vital decisions are made" (Marsh & Horns-Marsh, 1999, p. 152). Above all, we know that "Parents can contribute insights and knowledge that complement the professional skills of schools' staffs in ways that strengthen academic and social programs" (Comer & Haynes, 1991).

To support the idea of parent and community participation in the decision-making process, the National Parent-Teacher Association has included among its six Standards for Parent/Family Involvement Programs parent involvement in school decision making and advocacy. Ray (2005) emphasizes that our students come to school from a diversity of family structures, each of which has its strengths and challenges. Whether a family is of the traditional two-parent, single-parent, foster-parent, multigenerational, lesbian, or gay family structure, its members and other members of the community should be invited to participate in discussions and serve on advisory committees considering changes that may be directed toward the interdisciplinary instruction. Parents also need to understand the underlying theory, so they can help their children at home with the kinds of work that an interdisciplinary approach entails. Parents who speak other languages may have difficulty understanding the theory (Henson, 2015), especially when it is explained in English-only information sessions; therefore, explanations in other languages may need to be scheduled.

Bryk and Schneider (2003) have emphasized the need to build a trusting relationship among members of the school community to reduce "the sense of risk associated with change" (p. 43). Others (Henson, 2015; Ray, 2005; Ruso, 2013) make more specific suggestions for inviting parents to become active participants in the decision-making process in their schools. Any movement toward instituting the interdisciplinary approach will require cooperation, support, and mutual trust on the part of those involved. Working together, a team composed of teachers, administrators, and parents can effect changes that endure.

Lack of Adequate Research

As explained earlier, reports on interdisciplinary programs in schools have been and continue to be rare. Lagemann and Shulman (1999) voiced their concern about this lack of research and also the need to make changes in the methods—primarily an exclusive reliance on testing—that are used to evaluate the success of programs in schools of different sizes (e.g., arrangements such as team teaching and approaches that include interdisciplinary instruction).

Several departures from conventional education included the Dewey School at the Laboratory School of the University of Chicago from 1896 through 1903 (Mayhew & Edwards, 2011/1936). It focused on the inner motivation of students for its curriculum design, and it involved students in projects similar to those in an interdisciplinary program. However, it was not exactly an interdisciplinary approach as we know it today. "The main hypothesis was that life itself, especially those occupations and associations which serve man's chief needs, should furnish the ground experience for the education of children" (p. vi). A difference between the Dewey method and today's interdisciplinary instruction is that today we first establish goals and standards; students may then add other goals of their own once our goals are first made clear.

Later, there were missed opportunities to assess the effectiveness of such programs. In 1968, Roland Chatterton, a school district administrator in a suburban community on Long Island in New York State, produced and directed two unique documentary films illustrating a *multidisciplinary,* unit-centered instructional program that the teachers in his schools had developed. The films show a master teacher guiding a group of fifth-grade students through two research-oriented multidisciplinary units. Special-area teacher consultants in art, music, library and media, health, and physical education are observed assisting the classroom teacher and students with their research, projects, and reports.

The Chatterton films followed the students and teachers engaged in research, various lessons, and activities throughout a five- to six-week multidisciplinary unit. The films intentionally left the value of this approach for the viewer to decide. Although the documentaries are both inspiring and convincing, and the method's positive results are inferred by the film director, neither film reports any research that may have been undertaken by the school system to document the value of the approach. Therefore, viewers are left to wonder if any objective evidence was collected and if there was any indication that the approach was at least as effective as or possibly more effective than other methods. (Although some colleges and universities have copies of these unusual films, unfortunately the film company that produced them no longer exists.)

Current curriculums in many states clearly indicate that their departments of education advocate the interdisciplinary approach. However, until more serious research studies and formal reports on the method's actual use in schools are available, movement toward interdisciplinary instruction is likely to remain slow, and some teachers will continue to be reluctant to try the method in their classes.

Summary

Teachers who use interdisciplinary instruction find it professionally challenging. To be successful, we need to become secure in the lesson- and unit-planning processes and in classroom management. Interdisciplinary instruction requires an extensive fund of general knowledge, child development, and theories of learning. Individual differences in learning style also require us to adapt our instruction to the ways students are able to learn best.

Even with the emphasis on testing stimulated by legislation and other challenges, there continues to be interest in interdisciplinary instruction. Practical aspects of the interdisciplinary approach that follow in the remaining chapters include:

- Designing interdisciplinary units,
- Designing multidisciplinary units,
- Lesson-planning strategies, and
- Assessment planning.

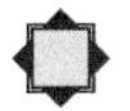

ACTIVITY

Melissa Cooper teaches the fourth grade in a small elementary school in her rural community. She and the other teachers in her school have always used fairly conventional teaching methods. She recently attended a professional workshop on interdisciplinary instruction and would like to try using it with her class. Ms. C. realizes that making such a change in her teaching will require some discussion with her administrators and that any changes she makes could affect the other teachers in her school.

Ms. C. is considering what she will need to do before she undertakes such a change in her teaching in this small school. Help her to answer the following questions:

- What arguments should she propose to her administration for the change she wants to make?
- How should she approach other teachers who may be affected by any changes she makes in her teaching?
- What else should she consider in making the change?
- How would you respond to the three questions above if you knew that Ms. Cooper was teaching in a large inner-city school?

Designing Interdisciplinary Units

Overview

This chapter explains a process for planning interdisciplinary units. Examples are provided for each step in the process. The chapter responds to the following questions about the planning process:

- What are the basics in the planning of an interdisciplinary study?
- Interdisciplinary units are always within a context—a school, classroom, and students; what contextual factors need consideration in the unit-planning process?
- Is there a recommended form to use when designing an interdisciplinary unit?
- What is the sequence of steps involved in preparing an initial interdisciplinary unit plan?

Important Considerations When Planning an Interdisciplinary Unit

Planning an interdisciplinary unit requires considerable time and skill. Interdisciplinary units are especially suitable for students in elementary schools where all the students work under the direction of one teacher who assumes responsibility for instruction in all or most academic subjects. Poorly planned units generally resemble an assortment of loosely connected lessons and activities that may lack clear objectives and direction, the kind of unit planning Jacobs (1989) refers to as the *potpourri approach*. When a unit is *not* well planned with well-aligned goals—standards, understandings, knowledge, skills, dispositions—and essential questions, unit assessments, and a learning plan, the results are likely to be disappointing.

Student Involvement in the Planning Process

In a democratic classroom, students should be given opportunities to participate in the design of an interdisciplinary study and to have their questions, suggestions, and special interests incorporated as a unit develops. However, the teacher needs to assume the major responsibility for the plan and for guiding the planning process to ensure that all applicable disciplines are included that will assist thorough exploration of the topic.

Students also need to be helped to note the relationships between the various disciplines and the central topic, theme, or problem of their study. Although our long-term goal should aim to help students become independent in planning their studies, it is important to monitor their involvement carefully and proceed slowly until the students have developed adequate skill with the process. Gardner (1995) emphasizes this idea:

> The educator of the future needs to walk a fine line—always encouraging the youngster to stretch, praising her when she succeeds, but equally important, providing support and a non-condemnatory interpretative framework when things do not go well. Eventually, aspiring creators can supply much of this support, scaffolding and interpreting framework for themselves. (p. 15)

Encouraging Students to Develop a Variety of Abilities

All students are unique in their mental makeup, learning styles, and abilities. Gardner's (1993) proposition that "people have different cognitive strengths and contrasting cognitive styles" (p. 6) suggests that students should have opportunities to develop simultaneously in more than one cognitive area. Therefore, if we consider their *multiple intelligences*, young students should be encouraged to undertake inquiries and to use reporting methods that do not depend exclusively on their linguistic ability. Instead, music, art, drama, movement, natural exploration, critical thinking, and thoughtful questioning can also be employed by students to investigate and to demonstrate their mastery and application of knowledge.

A model program, the *Key School*, used a multiple intelligences approach to the curriculum. According to Gardner (1993a), students in that program participated on a regular basis in activities involving computing, music, and bodily–kinesthetic intelligence, in addition to exploring topic-centered curriculums that embodied the standard literacies and subject matter. Each student participated in an apprenticeship-like *pod,* where he or she worked with peers of different ages, and with a competent teacher to assist them in mastering a craft or discipline of interest. Students at the Key School investigated several multidisciplinary topics each year, including those with titles such as *Patterns*, *Connections*, *the Renaissance, Then and Now*, and *Mexican Heritage*.

For many elementary students, inquiries that rely exclusively on reading can be difficult, particularly if relatively few resources on the unit topic are available for them to read independently. In the primary grades, we need to offer an environment with a rich and abundant supply of varied types of reference materials and learning activities, similar to a Montessori *prepared environment* (Lillard, 1972; Montessori, 1912/1964). This type of environment fosters active involvement with learning materials and increased participation in activities. When very young students are developing concepts, hands-on learning activities are more helpful than using abstract materials which rely heavily on their linguistic and mathematical abilities. These hands-on, concrete opportunities are especially important for special-needs students. Older students in the middle elementary grades are often able to read for information more independently and will be able to rely more on this skill. All students can learn through listening activities, viewing presentations, watching videos, and interactions with others.

Students who have specific talents—artistic, musical, physical, linguistic, mathematical, and so on—should be challenged to undertake forms of inquiry that use their special abilities. Those who can read for information and prepare written reports should be encouraged to do so. Some students, even in the lower elementary grades, may also be able to complete aspects of genuine research during their units. As an interdisciplinary unit reaches its conclusion, culminating activities can help the students summarize the concepts they have gained from their study.

The Context for Learning: What Are Its Components?

All learning takes place in a context. So, before beginning the interdisciplinary unit-planning process, it is important to consider the context for learning in which the new unit will be taught. This is one of the most important factors in the process of planning for any instruction. The context includes consideration of students' developmental abilities, their background knowledge, academic skills, special talents, interests, limitations, multiple intelligences, behavior, and ability to interact with one another. It also includes the availability of materials and equipment as well as the physical classroom environment and our own teaching skills.

Cognitive Development: Levels and Abilities

We first need to consider the critical match between the cognitive abilities of the students in our classes and the new facts, concepts, generalizations, and important understandings we hope they will gain from a new interdisciplinary study. Estimating students' thinking and reasoning abilities prior to teaching helps to minimize the chance that they will meet with frustration. Even before the second or early third grade, some students develop fairly sophisticated thinking and reasoning abilities, especially if they have had adequate instruction and opportunities to interact with adults and competent peers.

Nevertheless, as suggested earlier, students in the early elementary grades will benefit from direct, hands-on experiences. These concrete experiences can easily be brought to primary-level interdisciplinary studies in a number of ways. Young students can conduct their own inquiries and experiments in science by using concrete materials to help them develop unit concept goals. They improve their spatial skills by working with art media and designing projects to show some of the concepts they are gaining. Young students can paint murals; make collages and dioramas; and work with papier-mâché, Play-Doh™, and modeling clay to form artifacts and other constructions related to their interdisciplinary unit topics.

We can also provide concrete experiences for all students by organizing field trips, especially to places where they are permitted to interact physically with real objects as well as make observations. Music is also a pathway to learning for many students, and we can offer opportunities to learn about the world through singing, experimenting with simple musical instruments, and listening to recordings. The only techniques that are not defendable for young students, from a developmental viewpoint, include substituting excessive teacher demonstrations, lectures, and whole-class oral reading exercises for the kinds of concrete learning experiences young students are capable of handling for themselves.

Knowing students both developmentally and academically is always more difficult early in the school year than later on. Even so, in the early months we should try to estimate their readiness for the interdisciplinary unit topics we plan to teach. Piaget (1955, 1966, 1970, 1973, 1974, 1976) often stressed the importance of recognizing that, at all age levels, students' thinking characteristics have a significant effect on the kinds of academic work that they can do. Piaget's research also led him to conclude that thinking and reasoning in the primary grades was dominated by *preoperational thought*—a pattern of thinking that tends to be egocentric, centered, irreversible, and non-transformational (Phillips, 1981; Piaget & Inhelder, 1969). For many years, Piaget's unchallenged research led us to believe that all young children were highly egocentric and that their thinking was extremely centered during the early childhood years.

Since Piaget completed his work, contemporary researchers—sometimes referred to as *neo-Piagetian* and *post-Piagetian* researchers—have found that Piaget had underestimated the abilities of children in the preschool and early elementary years (Flavell, 1985). These researchers have found young children to be less egocentric than Piaget believed. Also, Piaget never considered the impact of social interaction as seriously as Vygotsky (1986) and the post-Piagetian researchers. In chapter 1, several of these researchers were cited, including Bruner (1990), Case (1985), Checkley (1997), Forman, Minick, and Stone (1993), Gardner (1991, 1993a), and Wertsch (1985).

Piaget's work can still provide us with important information about children's intellectual growth and development, but one fact is clear: Contrary to Piaget's belief, intellectual development appears to proceed continuously, and cognitive development is influenced considerably by our culture and by instruction. Santrock (2012) affirmed this notion: "Most contemporary developmentalists agree that children's cognitive development is not as grand stage-like as Piaget thought" (p. 383). Information is processed, and learners improve steadily in their ability to absorb and store knowledge from their environment (Berk, 2008). Interdisciplinary units for students in the middle and upper elementary grades can follow the same basic structure as those designed for younger students. However, they will differ in both the quantity and the level of work that is required. (Note that *multidisciplinary* units, which are explained in chapter 4, offer an alternative approach to unit studies for students in the upper elementary grades and middle school.)

Affective and Psychomotor Development. Development in the affective and psychomotor domains should also be considered as a part of the context for learning. Knowledge of students' dispositions, their individual feelings, attitudes, temperaments, and ways of interacting with others is valuable when we are planning a unit. Information about motor coordination, health, and physical development is also important, particularly when we are planning outdoor activities, field trips, or are planning to include food in the unit.

Background Knowledge. Equally important, we need to learn as much as possible about our students' experience and knowledge backgrounds. New information in a study can be assimilated only if it builds on students' existing knowledge base. To minimize frustration and failure, we must ensure that students have a foundation for any new material they are expected to learn.

Other Factors. Additional factors to consider are students' interests and academic skills, especially skills in reading, writing, listening, speaking, and research abilities. The availability of adequate supplies of appropriate learning-resource materials is critical to interdisciplinary instruction. In addition to books, other media resources are required for thorough investigations of most topics. These resources include relevant magazines and newspapers; computer software; teacher-prepared presentations; video programs; and access to the Internet and networking facilities.

We must ensure that students have the equipment, technology, and materials required for their research, constructions, art projects, and science experiments. A detailed description of the thinking process that a group of teachers may experience as they work together to select a unit topic is given in Perkins's interesting and informative scenario on this important task (Jacobs, 1989, pp. 67–76). In the scenario, a group of teachers is meeting to select a topic for their interdisciplinary unit. After choosing a topic and determining the unit goals and assessment strategies, a web design of the unit can be prepared to indicate the overall learning plan—the lessons and activities—that may be found useful in helping students to meet the unit goals.

In summary, planning for any instruction, including interdisciplinary units, must take into consideration the context in which the learning takes place. This context includes many factors that need to be considered while developing an interdisciplinary unit plan. Among these factors are students' cognitive, affective, and psychomotor development as well as their academic skills, interests, background knowledge, multiple intelligences, school facilities, and available equipment and supplies.

Interdisciplinary Unit Plan Outline and Design

Most teaching-methods textbooks include unit-plan outlines. Perusal of those outlines reveals that there is little consensus for both the format and the planning process. For example, the emphasis in one text may be on unit goals and assessments; another may simply list resources; and still another may suggest that units are only a collection of lesson plans or hands-on activities.

The unit-plan format recommended in this text includes:

- learning standards—the *Common Core State Standards* (CCSS)—and any required state content standards that are related to the unit goals and assessments;
- the unit goals—*understandings, knowledge, skills,* and *dispositions*;
- essential questions of the study;
- the unit assessment plan;
- a learning plan that includes both a graphic web design of the plan and descriptions of lessons, research, experiments, field trips, and other activities to be included in the unit;
- a list of essential materials; and
- a reflections section that is completed after teaching the unit.

These will provide the framework for, give direction to, and guide development of the study.

A three-part process for designing the unit plan is guided by the *backward design* process (Wiggins & McTighe, 2012) described earlier in chapter 1. The interdisciplinary unit-plan outline contains new elements and those that have been included in outlines known to most elementary and middle school teachers, such as those in the *topic study* unit plan by Charbonneau and Reider (1995) and the Jacobs model (1989). The sections that may be less familiar are the Common Core State Standards and essential questions sections.

The first time we plan an interdisciplinary unit, it may be described as an *initial* unit plan. This plan is the preliminary plan for a unit *prior to teaching it for the first time*. This plan differs from a plan that has already been taught. For example, in an initial unit plan, instead of complete lesson and activity plans, the unit learning plan needs to include either brief or detailed *descriptions* of lesson and activity ideas in the sequence likely to be used when teaching the unit. The reason why preparing complete lessons can be delayed is simply that after introducing a unit, it may be decided that some of the anticipated lessons or activities will not be used at all. The descriptions will provide enough information so that complete lesson plans can be prepared, if and when it is decided that they will *actually* be included in the study. It is, therefore, not necessary to write complete lesson plans at this point; as the unit progresses, some of the original ideas for lessons and activities may be considered inappropriate to include in the study for a particular student group.

Once the initial unit has been planned, the first complete lesson that needs to be developed is the lesson that will be used to introduce the unit to the students. The introductory lesson should be designed in a manner that elicits the students' previous knowledge about the topic. It should also introduce the essential questions of the unit to students and encourage them to raise other related questions they would like to include in the study. We want to stimulate students' interest in the study at this early point. Their reactions during this first lesson can help to guide us as we make decisions about how to proceed. This lesson or one that follows may also be designed to gain additional student input in the unit design. The result of the introductory lesson should also help us to decide if some of the ideas we have in our lesson descriptions or activities for the unit plan will not be needed. Other activities that need to be considered in the ongoing planning process may also be suggested by the students, as long as the activities address the unit's goals.

Lesson planning is more thoroughly discussed in chapter 5. In that chapter are guidelines for a number of different lesson-planning protocols that may be helpful when developing complete lesson plans for different purposes. It is important to keep in mind that interdisciplinary units are flexible and dynamic, always open to modification. Each time the same unit is taught to a new group of students, plans for additional lessons and activities can be added to the design if needed, and reflections about possible modification can be added to help guide its development in the future.

The process explained below offers information needed to design an initial interdisciplinary unit plan. The steps followed during the discussion include elements found in the unit plan outline listed in Exhibit 3.1.

This basic outline can be used to design interdisciplinary unit plans for students at all elementary grade levels. The outline will be followed as the template for the discussion of the interdisciplinary unit-planning process in the remainder of this chapter. The discussion will explain and illustrate with examples a three-part process involved in designing an *initial* plan. This process differs in some ways from more conventional unit-planning practices. Those differences are indicated in Exhibit 3.2.

Exhibit 3.1 Interdisciplinary Unit Plan Outline.

Topic:
Level:
Estimated Length:
Learning Standards:
Goals:
Understandings:
Knowledge:
Skills:
Dispositions:
Essential Questions:
Assessment Plan:
Learning Plan:
Unit Web Design
Descriptions of Lessons and Activities
Materials:
Resources:
Reflections:

Exhibit 3.2 Differences between Conventional and Recommended Practice in Designing Interdisciplinary Unit Plans.

Process	Conventional Practice	Process	Recommended Practice (Backward Design)
Preliminary	*Determine the topic, theme, or problem.*	*Preliminary*	*Determine the topic, theme, or problem.*
Step 1	-Plan a sequence of learning experiences—lessons and activities. -Determine and list the unit materials.	Part I	-Determine the unit learning standards -List the unit goals: the understandings, knowledge, skills, and dispositions to be developed. -List the essential questions of the study.
Step 2	Determine the unit learning standards and objectives.	Part II	Prepare the unit assessment plan, and ensure that it is aligned with the goals of the unit.
Step 3	Determine unit assessment strategies.	Part III	Design a learning plan for the unit: -Construct a unit web design indicating the interdisciplinary content of the unit. -Write descriptions of the lessons and activities. -Ensure that the lessons and activities in the learning plan are aligned with the unit goals and assessments. -List materials needed for the unit.

Although we can use our individual preferences for sequence when planning the various components of a unit, it is essential that all the unit sections align with one another once the plan is completed. These include the learning standards; the unit goals—understandings, knowledge, skills, and dispositions—to be developed; the essential questions; the assessment plan; and the learning plan. See an example below in which a learning standard, understanding, and an essential question align with one another for a fourth-grade unit plan, *A Community Study.*

A Word about Learning Standards

To save teachers time, some school districts prefer an abbreviated method of listing learning standards in their unit and lesson plans. On its website, the *Common Core State Standards* (CCSS) document suggests that a standard can be cited by its strand, grade level, and standard number—or number and letter. For example, the acronym RI.5.4 indicates "**R**eading for **I**nformation, Grade **5**, Standard **4**". The acronym of SL.4.4, as in the example below, indicates "**S**peaking and **L**istening, Grade **4**, Standard **4**". The abbreviated method is used throughout this book. The Common Core State Standards are available online to read and download (http://www.corestandards.org/read-the-standards/).

Note that the state standards examples in this text are those required in New York State; standards of other states can easily be substituted if the state requires them.

EXAMPLE

Learning Standard

Report on a topic or text, tell a story, or recount an experience in an organized manner, using appropriate facts and relevant, descriptive details to support main ideas or themes; speak clearly at an understandable pace. (*CCSS, SL.4.4*)

Goals

Students will understand that:

Communities are social units organized and shared by people who may be from various cultural, ethnic, and religious backgrounds.

Essential Questions

What is a community?

Why would people want to live in our community?

Assessment Plan (in part)

The essential questions and related local community questions of the unit will be divided among the students for individual research and preparation of written reports of findings. Four groups will be formed for students who have researched the same essential and the related local community questions. Students in each group will share their individual findings, and each group will prepare a presentation for the class summarizing those findings. Rubrics will be prepared to assess the individual written reports and group presentations.

In the example above, we can see that the students will be required to prepare individual written reports, and groups of students will organize presentations summarizing their findings to the essential questions and related local community questions. The standards, understandings, essential questions, and assessments are related. No matter where we begin to plan, whether it is with the learning standards for the unit, the goals—understandings, knowledge, skills, and dispositions—or the essential questions, it is critical to ensure that once those components of the unit have been determined, their relationships to one another are clear. For illustrative purposes, examples will be given in the discussion that follows from the same community study designed for fourth-grade students. (Note that the complete initial unit plan for this study can be found at the end of this chapter.)

Before beginning the planning process, we should first consider the *context for learning* in which the unit will be taught. This context includes information about the students' previous study and background for the new unit, their thinking, academic abilities, social characteristics, special needs, and talents. Also, the actual environment of the classroom and school and the availability of materials and equipment will need to be considered.

EXAMPLE

It is early fall, and the students in this heterogeneous group of fourth graders are mainly at the concrete operational levels in their thinking and reasoning abilities. They have had some experience researching short-duration topics and reporting their findings.

They will need authentic experiences whenever possible to help them develop the understandings and knowledge the study will involve. Some students in the group can read for information; some have not yet developed independent reading levels adequate for the books and other resources available on this topic.

Socially, the students get along well with one another; there are only occasional disagreements and rarely any serious behavioral problems. Three students have special needs: two have been diagnosed with specific learning disabilities, and one has a serious vision problem. Two students are talented in art, and several students play musical instruments. Last year, the class completed a unit that focused on learning about communities around the world, a study that helped the students to gain some understanding of the "community" concept.

Next, the task for planning each section of the interdisciplinary unit plan is explained. Each explanation is followed with examples from the community study unit plan. Before beginning the planning process, it is important to know how topics, themes, or problems are selected for elementary and middle school state curriculums and by textbook publishers. Two developmentally based approaches to this task that are used by publishers of elementary textbooks follow. The same two approaches are also evident in state curriculum guides and lists of learning standards. Using the first approach, the *expanding environments*—or *widening horizons—approach*, topics are ordered according to students' developmental levels. Young children initially study topics that are within their range of personal experience and about which they have considerable prior knowledge. For example, in the primary grades, social studies topics begin with the study of self and family; later, students study their school and neighborhood. Older students study regions, states, nations, and cultures in the Eastern and Western hemispheres. To use the widening horizons approach in selecting topics for a particular grade level, we can usually rely on those that are listed in state curriculum guides and textbooks in science, social studies, and other disciplines.

Some educators have criticized the exclusive use of the expanding environments approach for selection of interdisciplinary unit topics. For example, Ravitch (1987) contends that by following that approach, teachers limit students to simple, familiar topics that may fail to challenge or motivate them. This concern is reasonable today because many young children are exposed to the wide range of information offered via television and other media well before they enter school. However, if we keep this idea in mind when selecting topics to study, the widening horizons approach can still provide a general guide.

The second approach to selecting topics involves the development of concepts. In Bruner's (1963) *spiral curriculum*, children may be exposed to the same concepts and basic ideas at each grade level. In 1963, Bruner stated, "A curriculum as it develops should revisit these basic ideas repeatedly, building upon them until the student has grasped the full formal apparatus that goes with them" (p. 13). Each year, new and more complex aspects of these concepts and ideas can be introduced as students become developmentally ready to understand them. For example, the concept of *community* can be taught at every grade level. As students become intellectually ready, they can be exposed to more sophisticated interpretations of this concept. Bruner's approach is compatible with and complements the expanding environments approach. Whereas the expanding environments approach centers on the selection of the *topics* to be selected, the spiral curriculum approach involves developing fundamental key *concepts* and the *understandings* those topics can help to develop.

The spiral curriculum approach supports *backward design,* the approach to unit planning discussed earlier and recommended by Wiggins and McTighe (2012). Using backward design, the study of any topic needs to assist in developing *enduring understandings* by engaging students in investigating *essential questions* regarding a particular topic. (See Chapter 1, Exhibit 1.2 for examples of enduring understandings and essential questions.)

A number of appropriate topics, themes, and problems for each grade level are usually listed in state curriculum guides. For example, in New York State, there are *Core Curriculum* guides for each subject area; the guides clearly explain the content that is expected to be taught at each level. Other states have similar publications. Teaching the topics listed in the guides helps to ensure that students are exposed to the information they need in order to meet state standards. The guides are not intended to restrict us from teaching about other topics. Over the course of an academic year, it may be possible to study additional topics, themes, or problems other than those included in state guides.

A title for a unit can be displayed in the classroom during the study. The title selected for the unit example in this chapter, *A Community Study,* is simply the same as the topic. However, another title may be assigned; it could be one suggested by students that reflects the topic. Determining a distinctive unit title can usually be accomplished easily. Students will often be able to think of a title they like. Offering students a chance to suggest their own title is a good way to stimulate their interest and help them become invested in the study. In reality, the study belongs to them, so feeling a sense of ownership is important. The students can suggest titles during a class meeting, or individuals can write suggested titles on slips of paper and put the slips in a suggestion box. A class vote can be taken to select the final title. Students can also create artwork for the title so that it can be displayed in the classroom throughout the study. The title can be made from cutout letters, written with crayon, painted on a long strip of paper, or made from other suitable materials.

The length of the unit will depend on the topic and other factors, such as curriculum requirements, the concepts to be developed, and the amount of interest it engenders in students. Interdisciplinary units for early childhood may range in length from a few days to one or more weeks. In other elementary grades, most interdisciplinary studies usually take at least three or four weeks; many require more time. In middle school, a unit may require four to six weeks or more. An example of the topic, level, and estimated length of the communities unit plan follows.

EXAMPLE (A COMMUNITY STUDY)

This topic was selected because it offers the students a number of opportunities to become involved in a research experience related to a familiar topic that is designed for students at the fourth-grade level. (Modification of the plan will be needed if the unit is used for third grade.)

Level: Grade 4

This unit is designed for students in the fourth grade. (It can be adapted for third grade.)

Estimated Unit Length: 3–5 weeks

After selecting a topic for the unit, other sections of the unit plan can be prepared. The order for developing the different sections is optional, but it is again emphasized that the various sections must be aligned with one another once the unit plan is completed.

Unit Goals

Prepare a list of goals. The unit goals include (1) the learning standards, (2) understandings, (3) knowledge, (4) skills, and (5) dispositions the unit will aim to develop and achieve as its anticipated outcomes—or desired results. Each will be explained briefly with examples.

Learning standards are the overall, long-term goals toward which the unit is expected to contribute. The Common Core State Standards (CCSS) are national standards that have been adopted with optional additions by most individual states and local school systems. Some states and school districts may also require state or local content standards for various subjects that were developed previous to the CCSS. If so, those standards will need to be included along with the CCSS standards. It is always important to ensure that only standards the interdisciplinary unit actually addresses should be listed in the plan.

Prepare a list of the major learning standards the unit will address. The selected standards will give direction to the study; the individual State Learning Standards in the disciplines related to the topic of the unit, the Common Core State Standards in Language Arts and Literature and Common Core Mathematics Standards need to align with the assessment strategies described in the assessment plan and indicated by the lessons and activities in the learning plan. They must also align well with the important understandings, skills, and dispositions to be developed. An abbreviated example from the Community Study unit plan follows.

EXAMPLE

Students will:

- Describe the overall structure (e.g., chronology comparison, cause/effect, problem/solution) of events, ideas, concepts, or information in a text or part of a text. (*CCSS, RI.4.5*)

Understandings are the important learnings that are anticipated to be the results of the unit of study. Understandings listed in a unit are usually expressed as *enduring understandings.* Other, unit-specific goals may be included that reflect ideas the students contribute; those understandings may not meet the criteria for an enduring understanding. An enduring understanding is one that expresses a *big idea*, a known truth that can be generalized to more specific examples. The examples below represent an enduring understanding included in the communities unit plan. Both examples reflect the big idea, "Community," an important concept to be developed further in this unit.

EXAMPLE

Students will understand that:

Communities are social units organized and shared by people who may be from various cultural, ethnic, and religious backgrounds.

Knowledge suggests basic information students will be expected to remember as a result of the study.

EXAMPLE

Students will know:
Key terms and concepts related to the community study, such as "democracy" and "citizenship."

Skills include abilities such as reading, writing, speaking, listening, mathematics, and researching topics.

EXAMPLE

Students will further develop their skills in:
Planning for investigations.

Dispositions are the attitudes and social skills that are necessary for cooperation with others.

EXAMPLE

Students will demonstrate:
Behavior that is respectful and cooperative when working in groups.

Essential Questions

Essential questions are the major questions that will guide the inquiry during the study of the topic. Wiggins and McTighe (2012) describe an essential question as one that:

> . . . lies at the heart of a subject or a curriculum (as opposed to being either trivial or leading), and promotes inquiry and uncoverage of a subject. Essential questions thus do not yield a single straightforward answer (as a leading question does) but produce different plausible responses about which thoughtful and knowledgeable people may disagree. (p. 342)

Essential questions are, therefore, the focus questions upon which the study is based. Prepare essential questions designed to help students gain insight into the big ideas they should gain from their unit. Essential questions must be related to the goals of the unit—its understandings, knowledge, skills, and dispositions. In this section, only those defined as *essential questions* are listed; other questions that will help students to research their topic (as well as questions students suggest) can be added when a teacher believes them to be important, as long as they are also addressed in the unit work.

EXAMPLES

- What is a community?
- Why would people want to live in our community?

Alignment is critical among the various unit goals and its essential questions. In the example below, the comparison of a learning standard, understanding, and essential question from the communities unit plan, it is clear that they align with one another as in the following:

EXAMPLE

- *Learning Standard*: Students will conduct short research projects that build knowledge through investigation of different aspects of a topic. (*CCSS, W.4.7*)
- *Understanding*: Students will understand that communities are social units organized and shared by people who may be from various cultural, ethnic, and religious backgrounds.
- *Essential Question*: What is a community? Why would people want to live in our community?

Assessment Plan

When an interdisciplinary unit is taught, the assessments in each lesson and activity will provide information regarding their contributions to the development of the unit goals. However, more comprehensive measures will be needed for the unit as a whole. Those measures are the student requirements and performances stated in a unit assessment plan. Using those assessments, we can determine the ability of students to respond to the unit's essential questions and the extent to which they have addressed the standards and other goals of the unit.

We want to know if students can recall information from their unit work but, more importantly, we need to know whether they can apply their newly gained understandings, knowledge, and skills to new situations. Assessments can include the usual quizzes, examinations, and papers. Other assessment techniques will need to involve applications, interpretations, and creative work products. Creative assessment techniques may include student performances, preparing original designs, completing projects using various art media, keeping journals, constructing original models, designing presentations, planning and conducting original experiments, and so on.

Observations of students can help to assess dispositions goals, such as their ability to work together, share materials, use equipment properly, and assess their own work realistically. Students' products can become part of individual portfolios that include both completed work and work that is in progress. OpenSchool ePortfolio, a free iOS app from Apple's iTunes, allows teachers to create and assign student projects; take pictures, video, and audio recordings of student work and upload them right to a student's ePortfolio; and use the built-in rubric maker to view Common Core State Standards as well as other standards that are pre-leveled to facilitate authentic assessment (Henson, 2015, p. 75). A similar app, Desire2Learn ePortfolio, is available for Android users from GoogleApps. Wikispaces for Education and Weebly offer ePortfolio website-based platforms for all users.

It is important to specify in the assessment plan how the unit goals, essential questions, and learning standards will be addressed. The example below is part of an assessment plan from the communities unit plan.

EXAMPLE

The essential questions and related local community questions of the unit will be divided among the students for individual research and preparation of written reports of findings. Four groups will be formed for students who have researched the same essential and the related local community questions. Students in each group will share their individual findings, and each group will prepare a presentation for the class summarizing those findings. Rubrics will be prepared to assess the individual written reports and group presentations.

Lessons and activities will be conducted to help students with their individual research, note-taking, and written reports, to gain and demonstrate through art and constructions additional information about their community, including its settlement, development, history, government, and local services. Mathematics lessons will include written problems related to the community study. A unit examination will be administered to test vocabulary and terms related to the study; notes students record following group presentations; and concepts from lessons and activities provided by the teacher. Observation will be used to assess the students' research-skills development and ability to work together and share materials. The written reports, group presentations, examination, and observations will assist in the assessment of students' progress in meeting the learning standards, essential questions, and goals of the interdisciplinary unit.

Learning Plan

The learning plan for an interdisciplinary unit includes two parts: a *web design* and *descriptions of lessons and activities.*

The Web Design. The web design is a graphic indicating the disciplines that will be involved in the unit as well as brief descriptions of lessons and learning activities that address the standards, essential questions, and other goals of the unit. A web design can be prepared by hand or with a computer by using drawing software or drawing tools available in some word-processing programs. Software is also available that is specifically designed for web construction (e.g., the previously mentioned *Inspiration,* from Inspiration Software in Portland, Oregon).

Web designs can be charted in two ways. One approach uses a *unidirectional design pattern,* one that begins with the topic at the center of the web design. Circling the topic are the different disciplines that the unit will involve. Radiating out from each discipline are related lessons and activity ideas. Pappas, Kiefer, and Levstik (2006) and Stephens (1974) use variations of the unidirectional arrangement for their web designs. See the model for this type of design in Exhibit 3.3 and an example of a unidirectional web design for the topic *Transportation through the Ages* in Exhibit 3.4.

Exhibit 3.3 Model for a Unidirectional Web Design.

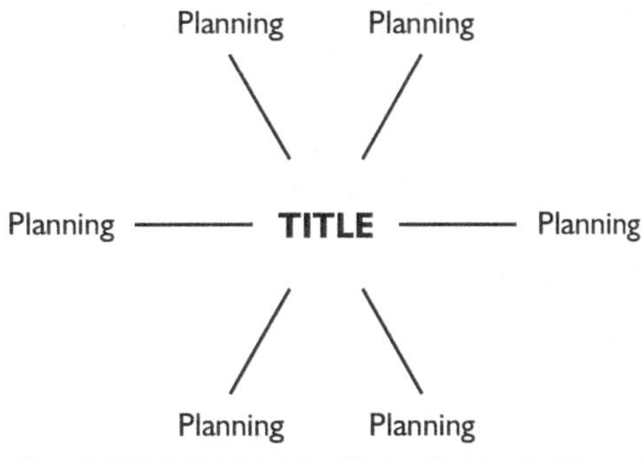

Exhibit 3.4 A Unidirectional Web Design for a Transportation Unit.

TRANSPORTATION THROUGH THE AGES

SCIENCE & TECHNOLOGY

- Air, sea, and land: Have students survey machines we use for transportation and their elementary principles of operation.
- The travelers' forecast: Learn why and how weather affects transportation.
- Prepare a lesson on how energy is used in transportation.
- Learn how animals have been used in transportation.

ECONOMICS

- Study the reasons we choose one means of transportation over another.
- Determine the most affordable way for a family of four to travel to Disney World.

ART

- Have students work in groups and produce constructions of their ultimate fantasy travel machine.
- Assemble a collage of old magazine photos with transportation themes.

LANGUAGE ARTS

- Read narratives of journeys set in different time periods.
- Write narratives using story elements based on transportation themes.

MUSIC

- Learn traditional sea chanteys.
- Listen to songs about train travel.

MATHEMATICS

- Study, through a simple graphing activity, the relationship between speed and time and distance.
- Have students conduct a statistical survey of school employee commuting times and distances, and prepare a graph of the results.

HISTORY

- Learn about Marco Polo's journey to China.
- Study why and how nomadic cultures travel.
- Study how changes in transportation affected the settlement of the West.
- Prepare a lesson on Ellis Island and the Statue of Liberty.
- From footpaths to freeways: Learn how some crowded highways began as Native American trails.

GEOGRAPHY

- Study places famous in the history of transportation, like the Golden Gate Bridge, the Continental Divide, and the Panama Canal.
- Have students predict the importance of location (e.g., if they had to choose where to put a new amusement park or build an new airport).
- Learn that the shortest distance between two points on the globe is a circle.
- Learn about different types of maps and how they are used.

ENVIRONMENTAL STUDIES

- Study how various forms of transportation can make the air and water dirty.

Courtesy of David Kennedy

Careful examination of the unidirectional design will reveal a weakness in this method from the perspective of interdisciplinary instruction. The unidirectional design fails to indicate any of the interdisciplinary relationships that exist among the various disciplines, lessons, and activities.

Adding interconnecting lines creates a branching or *multidirectional* design, one that has the appearance of a true web. Charbonneau and Reider (1995) and Jacobs (1989) use web designs that are multidirectional. Multidirectional web designs show graphically the interrelatedness of the disciplines, lessons, and activities we plan to include in a study. See Exhibit 3.5 for a model of the multidirectional web design.

Exhibit 3.5 A Model for a Multidirectional Web Design.

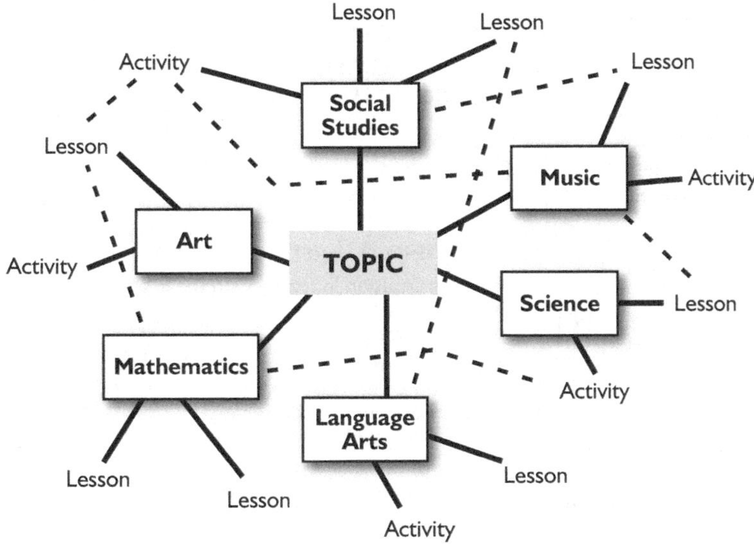

Exhibit 3.6 on the following page is an example of a web design for the topic *The U.S. Constitution*. Additional examples can be found in the appendix. Before beginning to construct the web design, it can also be helpful to prepare three lists: (a) a list of disciplines, (b) a list of interdisciplinary areas of concern, and (c) a list of instructional media, strategies, and techniques. These lists can assist us during the process of brainstorming ideas for lessons, activities, and performances that address the unit objectives and ensure unit interdisciplinarity.

At first, including abstract areas—such as political science, global issues, and future studies—in these lists for students in the primary grades may seem questionable. However, young students have a natural curiosity about people in other parts of the world and often express concern about the natural disasters, conflicts, and environmental problems they hear about. Although very young students may have some difficulty comprehending global issues, teachers can offer

Exhibit 3.6 A Multidirectional Web Design.

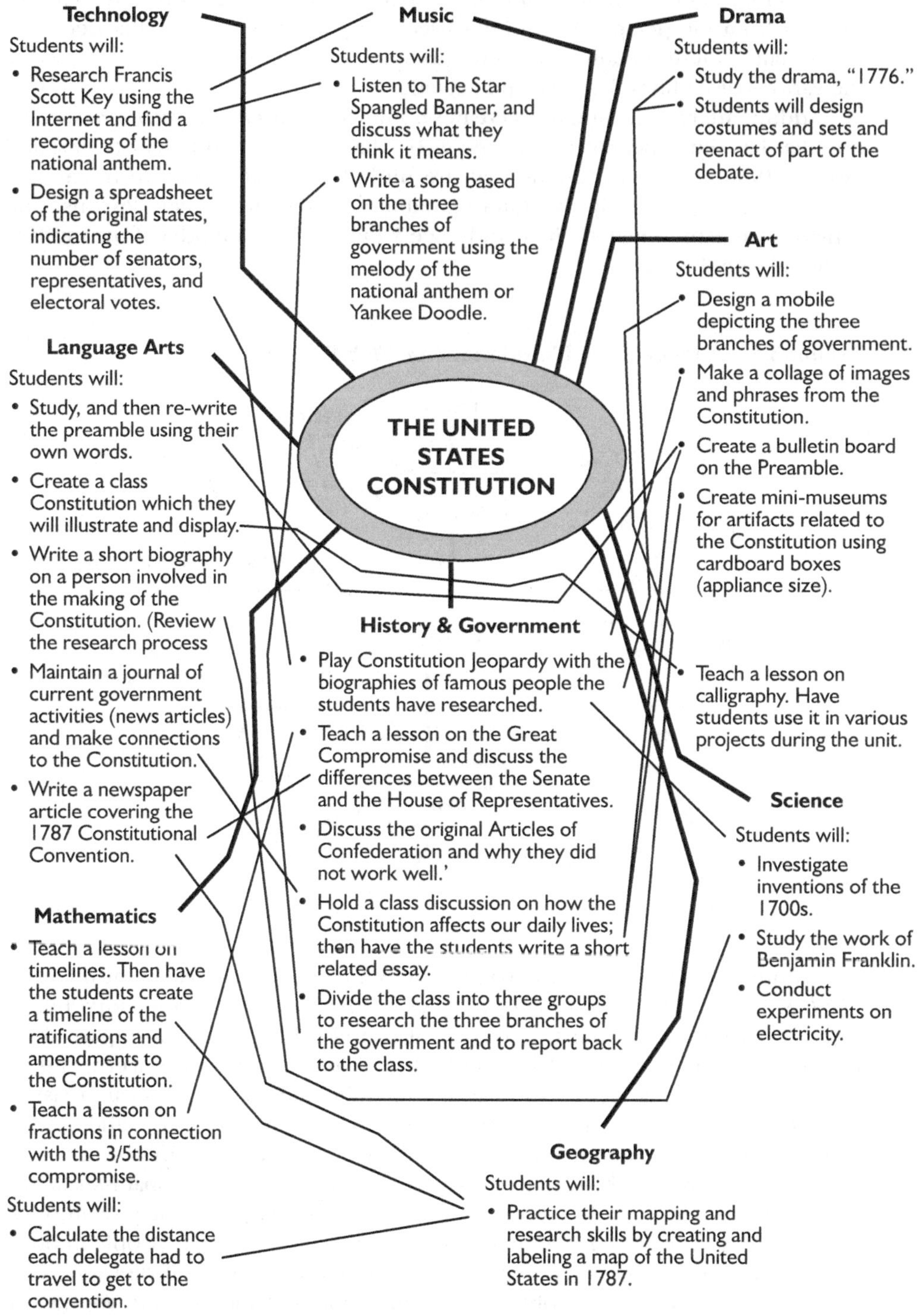

THE UNITED STATES CONSTITUTION

Technology

Students will:

- Research Francis Scott Key using the Internet and find a recording of the national anthem.
- Design a spreadsheet of the original states, indicating the number of senators, representatives, and electoral votes.

Music

Students will:

- Listen to The Star Spangled Banner, and discuss what they think it means.
- Write a song based on the three branches of government using the melody of the national anthem or Yankee Doodle.

Drama

Students will:

- Study the drama, "1776."
- Students will design costumes and sets and reenact of part of the debate.

Art

Students will:

- Design a mobile depicting the three branches of government.
- Make a collage of images and phrases from the Constitution.
- Create a bulletin board on the Preamble.
- Create mini-museums for artifacts related to the Constitution using cardboard boxes (appliance size).
- Teach a lesson on calligraphy. Have students use it in various projects during the unit.

Language Arts

Students will:

- Study, and then re-write the preamble using their own words.
- Create a class Constitution which they will illustrate and display.
- Write a short biography on a person involved in the making of the Constitution. (Review the research process
- Maintain a journal of current government activities (news articles) and make connections to the Constitution.
- Write a newspaper article covering the 1787 Constitutional Convention.

History & Government

- Play Constitution Jeopardy with the biographies of famous people the students have researched.
- Teach a lesson on the Great Compromise and discuss the differences between the Senate and the House of Representatives.
- Discuss the original Articles of Confederation and why they did not work well.'
- Hold a class discussion on how the Constitution affects our daily lives; then have the students write a short related essay.
- Divide the class into three groups to research the three branches of the government and to report back to the class.

Science

Students will:

- Investigate inventions of the 1700s.
- Study the work of Benjamin Franklin.
- Conduct experiments on electricity.

Mathematics

- Teach a lesson on timelines. Then have the students create a timeline of the ratifications and amendments to the Constitution.
- Teach a lesson on fractions in connection with the 3/5ths compromise.

Students will:

- Calculate the distance each delegate had to travel to get to the convention.

Geography

Students will:

- Practice their mapping and research skills by creating and labeling a map of the United States in 1787.

Courtesy of Virginia Mullis and Lori Oliver

explanations and be willing to discuss these issues, using terms that the students can understand. These explanations may help allay the fears that young children sometimes develop about world problems. An example of possible categories is shown in Exhibit 3.7.

Exhibit 3.7 A List of Disciplines, General Areas of Concern, Media, Teaching Strategies, and Techniques.

Aids to Brainstorming		
Disciplines	**Concerns**	**Media, Strategies, and Techniques**
Anthropology	career education	art projects
Economics	citizenship	audio recordings
Geography	civics	charts and graphs
History	consumerism	computer programs/software
English/Language arts	current events	constructions
listening	ecology	demonstrations
reading	family living	dioramas
speaking	future studies	experiments
writing	global studies	field trips
Mathematics	health	films/videos
Performing Arts	human behavior	DVDs/CDs
dance	human rights	group discussions
drama	Internet	Internet resources
music	learning styles	interviews
Psychology	political science	multimedia
Science	multicultural studies	murals
Sociology	space exploration	presentations
Technology	substance abuse	reports
Visual arts	values clarification	research
		skills lessons
		surveys
		timelines

In the primary grades, students also enjoy thinking about both the past and the future. Except for immediate events, history is in the past, which sometimes makes it a difficult subject for the very young to fully comprehend. Nevertheless, early childhood units can include aspects of history. Today, we know that by selecting a variety of materials—not only textbooks, but also visuals, manipulative materials, models, and so on—as well as providing opportunities for students to use a variety of media and their individual working styles, it is often possible to help them master concepts once thought to be beyond their understanding.

In these early grades, students can usually relate better to historical events and concepts when they are discussed by using terms such as *long ago* and *a long time before we were born*. Young students can relate personally to these terms because they have special meaning for them. The concept of *future* can also be problematic for young minds. Still, young students are naturally interested in what the future will be like for them; they can and should be encouraged to think about it. Both the past and the future become more meaningful when students use learning aids, such as timelines, to plot historical events. Timelines can easily include each student's birth date as a meaningful personal reference point for the historical events that are studied.

Some disciplines and interdisciplinary areas overlap or include similar material. For example, human relations and conduct are components of psychology, sociology, and anthropology. Human relations and values clarification issues are both included in multicultural studies. Other categories or items can be added to the lists in Exhibit 3.7 to reflect new areas, special interests, and concerns.

The web design is a simple drawing that shows at a glance what the unit includes. It also serves as a reminder when more detailed descriptions of each lesson or activity are prepared for the unit learning plan. Later, complete lesson plans can be written for the ideas that are actually needed when the unit is taught. The start of a web design for the community study unit is shown in Exhibit 3.8. It includes only a few ideas that have been charted as the brainstorming step begins in planning the unit.

In the design, the main topic is centered, with several possible disciplines surrounding it. Because we are just beginning to plan, only a few activities are listed in the web, including several ideas in social studies and one related to English/language arts. So far, we have planned to

- introduce the unit and its essential questions to the students;
- elicit from the students questions about the local community related to the essential questions; and
- assign students with the tasks of researching the questions, conducting a review of the research process, note taking; and documentation of sources.

A resource center will be developed with some materials for the students to consult.

Exhibit 3.8 Initial Step in the Design of an Interdisciplinary Unit.

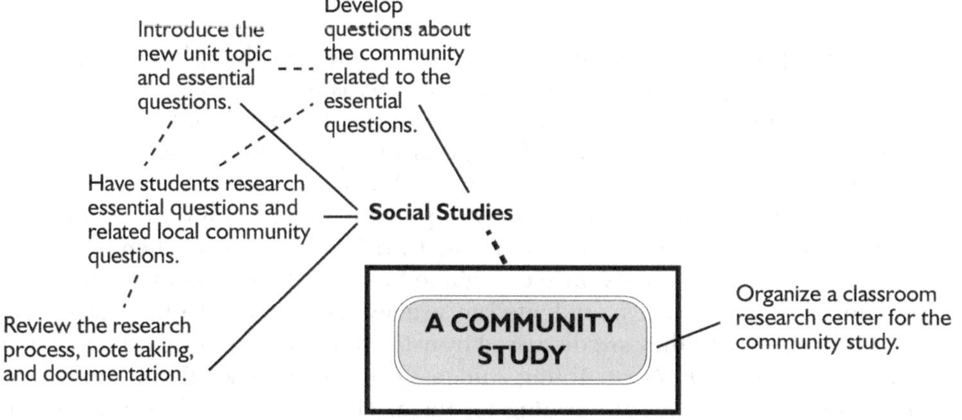
Introduce the new unit topic and essential questions.
Develop questions about the community related to the essential questions.
Have students research essential questions and related local community questions.
Review the research process, note taking, and documentation.
Social Studies
A COMMUNITY STUDY
Organize a classroom research center for the community study.

The brainstorming step and construction of the web design help to provide an idea bank and overview of ideas the teacher has in mind when planning the initial unit. As the Community Study web continues to grow, additional ideas are charted. Interconnecting lines are added to indicate some of the interdisciplinary relationships among the various lessons and activities. As indicated in Exhibit 3.9, additions (boxes with broken lines) to the original web design indicate that the students will be required to prepare written reports of their research on essential and related local community questions: they will work in groups to summarize their findings to those questions, present their summaries to the class, and complete a project related to their questions. Among other possibilities, project options can include

Exhibit 3.9 Additions to the Initial Design for an Interdisciplinary Unit.

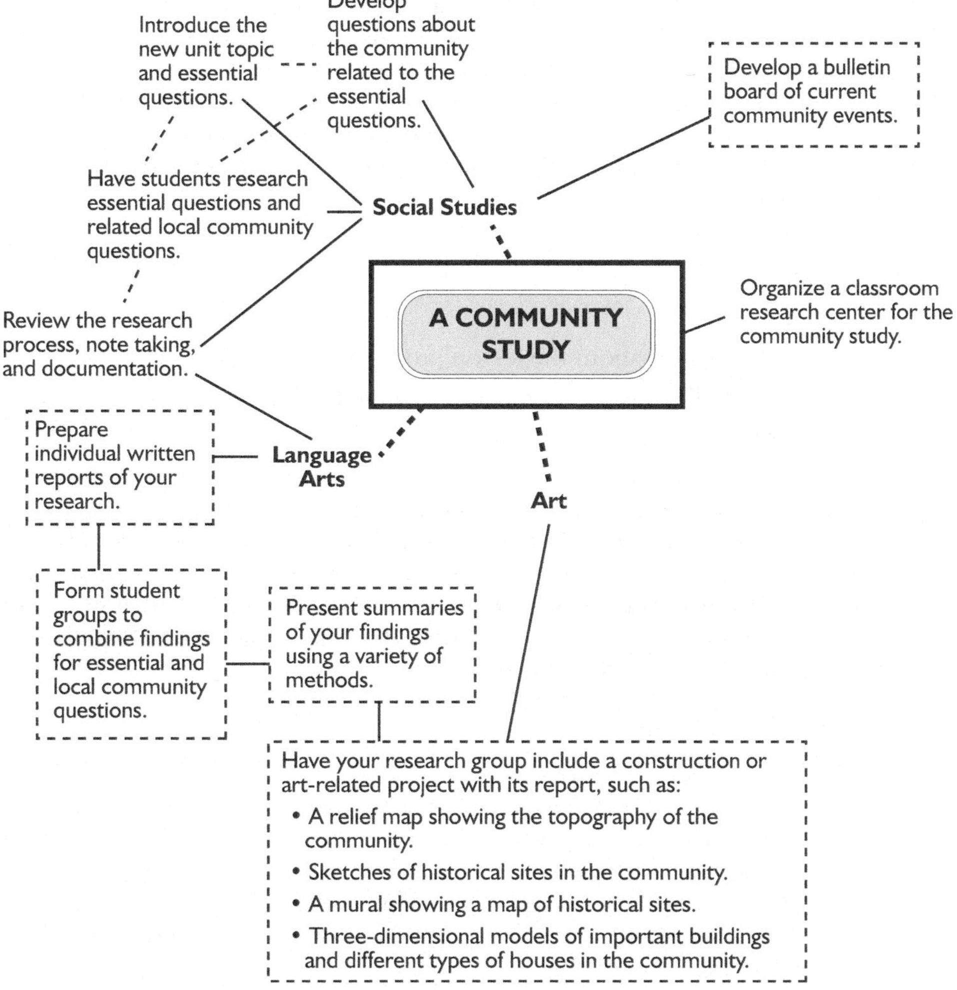

Introduce the new unit topic and essential questions.
Develop questions about the community related to the essential questions.
Develop a bulletin board of current community events.
Have students research essential questions and related local community questions.
Social Studies
A COMMUNITY STUDY
Organize a classroom research center for the community study.
Review the research process, note taking, and documentation.
Prepare individual written reports of your research.
Language Arts
Art
Form student groups to combine findings for essential and local community questions.
Present summaries of your findings using a variety of methods.
Have your research group include a construction or art-related project with its report, such as:
• A relief map showing the topography of the community.
• Sketches of historical sites in the community.
• A mural showing a map of historical sites.
• Three-dimensional models of important buildings and different types of houses in the community.

PowerPoint presentations, digital portfolios, and videos of panel discussions and dramatizations. Students can upload their projects on class websites or those they create themselves for sharing with parents. A bulletin board will be reserved for a display of community current events that occur during the study.

Descriptions of Lessons and Activities

The lesson and activity ideas shown in the web design are stated in such a succinct manner that, later, it may be difficult to remember exactly what we initially had in mind; the sequence for teaching the various items in the web is also not clear. Therefore, in this section of the unit plan each idea is expanded upon in the sequence that is thought to be most logical. Whereas the web design is an overall view or schematic of the unit and its interdisciplinary connections, the descriptions provide more details that will be included later on when the complete lesson or activity plan is designed. Each description explains the idea of the lesson or activity, usually in only a sentence or two, and some information about how it may proceed when taught. All descriptions are then placed in the sequence estimated for teaching during the period of the study.

The standards, goals, and assessments will be stated in the complete lesson plans that will need to be designed later before the lesson is taught. Teachers who would like to include additional information in the descriptions might consider adding some or all of the following items:

- Learning standard(s)
- Goal(s)
- Key question(s)
- Additional details about the lesson procedure
- Multiple intelligence areas addressed in the lesson
- Assessment plan

It is likely that most teachers will select the brief method, which avoids having to prepare lengthy descriptions of lessons that they may eventually decide not to include as the unit proceeds. Below are unit-plan examples for each of the two methods for writing a lesson or activity description and a description of an optional classroom research center for the community unit. (Note that in order to avoid repeating the words *lessons* and *activities,* the descriptions following the example below refer to both as lessons.)

EXAMPLES

Two **Brief** Descriptions in Sequence

- Introduce the unit and four essential questions to students. Help students generate additional questions of their own.
- Follow the K-W-L protocol to involve students in raising questions about their local community related to each of the unit's essential questions. Explain that the questions will be divided among the students for individual research after a review of the process they will be following.

A **Detailed** Description

The first lesson will introduce the community study unit and prepare the students for their study. The key question for this initial lesson is: What do we already know about communities? To begin the lesson, students will be asked what they have learned about communities from their previous studies in the second and third grades. The information they provide about communities will be recorded (on the blackboard or interactive white board) and later transferred to charts that will be on display during the study.

Next, students will be asked if they have any questions they would like to include in addition to the essential questions. Those questions will also be added to the list of essential questions; both will be displayed throughout the study. This introductory lesson addresses aspects of the following learning standards: Conduct short research projects that build knowledge about a topic (*CCSS, W.3.7*) and engage effectively in a range of collaborative discussions (one-on-one, in groups, and teacher-led) with diverse partners on third-grade topics and texts, building on others' ideas and expressing their own clearly (*CCSS, SL.3.1*).

Because the lesson involves a discussion, it will mainly involve students' linguistic intelligence. The lesson will be assessed primarily through teacher observation during the discussion of the essential questions to determine students' understanding of the intent of the questions and the goals of the study.

Additional lesson and activity ideas are included in the completed web design. See Exhibit 3.12 for the completed web design for the community study unit plan at the end of this chapter.

Optionally, in addition to lessons and activities, a classroom research center can be set up for a unit with a selection of reference materials for the students to use, or a typical, more conventional learning center that teachers have used for many years to provide students with independent work that extends practice with the concepts students are studying during the unit. Activities in the center need to address the unit's goals, and once the center activities have been introduced by the teacher, they should be capable of completion by students with minimal or no additional help. Depending on the actual activities included, learning centers can enable experiences that are stimulating and involve most of students' multiple intelligences.

In summary, lesson and activity descriptions add to the basic information provided in the unit web design, and they help to facilitate the preparation of complete plans for those ideas that are actually used while teaching the unit. (Review Exhibit 3.10, Planning for Field Trips, on p. 62 and Exhibit 3.11, Descriptions of Learning Centers and Classroom Research Centers, on pp. 62–63 for additional information about planning for those activities.)

Unit Materials

List major materials needed for the unit in this section of the unit plan. The list should include materials to be used with and by students and the *types* of texts, trade books, and other materials that will suffice until the unit is first taught.

Exhibit 3.10 Planning for Field Trips.

A field trip activity will take more than one class session. Before designing an introductory lesson plan for the unit plan on spring, the following three-phase procedure is recommended.

A logical organization for a field trip is similar to the process followed in any research activity. It involves three phases—planning (preparation for the trip), researching (the field excursion), and reporting (a follow-up session to review what has been learned). The three phases are explained below.

Before taking a field trip, students plan their excursion with guidance from their teacher. Questions about what students would like to learn at the field site are elicited from students and recorded for reference during the trip. Teachers may want to add other questions that they feel are important. Each student should have a copy of the questions raised during the discussion to take along on the field trip. Permission slips are distributed with instructions for returning them before the day of the trip. Several parents are usually invited to assist on the day of the trip.

On the day of the field trip, students attempt to gain answers to their questions and to learn other related information while at the field site. They use their lists of questions at the site and note answers to their questions.

Finally, when students return to their classroom, they discuss and record what they gained from the trip. This discussion is guided by the initial questions that were raised. Some questions may not have been answered; other information that was not planned for can be included during the discussion. The teacher then assists the students in summarizing what they learned from their field trip. This summary may take the form of an outline that students then copy for their records.

Exhibit 3.11 Descriptions of Learning Centers and Classroom Research Centers.

The designation *learning center* can connote diverse meanings to different teachers. In contrast to classroom research centers (described below), many learning centers do not involve research, relate to a specific interdisciplinary unit topic, or provide a supply of research materials. Following direct instruction, typical *learning centers* are planned to give students additional practice with skills they have recently been taught; others may be intended to stimulate creative work with activities, such as creative writing. These learning centers can be developed using a simple bulletin-board display with pockets. The pockets hold cards with written directions for the tasks or problem-solving activities for students to work on independently. Students can select a task card to take with them, to complete when they have time during another part of the school day.

Some early childhood teachers prepare several *centers* in the classroom with a variety of learning activities and materials as part of the regular curriculum. Typically, there may be four centers; the students are separated into several groups that then rotate, taking turns in each of the centers under supervision of the teacher or an assistant.

Classroom Research Centers

Classroom research centers differ from other types of learning centers. They are usually included in the design of an interdisciplinary unit to provide students with a collection of resources that are available on the unit topic. Students make use of the center as they pursue answers to the unit essential questions and other questions of their study. The resource materials in the center are initially selected and arranged by the teacher to be at different reading levels and to permit all or most students to use them with minimal assistance. This type of center does not replace instruction or teach the research skills students need to make use of the materials that are included, but using the materials does provide additional practice with those skills the students have already learned and are capable of using independently.

Because a classroom research center is primarily for student research, it usually includes a variety of textbooks in social studies and science, trade books, magazines, and other materials having information on the unit topic. Materials and equipment may include computers/computer software and materials on an interactive whiteboard including videos, PowerPoint presentations, charts and diagrams; science equipment; art supplies; and picture collections. The center is initially set up by the teacher; later, students can add other items that they find useful from the school media center, library, or elsewhere as they explore the unit topic. Classroom research centers can also include some creative activities. If so, supplies needed for projects and artwork should be included in the center.

Ideally, a classroom research center is set up in a designated part of the classroom where tables and shelves can house the center materials. Space may be provided for students to work at the center, or they can be directed to take the materials from the center to their seats or another part of the room or even to the school's computer lab. The specific form used for a classroom research center depends on available classroom space. If space is limited, classroom research-center resources can be displayed on a shelf under the windows or in another convenient area.

Developing a classroom research center requires a considerable amount of planning and preparation. Following are several important steps to help ensure its effectiveness:

- Provide a sign that clearly defines the center and includes any specific rules that students will need to use it effectively.
- Determine and locate the research materials to be included for students. The materials will be based on the goals and essential questions of the unit.
- If creative activities are also included in the research center, task cards should be prepared for the activities, which students either elect or are required to complete. *Task cards* provide specific directions needed to complete an activity. The sample task card shown below has directions for a group of fourth-grade students who are studying an interdisciplinary unit on deserts in the United States.

Desert Collage

In this activity, you will make a collage to show what you have learned from watching a video on the Mojave Desert.

Directions:

1. Use a computer to watch the video, *The Mojave Desert.* (At the time of this writing, several desert videos were located at: https://search.yahoo.com/yhs/search?type=avastbcl&hspart=avast&hsimp=yhs-001&p=video+on+mojave+desert)
2. Using materials from our scrap box, prepare a collage that shows something specific you feel you have learned about the desert from watching the video.
3. Take a sheet of construction paper from the supply section in the center. Write your name on the back of the paper. Paste, glue, tape, and other supplies for your work are kept in our supply closet. Take paint and paint brushes if you would like to use them.
4. Be prepared to explain your collage and what it shows during one of our regular "forums" at the end of each day this week.

- Develop a record-keeping device for assessing students' use of the center activities and for monitoring their participation.
- Decide how to introduce the classroom research center to the class. A thorough introduction can clarify routines and guidelines for using the center resources and help to deter problems that can arise later on.

Most of the usual art supplies and other consumable materials need not be included. Examples from the communities plan are:

- A collection of reference materials—books, magazines, newspapers—for students' use during their research.
- Social studies texts provided by the school system.
- Computer software, multimedia presentations, and informational programs on DVD and other media.

Resources

When the unit is first taught, and each time the unit is retaught, up-to-date materials can be added to this section, which lists *specific* resources that provide background for the teacher. Include specific book titles and publishing information, addresses of current Internet sources (URLs), and specific software/DVD titles. The names of people who have been helpful as consultants or guest speakers can also be included. Some resources rapidly become outdated (particularly URLs), and new ones may become available each time the unit is taught.

Summary

Preparation of the various sections of the interdisciplinary unit plan as explained and illustrated above will generate all the information needed to write an *initial* unit plan. The *initial* interdisciplinary unit plans for a fourth-grade study of communities and a second-grade unit on spring are presented below. The format of both plans follows the outline in Exhibit 3.1.

In order to begin teaching *any* unit, a plan for the lesson that will be used to introduce it will need to be prepared. The design of the first lesson or activity is a key factor in determining the success of any interdisciplinary unit. Before beginning to plan the lesson, we will again need to consider the students' background knowledge, academic skill levels, and developmental characteristics as well as the social makeup of the class. The purpose of any introductory lesson is to inform students of the unit topic, attempt to engage their interest, and elicit their input for the new study. General principles of teaching and learning can help to guide the lesson design. Three especially important principles are listed below:

- To be adapted, new information must build on the students' existing knowledge base.
- Students need to construct their own knowledge, using their different cognitive strengths, through direct experiences whenever possible and through opportunities to interact with adults and competent peers.
- Motivation is stronger if unit activities and lessons capitalize on the students' interests, working styles, and learning styles.

Usually, one of the lessons indicated in the web design is further developed to introduce the new unit. The introductory lesson for the spring unit (Example 2 on pp. 70–78) involves introducing the unit topic and the essential questions of the study, and inviting the students to suggest other related questions. The complete plan for that introductory lesson is included in chapter 5 (on pp. 133–136); it is the sample lesson used to illustrate the K-W-L protocol.

The two initial interdisciplinary unit plan examples are included below for illustrative purposes. The sequence represents only one possible way to proceed in teaching each of the two units. The first example is an initial interdisciplinary unit plan for fourth grade on the topic, *A Community Study*. The second example, of an initial unit plan on spring, is a unit designed for a second grade. (Note that the shorter method for writing lesson descriptions is used in both examples.)

Two Examples of an Interdisciplinary Unit Plan

Example 1: A Community Study

Note that this topic was selected because it offers the students a number of opportunities to become involved in a research experience related to a familiar topic.

Level: Grade 4 (Although this unit is designed for students in the fourth grade, it can be adapted for third grade.)

Estimated Unit Length: 3–5 weeks

Common Core State Standards

Students will:

- Describe the overall structure (e.g., chronology comparison, cause/effect, problem/solution) of events, ideas, concepts, or information in a text or part of a text. (*RI.4.5*)
- Write informative/explanatory texts to examine a topic and convey ideas and information clearly. (*W.4.2*)
- Conduct short research projects that build knowledge through investigation of different aspects of a topic. (*W.4.7*)
- Paraphrase portions of a text read aloud or information presented in diverse media and formats, including visually, quantitatively, and orally. (*SL.4.2*)
- Report on a topic or text, tell a story, or recount an experience in an organized manner, using appropriate facts and relevant, descriptive details to support main ideas or themes; speak clearly at an understandable pace. (*SL.4.4*)
- Use the four operations to solve word problems involving distances, intervals of time, liquid volumes, masses of objects, and money, including problems involving simple fractions or decimals and problems that require expressing measurements given in a larger unit in terms of a smaller unit. Represent measurement quantities using diagrams such as number line diagrams that feature a measurement scale. (*MD.4.2*)

New York State Standards

Students will:

- Use a variety of intellectual skills to demonstrate their understanding of major ideas, eras, themes, developments, and turning points in the history of the United States and New York. (*New York State Learning Standard for Social Studies 1*)

Goals

Students will understand that:

- Communities are social units organized and shared by people who may be from various cultural, ethnic, and religious backgrounds.
- The physical environment and geographic location of a community influence its location, development, size, and the lives of people living within it.
- Being a good citizen of a community carries responsibilities, such as voting, participation in community affairs, and so on.
- People rely on governmental structures and public services in a community to maintain order and preserve democracy for its citizens.

Students will know:

- Key terms and concepts related to the community study, such as *democracy* and *citizenship*.
- Facts about the settlement, development, and historic foundations of their local community.
- Responsibilities of the citizens living in their community, such as voting.
- The purposes, structure, and functions of the services and government in their community.
- Holidays and celebrations observed in their community.

Students will further develop their skills for:

- Planning for investigations.
- Conducting research projects, developing reports, and presenting findings of investigations.
- Constructing, reading, and using local maps.

Students will demonstrate:

- Behavior that is respectful and cooperative when working in groups.
- Willingness to cooperate and share in decision making and the use of materials.

Essential Questions

The following questions form the basis of the community study:

- What is a community? Why would people want to live in our community?
- How does the place where people live affect their lives? How does living in our community influence our lives?
- What does it mean to be a good citizen? What does it mean to be a good citizen in our community?
- Is government necessary? Is government necessary in our community?

Assessment Plan

The essential questions and related local community questions of the unit will be divided among the students for individual research and preparation of written reports of findings. Four groups will be formed for students who research the same essential and related local community questions. Students in each group will share their individual findings, and each group will prepare a presentation for the class summarizing those findings. Rubrics will be prepared to assess the individual written reports and group presentations.

Lessons and activities will be conducted to help students with their individual research, note taking, and written reports, as well as assisting student in gaining and demonstrating through art and constructions additional information about their community, including its settlement, development, history, government, and local services. Mathematics lessons will include written problems related to the community study. A unit examination will be administered to test vocabulary and terms related to the study; what students have learned from the notes they have taken during group presentations; and the understanding of concepts from lessons and activities provided by the teacher.

Observation will be used to assess the students' research-skills development and their ability to work together and share materials. The written reports, group presentations, examination, and observations will assist in the assessment of students' progress in meeting the learning standards, answering the essential questions, and other goals of the interdisciplinary unit.

Learning Plan

Exhibit 3.12 Completed Web Design for an Interdisciplinary Unit.

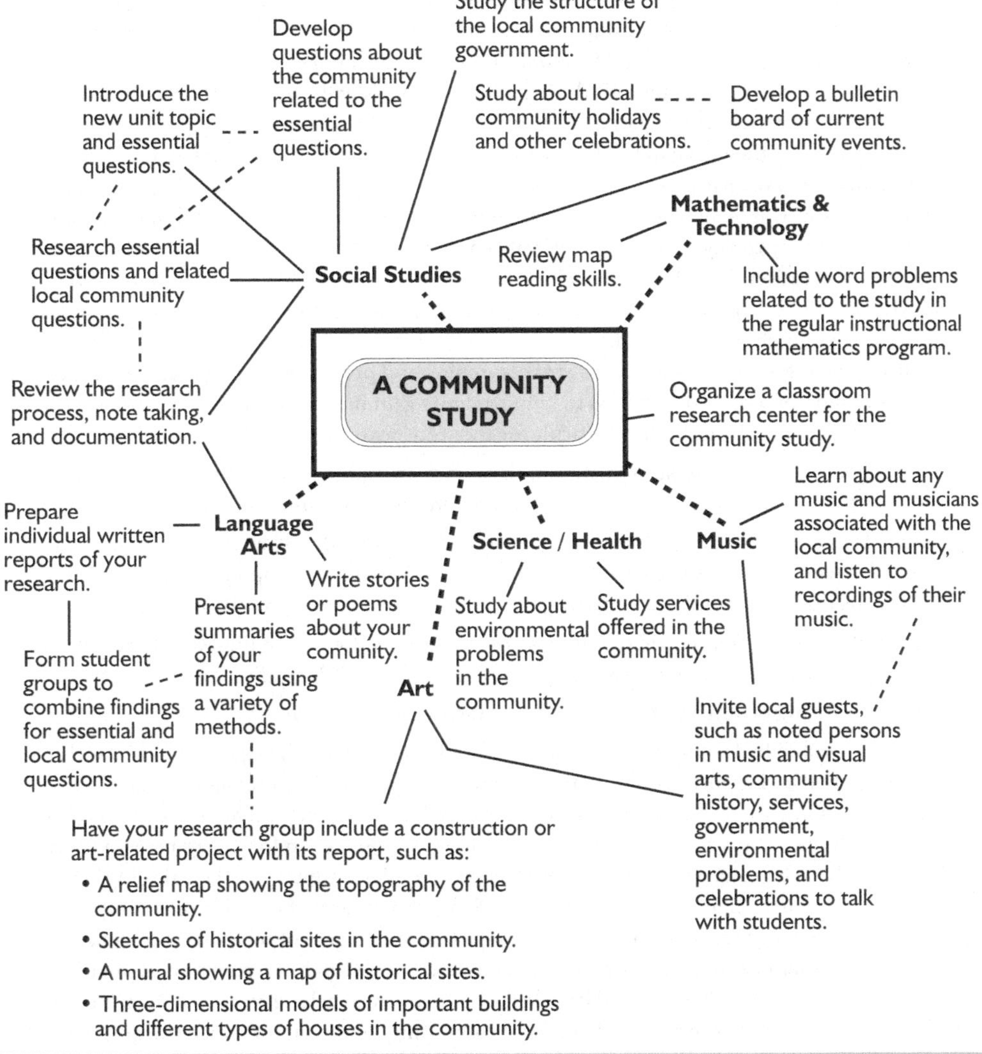
A COMMUNITY STUDY
Social Studies
Introduce the new unit topic and essential questions.
Develop questions about the community related to the essential questions.
Study the structure of the local community government.
Study about local community holidays and other celebrations.
Develop a bulletin board of current community events.
Research essential questions and related local community questions.
Review the research process, note taking, and documentation.
Mathematics & Technology
Review map reading skills.
Include word problems related to the study in the regular instructional mathematics program.
Organize a classroom research center for the community study.
Language Arts
Prepare individual written reports of your research.
Form student groups to combine findings for essential and local community questions.
Present summaries of your findings using a variety of methods.
Write stories or poems about your comunity.
Science / Health
Study about environmental problems in the community.
Study services offered in the community.
Music
Learn about any music and musicians associated with the local community, and listen to recordings of their music.
Invite local guests, such as noted persons in music and visual arts, community history, services, government, environmental problems, and celebrations to talk with students.
Art
Have your research group include a construction or art-related project with its report, such as:
• A relief map showing the topography of the community.
• Sketches of historical sites in the community.
• A mural showing a map of historical sites.
• Three-dimensional models of important buildings and different types of houses in the community.

Descriptions of Lessons and Activities

Introduce the unit and the four essential questions to students.

Follow the K-W-L protocol to involve students in raising questions about their local community related to each of the unit's essential questions. Explain that the questions will be divided among the students for individual research after a review of the process they will be following.

Before assigning students the questions they will be asked to research, teach one or more lessons to review the research process, note taking, and documentation of sources. (If this is the first time students are completing individual research on a topic, more than a single session will be needed to demonstrate and practice how to plan for their research and ways to search for information. Students who have previously completed individual research on topics may only need a brief review of the process.)

Divide the four essential questions of the study, along with their related local community questions, among the students for individual research. Several students will be assigned to research each pair of questions and to prepare individual written reports of their findings. Provide students with a target date to submit their written reports.

Schedule several research periods during which students will complete their individual research. During each session, monitor the group work and assist students where needed with any problems they have in locating sources and information on the Internet and in print. Continue to help students learn more about recording the information they are finding. (Students at this level who have not had previous experience with note taking may initially be asked only to develop a simple list of sentences with the information they locate. Basic documentation should minimally include the author, title, and reference source—the publisher or URL for Internet sources, and so on. During subsequent unit work, other documentation details should be added.)

During the interval, while students are researching and preparing their individual reports, devote time for lessons and activities to help students gain information about their local community that may be especially difficult for them to locate. Possible lessons include:

- Inviting local residents to speak with the class on such topics as community history, government, famous residents, and services offered in the community.
- Guided readings; listening activities (e.g., reading to students); reviewing photographs; and guided viewing of any available video sources on the history, development, governmental structure, environmental problems, important holidays, and community celebrations.
- As a part of the regular instructional program in mathematics, including word problems on themes related to the community study where they might fit logically.
- Creative writing of stories or poetry about living in their community.

After the individual reports have been completed and submitted, organize students who have researched and reported on the same essential and local community questions into four groups to combine their individual findings. Have each group select a chair and recorder. Provide time for the groups to summarize their findings in preparation for a class presentation.

Meet with each group after the students have prepared a summary of their findings in order to help them decide how they will report. Suggest a variety of possible reporting methods for the presentations, encouraging the groups to use a variety of methods, such as video, PowerPoint presentation, panel discussion, demonstration, mural, construction, dramatization, and so on. Also, each group will be asked to prepare and include as part of its presentation a project related to the essential and local community question for which the group is responsible. Possible projects may include:

- Construction of important historic sites, monuments, or buildings in the community. Students may create drawings, dioramas, or murals.
- A street map or topographical relief map of the community.
- Some other art-related project.

Provide time for the four groups to prepare their presentations, assisting where needed.

Schedule the group presentations. Have each group present its summary presentation and project in response to the essential and related community question the group members have researched. (Group reports will be assessed with a rubric.) After each group presentation, the class will be asked for the most important information presented. Their responses will be recorded on a chart or board, and all students will be asked to copy the information into their notebooks. (This information will form part of the content to be tested by the unit examination.)

Throughout the study, have a local newspaper available in the classroom for students to search for current events or other items about their community. Encourage students to contribute any articles they locate for a bulletin board display. Hold a brief discussion each day of any new articles posted.

Hold a summary and review session during which students will also be asked to write individual reactions to the community study unit. Reaction papers will be collected, summarized by the teacher, and presented to the class before the unit examination.

Administer the unit examination.

Materials

- Social studies texts provided by the school system.
- Copies of other publishers' social studies texts that include pertinent community information.
- Current literature for children that provides information on community living. (The books and other print materials are likely to vary each time the unit is taught.)
- Access to computers for Internet searches.
- Up-to-date maps of the local community.
- A collection of reference materials—books, magazines, newspapers—for students' use during their research (see below).

Resources

Berry, J. (2013). *Every kid's guide to laws that relate to kids in the community—A living skills book.* Wheaton, IL: Watkins.

Chicola, N. (2002). *Creating caring communities with books kids love.* Golden, CO: Fulcrum.

Pollack, B. (2004). *Our community garden.* Hillsboro, OR: Aladdin/Beyond Words.

Roberts, P. (2002). *Kids taking action: Community service learning projects, K–8.* Turner Falls, MA: Northeast Foundation for Children, Inc.

Sterling, K. (2007). *Living in rural communities.* Minneapolis, MN: Lerner Classroom.

Sterling, K. (2007). *Living in suburban communities.* Minneapolis, MN: Lerner Classroom,.

Sterling, K. (2007). *Living in urban communities.* Minneapolis, MN: Lerner Classroom.

Example 2: The Spring Season

Other Possible Titles: The Season of Spring, Signs of Spring, Spring Is Here, Changes in the Spring

Note that this topic was selected because it offers young students a number of opportunities to have direct experiences related to the concept and the process of "change," an important concept in both social studies and science.

Level: Grades 2–3 (Although this unit is designed for students in the second grade, it can also be adapted for students in other grades.)

Estimated Unit Length: 3–4 weeks

Common Core State Standards

Students will:

- Ask and answer such questions as who, what, where, when, why, and how in order to demonstrate understanding of key details in a text. (*RI.2.1*)
- Participate in collaborative conversations with diverse partners about second-grade topics and texts with peers and adults in small and larger groups. (*SL.2.1*)
- Follow agreed-upon rules for discussions (e.g., gaining the floor in respectful ways, listening to others with care, speaking one at a time about the topics and texts under discussion). (*SL.2.1a*)
- Tell a story or recount an experience with appropriate facts and relevant, descriptive details, speaking audibly in coherent sentences. (*SL.2.4*)
- Write informative/explanatory texts in which they introduce a topic, use facts and definitions to develop points, and provide a concluding statement or section. (*W.2.2*)
- Write narratives in which they recount a well-elaborated event or short sequence of events, include details to describe actions, thoughts, and feelings, use temporal words to signal event order, and provide a sense of closure. (*W.2.3*)
- Participate in shared research and writing projects (e.g., read a number of books on a single topic to produce a report; record science observations). (*W.2.7*)
- Recall information from experiences or gather information from provided sources to answer a question. (*W.2.8*)
- Create and present a poem, narrative, play, art work, or personal response to a particular author or theme studied in class, with support as needed. (*W.2.11*)
- Measure the length of an object by selecting and using appropriate tools such as rulers, yardsticks, meter sticks, and measuring tapes. (*MD.2.1*)
- Use addition and subtraction within 100 to solve one- and two-step word problems involving situations of adding to, taking from, putting together, taking apart, and comparing, with unknowns in all positions (e.g., by using drawings and equations with a symbol for the unknown number to represent the problem and measurement and data). (*OA.2.1*)
- Draw a picture graph and a bar graph (with single-unit scale) to represent a data set with up to four categories. (*MD.2.10*)
- Solve a simple put-together, take-apart, and compare problems using information presented in a bar graph. (*MD.2.10*)

District and State Standards

(Note that standards in this group represent possible standards developed by a local school district.)

Students will:

- Use the scientific approach to inquire about materials in order to discover their various properties.
- Gain an understanding about the changes that occur in their environment.
- Participate in the celebration of spring through creative writing and the performing and visual arts.
- Use various forms of measurement to denote changes in their environment.

Goals

Students will understand that:

- Seasonal changes are signaled by changes in the earth's environment.
- All living things have distinctive characteristics that distinguish them from one another.
- Living things need sunlight, nutrients, air, water, and shelter in order to survive and be healthy.
- Sound is produced by vibrating objects in the environment.

Students will know that:

- Scientific inquiry involves raising questions, hypothesizing about some phenomenon, investigating, organizing data collected, and reporting results to others.
- Some celebrations and holiday events, which people observe in different ways, are associated with the season of spring.
- Various phenomena, including the weather and seasonal changes, can affect people's feelings and inspire works of art, music, and literature.

Students will further develop their skills for:

- Developing plans for scientific investigations.
- Observing, collecting, and recording data about natural phenomena.
- Constructing graphs to record data.
- Using various instruments and materials needed for scientific investigations.
- Creating art with various media.
- Designing and constructing models.
- Creating original stories and poems.
- Following the conventions of grammar, syntax, spelling, and punctuation when writing.

Students will demonstrate:

- Appropriate behavior that is respectful of others in a variety of settings.
- Willingness to share in decision making and use of materials.

Essential Questions

The following questions form the basis of the spring study:

- How will we be able to tell that seasons are changing?
- How can we tell one living thing from another?
- What do all living things need to live healthfully?
- How is sound produced?

Assessment Plan

The following activities will provide specific assessments for the unit.

Students will paint a mural from drawings they sketch while on a field trip. The individual sketches and mural will summarize signs of spring they have observed, such as new flowers, leaves beginning to grow, and so on. The sketches and mural will indicate how well the students have detected changes in their environment that signal a change of seasons.

Students will examine and prepare records of the distinctive features of different plant specimens collected during a field trip. These investigations of plants will demonstrate that the students have noticed and can express the differences in the plants they examine.

Students will plant seeds and care for them to maintain healthy plants during the period of the unit. They will study an example of a bird that is found in their area during the spring season, the Carolina wren, pass a quiz on the needs of that bird, develop designs, and construct models for a birdhouse that would attract a wren. These activities will provide evidence that the students have gained insight regarding the survival needs of living things.

During a lesson on the cause of sound, students will discover and explain that sound is caused by a vibrating object by observing that each of several objects and instruments vibrate when they are made to produce sounds. The students will also listen to and identify sounds of nature that are typical in their local environment during the spring season. These activities will provide evidence that students know that sound is caused by vibrating objects and that they can use the differences they hear to distinguish different sounds in their environment.

The students will perform experiments on plants and study water samples taken from various locations in their local neighborhood. Students will prepare graphs of temperature changes and maintain records of precipitation during the period of the unit. The students' questions, experiments, and record keeping will indicate that they have gained insights about how to investigate a topic or problem.

After studying holidays that are celebrated in their community during the spring season, students will prepare a display of current events that reflect any of the holiday celebrations. The students will look for pictures and articles in their local newspaper to include, and they will help to arrange the display, which will show their ability to associate the spring season with special holiday celebrations.

Students will listen to stories, poems, and music having a spring theme. They will write their own stories or poems and prepare drawings that represent their reactions and thinking about the season of spring, and they will participate in a movement activity accompanied by music having spring as the theme. The listening lessons, creative writing, and art will help to indicate students' understanding that the spring season affects people, their literature, and art as well as their writing skills development.

Students will be observed for their interest, participation, listening skills, their general behavior, cooperation, and sharing of materials, and their accuracy in conducting experiments.

The teacher will maintain anecdotal records of observations about each student's general work habits, working and learning style preferences, cooperation when working with others, and ability to learn through experiential activities. Their creative writing and journals will help provide assessments of their English/language arts skills. Include observations of activities and lessons that appear to be most helpful in developing the unit objectives. Also, note the need for revisions in the unit plan—areas that need to be strengthened and additional activities that may be offered to meet students' individual learning styles.

Administer an examination at the conclusion of the unit to assess facts, concepts, and generalizations developed throughout the study. The examination may be given orally for students who have difficulty reading the questions. Students should achieve a minimum passing grade of 75 percent.

Learning Plan

Exhibit 3.13 Web Design for an Interdisciplinary Unit.

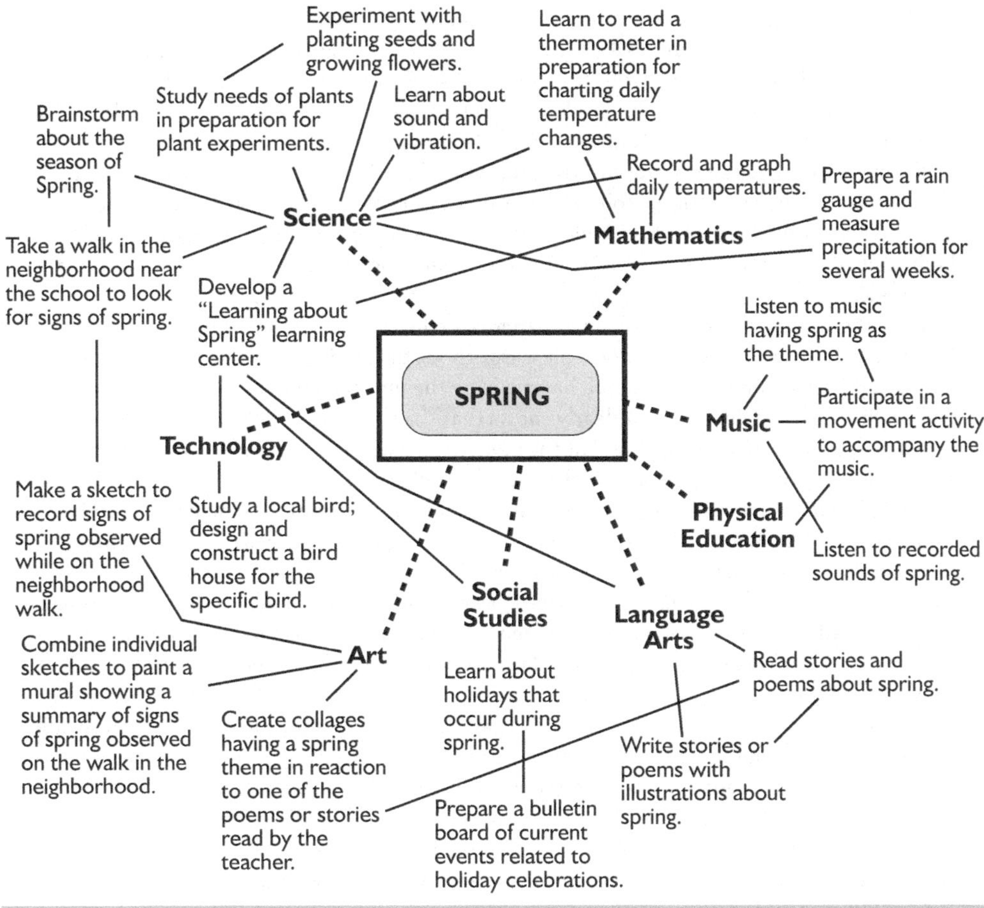

Descriptions of Lessons and Activities

Note that the lessons and activities in this study will take a period of time to complete; most will not be completed in a single session due to the time needed to complete projects and experiments. It may also be found that the sequence may need to change as the unit is taught for the first time.

During the initial lesson of the unit, the students will be introduced to the essential questions of the unit. The students will then be prepared for a short field trip to look for signs of spring and to collect plant and water samples in their local neighborhood. Students will be asked what they believe they already know about the spring season and what they would like to learn about spring. Their responses will be recorded on the first two sections of a K-W-L chart. The questions students raise will help to determine additional goals for the spring unit. The students will learn that they will be taking a walk in their local neighborhood to look for some signs of spring.

The second phase of the field trip experience will offer the students opportunities to be involved in the work of scientists. It will involve data gathering during the field trip in response to the questions and suggestions about the signs of spring that students have raised during the introductory lesson. On the day of the field trip—a walk through the neighborhood to look for signs of spring—students will take along drawing paper and pencils to make sketches of any signs of spring that they notice: animals, birds, insects, plants, and so on. Stop occasionally and encourage the students to observe for signs of spring and to make sketches. Also, have containers for students to collect specimens of plants and samples of water to take back to the classroom for examination.

Upon returning to the classroom, students will be asked to select one of their observations—a sketch made or sample collected of a sign of spring—and to write a one- or two-sentence explanation telling why they believe the sketch or sample indicates a sign of spring. Each student will have the opportunity to show a sketch or sample and to read the explanation aloud.

Have the students transfer and enlarge their sketches to a large sheet of mural paper. (Note that this will take time, periodically, throughout the study.) Involve the students in arranging their pictures on the mural. Later during the unit the students will be asked to explain how the completed mural clearly shows that the spring season has arrived. Using art media to record the signs of spring that the students have noted on a mural will develop a visual summary of the signs of spring that they have observed.

Students will be involved in activities that make use of the plant specimens brought back from their neighborhood walk. The key question to be explored for these investigations is: How can the plants and water samples we have collected be distinguished from one another? First, the students will have hands-on experiences examining the plant specimens. They will be encouraged to observe each plant specimen carefully to determine its size, colors, and other distinguishing features and to record their findings. A slide will be prepared for each of the water samples collected. Students will examine the different samples under a microscope and draw pictures of their observations to note and draw pictures for each sample to illustrate the differences in samples from different locations. These activities will give students opportunities to use equipment such as microscopes and measuring devices as they explore properties of plant and water specimens; they will also have experience writing explanations of what they learned about the different plants and drawing illustrations of the water samples they examine and to give reasons for their conclusions about what they have observed.

Give the students opportunities to conduct their own experiments to determine the basic needs of the plants collected while on their neighborhood walk. The key question for these experiments will be: How can plants be helped to live and grow healthfully? Begin by having the students suggest what they believe plants need to live. The students will probably have different ideas; it is possible that some students will not include all the essentials. Have the students maintain a journal that describes what they do with the plants and the observations they make over time; explain the form they will need to use for their journals. Collect the journals each week and provide feedback and suggestions to the students. Help individual students set up experiments to test their ideas about what plants need. It is likely that some may fail to control variables when conducting their experiments. When this happens, let the students perform their experiments, then raise questions to help them understand that they need to test one variable at a time. Replicate experiments when needed.

After students have determined the basic needs of plants, teach a lesson on planting flower seeds. The key question of the lesson is: How should plant seeds be sown in order to develop into healthy plants? Use marigold seeds because they will grow rapidly and easily under proper conditions. As a first step in this lesson, guide students in reading a selection in their science book or another source on planting seeds. After reading the selection, the students will be asked to explain the conditions needed for growing the seeds and be given time to collect necessary materials, such as soil and containers. Assist the students as they plant their seeds. Ask the students to observe the plants each day and keep a record by writing about or drawing the changes that they observe. Students should measure and chart the height of their plants each week after the seeds have sprouted. Later in the spring, the students can take their plants home when the marigolds are mature enough for transplanting. This science lesson offers students a concrete experience in raising and caring for growing plants.

The key question for another lesson is: How do we read an outdoor thermometer to determine the temperature? In preparation for this lesson, install an outdoor thermometer near one of the classroom windows, and teach students how to read the thermometer. Practice reading the thermometer with the students for several days. This will prepare the students for keeping a daily temperature record for the remainder of the unit on spring. Divide the students into three groups: one group will be responsible for reading and maintaining a list of temperature readings early in the morning; the second group should take readings at noon; and the third group should check temperatures at the end of the school day. Students will maintain records showing the date each measurement is taken.

Another lesson will also involve measurement and maintaining a record. Students will be asked to decide how they can determine the amount of rain that falls during a period of precipitation. Ask the students if they can think of any way they can determine how much rain has fallen after it has rained. It may be possible for the students to devise a method. Ultimately, however, a rain gauge will be needed, so a simple gauge using an untapered glass container with its depth measured in inches or centimeters will be sufficient. Have the students practice reading different amounts of water in the container. Locate the rain gauge in an outdoor area near the classroom for students to inspect after each period of precipitation. Have students record the amounts of water collected by the gauge in their notebooks following each period of precipitation throughout the unit. At the end of the unit, have students compute the total amount of precipitation that has fallen during their study of spring and record it on their graphs. Optionally, use the different amounts of precipitation to create other addition and subtraction problems for students to solve.

This activity will be needed to introduce (or review) graphing. Students will be asked: What do our records of the daily temperature and rainfall during our study of the spring season show us, and how can we show the information we have recorded in our notebooks?

After students have collected and recorded temperature and precipitation records in their notebooks for at least two weeks, teach the students how to prepare simple bar graphs to chart the daily temperature and rainfall readings they have been recording in their notebooks. Students should continue adding new readings to their graphs throughout their study. At the conclusion of the unit, ask the students to decide what the records tend to show about the temperature in spring and the amount of rain that has fallen. (Note that it is anticipated that there will be a gradual rise in the temperature if normal conditions prevail.)

Conduct a lesson on the natural sounds in our environment during the spring season using only the sense of hearing. Prepare a recording of natural sounds that prevail during the spring months, such as birds chirping, children playing outside, and water rushing in a stream. Have the students listen to each recording and write what they believe is the source of each sound on a sheet of paper. Then, hold a discussion during which students contribute their individual ideas about the sources. Finally, replay each sound and have the group decide which is the most accurate guess for the source of the sound.

Ask students what they think about or feel when they hear music that has a spring theme. Select recordings of music having spring as the theme. Include at least one classical and one other piece to play for the students. Have the students comment on what the music makes them think about or what feelings it evokes. After discussing some of the students' reactions, give them the choice of either writing in their journals about what the music makes them think about and feel or creating a poem or drawing a picture that represents their thoughts. Finally, assist the students in editing their writing, and give them the opportunity to present their final composition to the class.

Involve the students in an impromptu creative movement or dance activity accompanying the music to help them understand how we may react to music with our bodies. After listening to one of the pieces of music that has the spring theme, invite the students to describe and demonstrate ways to move to the music. Some students will be likely to consider rhythmic patterns; others may perform large muscle movements or acrobatics, so this activity may be safer in the environment of a gymnasium or outside. This lesson will provide opportunities for the students to discuss and interpret the music individually in a movement exercise.

The next lesson will be designed to help students learn how sound is produced. The question of the lesson is: How is any sound produced? In this lesson, various vibrating objects will be used to help students discover that all sound is caused by vibration. Several objects, such as a drum, a stringed instrument, a stretched rubber band, a tuning fork, and others will be sounded as students observe. The students will be asked to decide what happens to each of the objects when it makes a sound and write about their conclusions. Students will then read their responses to the class. If some students have noted a reason other than vibration, demonstrate again to help them note that it is the vibration of each object that creates sound.

Select and read an adaptation of a short story related to the spring theme. For example, *The Proud Little Apple Blossom* (Andersen) can be used for younger children. Follow the guided listening protocol when reading to the students in order to encourage their involvement in the lesson. After the reading, have students write their own story or poem about spring, and have the students illustrate their writing with a drawing or painting. As an alternative, have students create collages that reflect the story. Using their completed work, assist the students in preparing a bulletin board to display their collages. Encourage the students to make decisions about how to arrange the display.

Teach a lesson comparing two spring holidays to help students understand why we celebrate them, how different people observe them, and how the two holidays are alike and different. Select an appropriate video about each holiday for students to view and discuss. The visual presentations should be selected to provide the students with insights about how each holiday originated and the different ways people in our multicultural society celebrate them. Conduct the lesson by following the guided viewing protocol. (Guided viewing is explained in chapter 5 along with a sample lesson plan.)

Conduct a lesson on the Carolina wren—or another bird—that is found in the northeast during the spring season. The students will be helped to determine the characteristics and needs of a Carolina wren. (A good example of utilizing technology in a lesson plan is an excellent iPhone/iPad app, *iBird Pro*, which contains a wealth of information on all types of birds in the U.S., including illustrations of habitat range, nesting and feeding habits, many color photos, actual recordings of bird calls, and much more. The app is easy to use, for either teachers or students.)

Help the students to learn about the food, size, color, and nesting habits of the Carolina wren by preparing a PowerPoint presentation that includes photographs and information. The lesson will be conducted by following the guided viewing protocol during which guided questions are raised about this bird and its needs. After the presentation, involve the students in considering what materials and design would be necessary to build a birdhouse that would attract the wren.

Next, ask the students to create their own designs or divide the class into groups of three to develop designs for a proposed wren house model. Using their designs, have students construct model wren houses from cardboard, wood scraps, or other simple materials that are available. After the models have been constructed, give students an opportunity to explain their constructions orally to the class; the reasons for their particular designs should be included in their explanations.

Optionally, in addition to the above lessons, prepare a learning center equipped with at least ten activities for the students to complete independently. One activity could include examining additional samples of water taken from various sources in the local neighborhood and writing descriptions of and/or drawing pictures of what the students observe. If frogs' eggs are available, samples may be collected and placed in the learning center for the students to observe. If the eggs are included in the center, books or other materials at the students' reading levels on the development of frogs from eggs into tadpoles and adult frogs should be placed in the learning center. (As another technology-related example viewing of the video, *Life Cycle of a Frog!* [available on YouTube] might be assigned as a learning center activity.) Activities in the center may also include reading and preparing short reviews or reactions to other books, stories, and poems; creative writing; listening to music; and mathematical problem solving. Each activity should have a task card to explain directions. (Refer to Exhibit 3.11, Descriptions of Learning Centers and Classroom Research Centers, which appears earlier in this chapter.)

Materials and Equipment

- A video on the needs of plants (to show after children conduct their own experiments with plants)
- A selection of children's books on spring from the school and public libraries
- A teacher-prepared PowerPoint presentation on wrens
- Computer software and WebQuests featuring information on the seasons and nature
- Marigold (or other annual) seeds for planting
- Materials for experiments with plants
- Microscopes
- An outdoor thermometer
- A rain gauge
- A recording of spring sounds (teacher prepared)
- Recordings of music and environmental sounds
- Rulers
- A tuning fork
- A selection of resources, such as children's books on spring from the school and public libraries (see below).

Resources

ABC Teach. Spring activities. Retrieved from http://www.abcteach.com/directory/seasonalseasons/spring/

Andersen, H. C. *The proud little apple blossom* (adapted). Retrieved from http://www.apples4theteacher.com/holidays/spring/short-stories/the-proud-little-apple-blossom.html

Bobick, J. E., & Balaban, N. E. (Eds.). (2003). *The handy science answer book* (Rev. & expanded ed.). Detroit, MI: Visible Ink Press.

Brewer, D. (2001). *Wrens, dippers, and thrashes*. New Haven, CT: Yale University Press.

Fogliano, J. (2012). *And then it's spring.* New York: Roaring Book Press/Macmillan.

Gogerly, L. (2005). *Spring.* Vero Beach, FL: Rourke.

Huser, G. (2013). *Time for flowers, time for snow: A retelling of the legend of Demeter and Persephone.* Vancouver, BC: Tradewind Books.

Phillips, R. (1978). *Trees of North America and Europe*. New York: Random House.

Rosen, M. (1990). *Spring festivals.* New York: Bookwright Press.

Weinstein, E. W. (1999). Vernal equinox. Retrieved from http://scienceworld.wolfram.com/astronomy/VernalEquinox.html

Williams, J. (1997). *The weather book* (2nd ed.). New York: Vintage Books.

ACTIVITY

Allison Ramirez is a teacher in an urban community in the Midwest. She is planning an interdisciplinary unit on industrial growth in the United States for students in her fourth-grade class. Two of her ***understanding*** goals are:

- Students will understand that geographic factors and natural resources in the United States influenced the inventions, particularly in transportation and communication during the 1800s and 1900s.
- Students will understand that immigrants to the United States during the 1800s and 1900s made significant contributions to the growth and development of the United States.

Complete the following tasks that are related to the two understandings expressed in these knowledge-level general objectives for the unit:

1. Write an essential question related to each understanding.
2. Devise assessment plans to help determine the students' achievement of each understanding.
3. Locate learning standards from the Common Core State Standards that relate to each assessment.

Finally, write descriptions of a lesson or activity aimed at developing each of the two understandings.

Designing a Multidisciplinary Unit

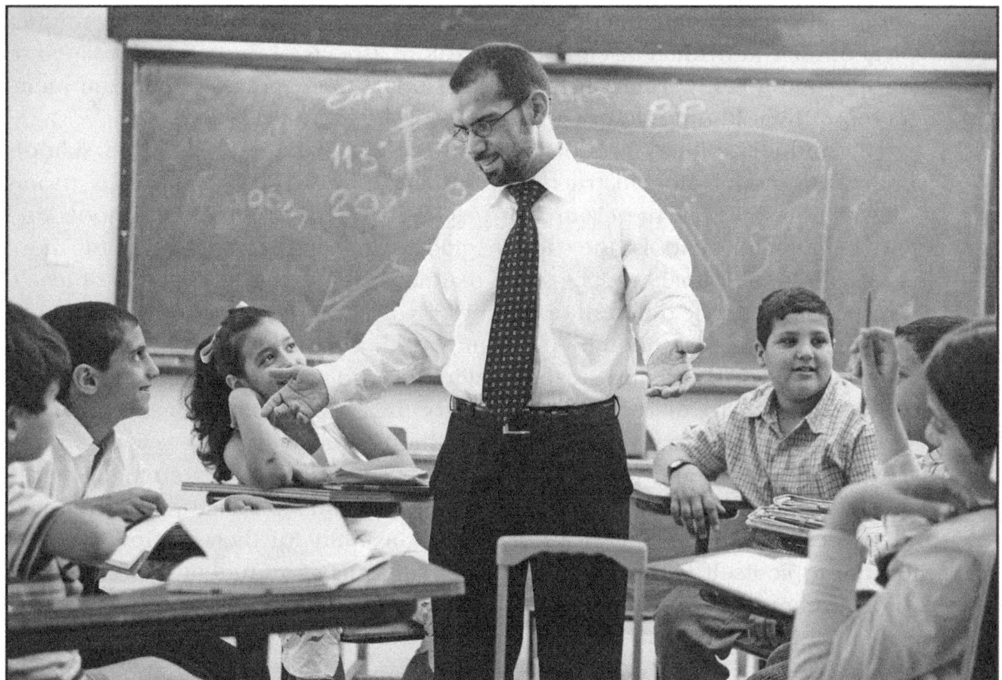

Overview

This chapter reviews the process for planning a multidisciplinary unit for students in departmentalized upper elementary grades and middle school and provides an example of an *initial* multidisciplinary unit plan. The discussion will respond to the following questions:

- How does multidisciplinary instruction differ from the interdisciplinary approach?
- Why is the multidisciplinary approach appropriate for older elementary and middle school students?
- How is a multidisciplinary unit organized and outlined?
- How is a multidisciplinary unit planned?

How Does Multidisciplinary Instruction Differ from the Interdisciplinary Approach?

In chapter 1, it was explained that in most fields, the significant difference between approaching a study from an *interdisciplinary* versus *multidisciplinary* point of view is that in multidisciplinary studies, a research team works together to plan the study of a topic in which the individual members have a mutual interest and some expertise to contribute. However, once the study is planned, the team members work independently from one another. They each use techniques typical of their individual disciplines to explore aspects of the research related to the topic under study. Then, at the conclusion of their research, the team members report their findings to other members of the group.

The multidisciplinary approach to instruction in departmentalized schools parallels this model. Most instruction in primary and early elementary classrooms is the responsibility of the classroom teacher. However, in middle schools and some elementary schools the upper grades are departmentalized. In those schools, multidisciplinary units may be planned cooperatively by a team of teachers responsible for the different disciplines involved in the study.

Once the unit is planned by the team working together, each teacher on the team independently assumes responsibility for and teaches the portions of the unit that pertain to his or her disciplinary area. For example, aspects of the research related to social studies becomes the responsibility of a teacher in that department; English and literature-related aspects of the topic are taught by the English/language arts teacher to the same group of students; likewise, art, music, and science teachers for the group have responsibility for their disciplines. Typically, the topic itself is then separated into subtopics for student committees to explore and report upon at the conclusion of the study. The team works together on culminating activities and final assessments to be used.

Why Is the Multidisciplinary Approach Appropriate for Older Elementary and Middle School Students?

As students mature, their changing developmental abilities allow them to undertake studies that are increasingly more sophisticated and demanding. Most students at the upper elementary and middle school levels have developed adequate research, reading, and writing skills for the academic work required by multidisciplinary studies. At these grade levels, we can usually find more independent reading material and a much larger variety of other resource materials appropriate for the topics students study.

Multidisciplinary studies are specifically adapted for students in departmentalized upper elementary grades and middle schools. These students are capable of working with others on committees that assume responsibility for subtopics of the study and investigate information afforded by the various disciplinary areas—history, geography, science, mathematics, economics, health, music, art, and so on. Each committee researches only that part of the study pertaining to its subtopic; students on each committee then attempt to determine answers to the essential and other questions related to the subtopic for which they are responsible. For example, in the multidisciplinary unit-plan example at the end of this chapter, the topic, *Principal Deserts in the United States,* is divided into four subtopics that include the four largest desert regions in the United States. Each committee is responsible for only one of those regions. At the conclusion of the unit, committees assemble and report their findings to other members of their class. Thus, the key features of the multidisciplinary approach are:

- In departmentalized schools, multidisciplinary units are planned and taught by teams of teachers (whereas interdisciplinary units are planned and taught by one classroom teacher who may elicit the cooperation of special-area teachers in art, music, media, and so on).
- The teaching team works together to decide the goals and assessments of the unit, the major assignments, the specific student committees the unit will require, and culminating activities.
- The study is then separated by the disciplines and taught separately by the various team members. One teacher will assume responsibility for introducing the new unit to the students and organizing students into research committees; this will often be the social studies teacher because multidisciplinary topics are often associated with that subject.
- After the unit is introduced, each teacher on the team will work with the same group of students during the regular scheduled classes for their disciplines. For example, the social studies teacher on a team will teach aspects of a unit that involve history, geography, economics, civics, and citizenship; the English/language arts teacher will include literature and elements of writing related to the unit topic; the science teacher will explore contributions from the sciences; and so on. Individual team members use methods and techniques that are suited to their disciplines.

In the next section of this chapter, multidisciplinary unit planning is explained in more detail and illustrated with examples. Note that because most of the components of the unit that are developed are identical to those for interdisciplinary units, this discussion will avoid repetition of detailed explanations of learning standards, goals, essential questions, and assessments that were included in chapter 3. Instead, the emphasis in this chapter will be on the aspects of those components that are unique to multidisciplinary units, such as organizing the study by discipline or subtopic and the structure of student committees.

Planning and Designing a Multidisciplinary Unit

Planning a multidisciplinary unit involves:

- Considering the context for learning in which the unit will be taught.
- Determining the topic, theme, or problem of the unit.
- Determining the unit goals—understandings, knowledge, skills, and dispositions that will be fostered.

- Determining the learning standards.
- Preparing the essential questions that will guide the study.
- Preparing the unit assessment plan.
- Preparing the unit learning plan: Constructing a unit chart that indicates the student research committees, areas for committee research, and disciplinary teachers' instructional tasks.
- Writing explanations of disciplinary teachers' instructional tasks and activities that the unit will include.
- Preparing a list of important materials that will be needed.

Exhibit 4.1 Outline for a Multidisciplinary Unit Plan.

Topic:
Level:
Estimated Length:
Learning Standards:
Goals:
Understandings
Knowledge
Skills
Dispositions
Essential Questions:
Assessment Plan:
Learning Plan:
Unit Chart
Disciplinary Teachers' Instructional Tasks
Activities
Materials:
Resources:
Reflections:

The organization of a multidisciplinary unit plan outline (Exhibit 4.1) is one that will be familiar to those who have previously followed other unit-planning outlines.

The process involved in planning a multidisciplinary unit mainly follows the *backward design* procedure (Wiggins & McTighe, 2012) that was described in chapter 1. Note that the sequence followed when planning the various components of a multidisciplinary unit plan can differ depending on individual teaching preferences and styles. For example, we can begin with any component of the unit: learning standards, goals, essential questions, lesson and activity ideas for the learning plan, and so on. However, when complete, all sections of the unit must be aligned.

Considering the Context for Learning

The context for learning—as explained in chapter 3—involves students' developmental, academic, and social characteristics as well as the available facilities and materials in the school. The majority of students in the upper elementary grades and middle school will have achieved what Piaget and Inhelder (1969) describe as *concrete operational thought.* This pattern of thinking and reasoning allows students to deal with more abstract concepts and systems of concepts, provided they have the opportunity to relate these concepts to personal or direct experiences. Although Piaget also believed that some students in middle childhood approach what he called *formal operational thought*—a type of thinking that involves genuine hypothetical thought—during their adolescent years, post-Piagetian researchers suggest this is not typical of most students at this level (Santrock, 2012).

Socially, older students usually enjoy working in groups with their peers where they can share tasks and become involved in making group decisions. Under our direction, students can learn to organize a research topic into manageable parts by discipline, essential and other unit questions, or by subtopic. An important part of planning the unit involves determining the disciplinary or topical student committees that can be formed for the study. The specific disciplines involved will depend on the learning standards and other goals as well as the essential questions to be addressed in the study.

Most older students can read better than students in earlier grade levels. It is, therefore, somewhat easier to provide them with a wider variety of more suitable independent reading and other resource materials. Their improved skills also enable them to make increasing use of the computer and other technology-related resources, local and distance networking, and Internet services. In middle school, students continue to need opportunities to acquire knowledge by using their diverse working and learning styles and multiple intelligences.

Following is an explanation of each component in a multidisciplinary unit. Examples are from a multidisciplinary unit plan on the topic, *Principal Deserts of the United States*. The unit is planned for students in a seventh-grade middle school and is adaptable for upper grade levels in departmentalized elementary schools. The examples are intended only to illustrate the planning process. Only a few examples for each component in the process are included with the explanations; the complete unit plan appears at the end of this chapter.

Topic, Theme, or Problem

Topics selected for students in the upper elementary grades and middle school should be kept broad to increase opportunities for student participation in the research activities. Excellent planning guides that have been developed by state departments of education and the National Council for the Social Studies can help in the selection process. In long-term planning, we should consult statewide and local curriculum guides and lists of the Common Core State Standards to assist us in making decisions about the topics to be investigated, assignments, and assessment methods. Often, a prescribed course of study is required, especially at the middle school levels (Kellough & Kellough, 2003).

Multidisciplinary topics can also be selected from disciplines other than those included in the social studies curriculum. Post, Ellis, Humphreys, and Buggey (1997) provide examples of several topics with an environmental focus. Environmental topics are not only important today but also are interesting to most students in the upper elementary grades and middle school, and they always involve more than a single discipline.

Regardless of the source of topics, several criteria may be helpful when making final decisions about the topics that need to be taught:

- Topics that will address specific learning standards should be included where they fit most naturally.
- The topic should be broad and inclusive. However, time constraints for teaching the unit, if any, should be considered because they may influence the type of topic that can be investigated (Criteria for Selection of Class Research Topics, 1966).
- To be sufficiently motivating, the topic selected should be of inherent interest to the students whenever possible. The scope of the study should also be flexible enough to allow for differences in individual interests, multiple intelligence areas, and learning styles.
- The unit topic should involve all the disciplines that can help to inform it.
- The availability of resource materials needed by students to investigate the topic should be considered. Required reading materials should be selected according to the students' independent reading levels.
- A topic should help to broaden students' understanding of their multicultural world and strengthen their sense of social justice and responsibility. The example below shows the topic, grade level, and estimated length of the Deserts unit.

EXAMPLES

Topic: Principal Deserts of the United States

Level: Middle School

For use at other grade levels this unit plan may need adaptation and modification. Seventh-grade social studies curricula commonly explore aspects of U.S. history and colonization. This example is designed mainly for students at that level; however, it can be modified for students in the upper elementary grades and middle school levels.

Estimated Unit Length: 5–6 weeks

Unit Goals

Goals of a unit include the understandings, knowledge, skills, and dispositions that the unit will address. Below are two examples from the Deserts unit for each type of goal.

Understandings. Understandings are the broad concepts to be developed during a unit. They can range from generalizable, enduring understandings to those that are topic specific. The examples below are topic specific, relating to the study of desert regions.

EXAMPLES

Students will understand that:

- Discovery and exploration of desert regions in the United States by European settlers impacted the lives of Native Americans living in those regions in both positive and negative ways.
- Plants and animals living in desert regions are those that are adapted to the severe conditions of a desert climate and those that have benefitted from irrigation projects.

Knowledge. Knowledge includes specific facts and other information that students are expected to gain from the study. Two examples follow.

EXAMPLES

Students will know:

- Terms and vocabulary related to their study of deserts in the United States
- Facts and historic information about the deserts included in the unit study

Skills. Skills that students will have opportunities to improve in any of the disciplines involved in the study are listed in this section. Three examples are listed below.

EXAMPLES

Students will improve their skills in:

- Designing investigations
- Preparing group presentations of research findings
- Following the conventions of grammar, syntax, spelling, and punctuation when writing

Dispositions. We would often like to see improvements in our students' cooperation, peer interactions, interest, and so on. These and other "dispositions" always affect their academic work. Following are two examples.

EXAMPLES

Students will improve the following dispositions:

- Gaining sensitivity to the problems that exploration of new regions can cause for people living in those regions
- Increasing their interest in the inquiry process

Learning Standards

After selecting a topic for the unit, prepare a list of the learning standards the unit will address. Those included in this text include the disciplinary learning standards required by some individual states and local school districts as well as the Common Core State Standards. The standards give direction to the study and suggest the important skills that will be further developed and assessed as a result of the study. Note that because learning standards are comprehensive, a unit may not address all aspects of a particular standard; those that are listed in the unit plan must be at least partly addressed. Two examples of learning standards from the Deserts unit follow.

EXAMPLES

Common Core State Standards

Students will:

- Write informative/explanatory texts to examine a topic and convey ideas, concepts, and information through the selection, organization, and analysis of relevant content. (*CCSS, W.7.2*)

New York State Standards
Students will:

- Use a variety of intellectual skills to demonstrate their understanding of the geography of the interdependent world in which we live—local, national, and global—including the distribution of people, places, and environments over the Earth's surface. (*New York State Learning Standard for Social Studies 3*)

Essential Questions

Prepare essential questions and other questions that are consistent with the unit learning standards and goals—understandings, knowledge, skills, and dispositions—of the unit, and define specifically what students should gain from their study. Essential questions must be consistent with the unit goals. Two examples from the Deserts unit follow.

EXAMPLES

- Why can some living things survive in deserts while others cannot?
- Are the deserts in the United States in trouble?

Assessment Plan

The assessment plan for a multidisciplinary unit describes the specific requirements of students that will be assessed during the study. Those assessments demonstrate how well students are able to respond to the essential questions of the unit and the extent to which they have met the learning standards and unit goals.

The assessments need to show how well students can apply their new knowledge in practical ways with applications, interpretations such as written reports, creative work, original designs and models, art projects, journals, presentations, experiments, and so on. Similar to the interdisciplinary unit assessments that were described in chapter 3, multidisciplinary studies also usually include examinations, papers, performances, and observations of students. Each assessment should address the learning standards and be associated with one or more of the unit's essential questions. See the partial example below.

EXAMPLE

Students will prepare portfolios that include their individual research reports, book reviews, sketches, and other items they developed during the unit study. The individual reports, committee work and reports, book reviews, and unit examination will provide for assessment of the unit goals as follows:

Students' individual written reports will provide evidence of their progress in researching and writing clear and organized reports of their research. The written reports will also permit assessment of individual students' responses to one of the unit's essential questions. Rubrics will be used to assess the book reviews.

Learning Plan

The unit learning plan includes two parts. First, a chart is constructed that outlines a list of possible student research committees, areas for committee research, and disciplinary teachers' instructional tasks for the teacher or teachers. Second, brief descriptions of each disciplinary teacher's instructional tasks in the unit chart are prepared.

Constructing the Unit Chart. A multidisciplinary unit plan chart substitutes for the type of web design included in interdisciplinary unit plans. When constructing the unit chart, the topic should be clearly stated, with titles of the student research committees to be organized for the study. The information that each of the committees should attempt to locate is included on the chart to provide the committees with an outline of material that may be possible to collect. A partially completed chart for the Deserts unit is shown in Exhibit 4.2 on the following page. Only a sample of the kinds of information are included in the example. The entire unit chart can be found in the completed Deserts unit plan example at the end of this chapter.

The chart also includes types of lessons and activities listed by discipline. These comprise the learning plan for the unit. In elementary classes, the classroom teacher assumes the responsibility for most instruction but may be able to arrange with art and music teachers to help with those aspects of the study. In a departmentalized school, the responsibilities are divided among the different team teachers and their respective disciplines. Optionally, lists can be prepared instead of constructing a unit chart because the chart for some topics can become overcrowded and difficult to read.

Writing Descriptions of Disciplinary Teachers' Instructional Tasks

Instead of designing complete instructional plans in the multidisciplinary unit plan design, brief descriptions of the disciplinary teachers' instructional tasks indicated in the unit chart can be written. The descriptions only suggest the lesson plans that need to be developed by the classroom teacher or various members of the teaching team. Using the descriptions, complete lesson plans can be designed when they are needed. (Note that lesson planning is discussed in chapter 5. In that chapter, there are guidelines for lesson planning using several different procedural protocols for different types of lessons.) An example task for the English/language arts teacher and an activity from the Deserts unit follow.

EXAMPLES

Disciplinary Teachers' Instructional Tasks

English/Language Arts Teacher

Select and introduce related literature on the desert theme to the students, such as *The desert: Lands of lost borders* by M. Welland (2015). The most current writings will need to be researched for this purpose. The teacher will select one or more readings to read and discuss with students in class. Students will be responsible for selecting a book and preparing a book review according to instructions to be outlined by the English/language arts teacher.

Activities

Individual Book Reports

Each student will read and prepare a review of a book from the library (either fiction or nonfiction) related to desert life. The book can be either prose or poetry. Students will need to write a review that encourages other students to read the book, or they can prepare a story map or plot profile for a work of fiction. The book reviews will help to indicate students' ability to read, analyze, and critically review a book on the desert theme. Students will also be demonstrating their ability to organize their ideas and write clearly. Rubrics will be used to assess individual book reports.

Exhibit 4.2 A Partially Completed Unit Chart for a Multidisciplinary Unit Plan.

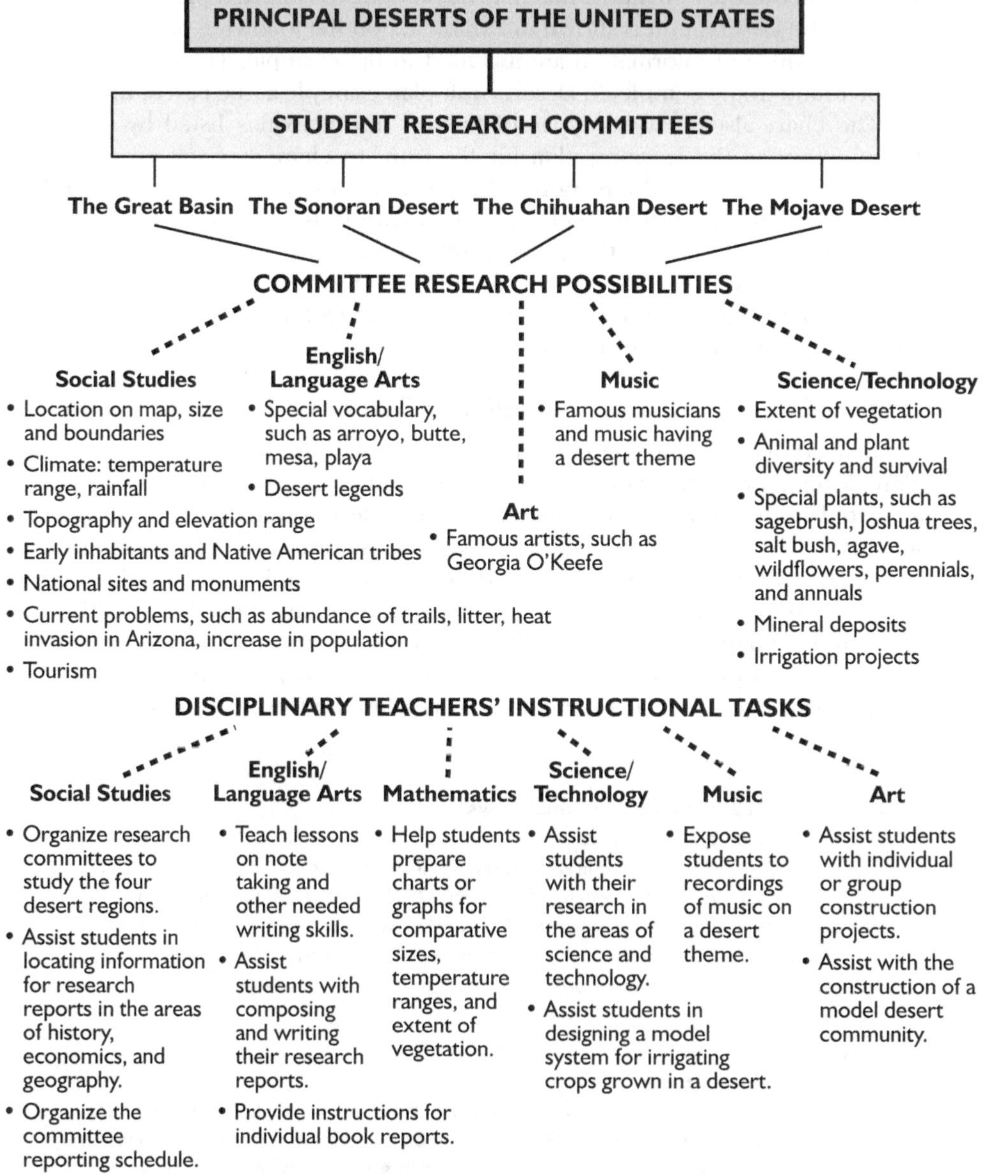

PRINCIPAL DESERTS OF THE UNITED STATES
STUDENT RESEARCH COMMITTEES
The Great Basin
The Sonoran Desert
The Chihuahan Desert
The Mojave Desert
COMMITTEE RESEARCH POSSIBILITIES
Social Studies
• Location on map, size and boundaries
• Climate: temperature range, rainfall
• Topography and elevation range
• Early inhabitants and Native American tribes
• National sites and monuments
• Current problems, such as abundance of trails, litter, heat invasion in Arizona, increase in population
• Tourism
English/ Language Arts
• Special vocabulary, such as arroyo, butte, mesa, playa
• Desert legends
Art
• Famous artists, such as Georgia O'Keefe
Music
• Famous musicians and music having a desert theme
Science/Technology
• Extent of vegetation
• Animal and plant diversity and survival
• Special plants, such as sagebrush, Joshua trees, salt bush, agave, wildflowers, perennials, and annuals
• Mineral deposits
• Irrigation projects
DISCIPLINARY TEACHERS' INSTRUCTIONAL TASKS
Social Studies
• Organize research committees to study the four desert regions.
• Assist students in locating information for research reports in the areas of history, economics, and geography.
• Organize the committee reporting schedule.
English/ Language Arts
• Teach lessons on note taking and other needed writing skills.
• Assist students with composing and writing their research reports.
• Provide instructions for individual book reports.
Mathematics
• Help students prepare charts or graphs for comparative sizes, temperature ranges, and extent of vegetation.
Science/ Technology
• Assist students with their research in the areas of science and technology.
• Assist students in designing a model system for irrigating crops grown in a desert.
Music
• Expose students to recordings of music on a desert theme.
Art
• Assist students with individual or group construction projects.
• Assist with the construction of a model desert community.

Materials and Resources

The materials and resources needed for the unit include: (a) materials that will be used with or for students and (b) informational resources for the teacher. It is not necessary to list every item currently available in the *initial* unit plan. A simple list of the kinds of texts and trade books, computer software, teacher-prepared presentations, videos and Internet items, and other potential materials is sufficient for the plan at this point. Addresses of Internet resources (URLs) and names of people who can serve as consultants or as guest speakers can also be listed. Some materials (such as URLs) rapidly become dated, and new items are usually available each time the unit is retaught. Most of the usual art and other consumable materials need not be listed. Several examples follow.

EXAMPLES

- Art materials for projects and report covers
- Hodge, D., & Stephens, P. (2008). *Who lives here? Desert animals.* Toronto, Ontario: Kids Can Press, Ltd.
- *Chihuahuan Desert.* Retrieved from http://mbreiding.us/ert/Arizona/desertecology/chihua.htm
- Chihuahuan Desert home page of the University of Texas. Retrieved from http://museum2.utep.edu/chih/chihdes.htm

An Initial Multidisciplinary Unit Plan Example

Topic: Principal Deserts of the United States

Level: Grade 7

This unit plan is designed for students in grade 7. Seventh-grade social studies curricula commonly explore aspects of U.S. history and colonization. Although this example is designed mainly for students at that level, it can be modified for students at other grades at the middle school level.

Estimated Unit Length: 5–6 weeks

Common Core State Standards

Students will:

- Determine a theme or central idea of a text and analyze its development over the course of the text; provide an objective summary of the text. (*RL.7.2*)
- Produce clear and coherent writing in which the development, organization, and style are appropriate to task, purpose, and audience. (*RI.7.4*)
- Write arguments to support claims with clear reasons and relevant evidence. (*W.7.1*)
- Write informative/explanatory texts to examine a topic and convey ideas, concepts, and information through the selection, organization, and analysis of relevant content. (*W.7.2*)
- Produce clear and coherent writing in which the development, organization, and style are appropriate to task, purpose, and audience. (*W.7.4*)

- Conduct short research projects to answer a question, drawing on several sources and generating additional related, focused questions for further research and investigation. (*W.7.7*)
- Understand that statistics can be used to gain information about a population by examining a sample of the population; generalizations about a population from a sample are valid only if the sample is representative of that population. Understand that random sampling tends to produce representative samples and support valid inferences. (*M.7.SP.1*)
- Gather relevant information from multiple print and digital sources, using search terms effectively; assess the credibility and accuracy of each source; and quote or paraphrase the data and conclusions of others while avoiding plagiarism and following a standard format for citation. (*W.7.8*)
- Draw evidence from literary or informational texts to support analysis, reflection, and research. (*W.7.9*)
- Engage effectively in a range of collaborative discussions (one-on-one, in groups, and teacher-led) with diverse partners on grade 7 topics, texts, and issues, building on others' ideas and expressing their own clearly. (*SL.7.1*)
- Present claims and findings, emphasizing salient points in a focused, coherent manner with pertinent descriptions, facts, details, and examples; use appropriate eye contact, adequate volume, and clear pronunciation. (*SL.7.4*)
- Include multimedia components and visual displays in presentations to clarify claims and findings and emphasize salient points. (*SL.7.5*)
- Demonstrate command of the conventions of standard English grammar and usage when writing or speaking. (*L.7.1*)
- Demonstrate command of the conventions of standard English capitalization, punctuation, and spelling when writing. (*L.7.2*)

New York State Learning Standards

Students will:

- Use a variety of intellectual skills to demonstrate their understanding of major ideas, eras, themes, developments, and turning points in the history of the United States and New York. (*Socials Studies, Standard 1*)
- Use a variety of intellectual skills to demonstrate their understanding of the geography of the interdependent world in which we live—local, national, and global—including the distribution of people, places, and environments over the Earth's surface. (*Social Studies, Standard 3*)
- Understand and apply scientific concepts, principles, and theories pertaining to the physical setting and living environment and recognize the historical development of ideas in science. (*Mathematics, Science, and Technology, Standard 4*)
- Be knowledgeable about and make use of the materials and resources available for participation in arts in various roles. (*Arts, Standard 2*)

Goals: This unit will assist in developing the following understandings, essential questions, skills, and dispositions.

Students will understand that:

- Discovery and exploration of desert regions in the United States by European settlers impacted the lives of Native Americans living in those regions in both positive and negative ways.

- Plants and animals living in desert regions are those that are adapted to the severe conditions of a desert climate and those that have benefitted from irrigation projects.
- Major problems facing our deserts today include heat invasion in Arizona, an overabundance of trails, litter, threats to animal and plant life, and the dramatic increase in population.
- Some people find living in a desert advantageous to their health; others, particularly writers, artists, and musicians, are stimulated in their creative work.

Students will know:

- That the principal desert regions in the United States vary in significant ways, such as size, location, natural resources, life forms, temperature, and rainfall.
- Terms and vocabulary related to their study of deserts in the United States
- Facts and historic information about the deserts included in the unit study

Students will improve their skills in the following:

- Designing investigations
- Locating and reading informational sources
- Collecting and recording data from informational sources
- Reading and interpreting maps
- Preparing group presentations of research findings
- Writing individual reports of research findings
- Constructing charts and graphs
- Creating art with various media
- Designing and constructing models
- Following the conventions of grammar, syntax, spelling, and punctuation when writing
- Following the conventions of English when speaking

Students will improve the following dispositions:

- Working cooperatively and courteously with others in group situations
- Gaining sensitivity to the problems exploration of new regions can cause people living in those regions
- Developing the desire to search for understanding
- Increasing their interest in the inquiry process

Essential Questions

The following unit questions form the basis of a study of *the Great Basin, Sonoran Desert, Chihuahuan Desert,* and *Mojave Desert,* four principle deserts of the United States:

- What effect did the discovery of deserts in the United States by European settlers have on the native people who were living in them at the time?
- Why can some living things survive in deserts while others cannot?
- Why are the deserts in the United States in trouble? What major problems are confronting them?
- How are people affected by living in a desert environment?

Assessment Plan

Students will prepare portfolios that include their individual research reports, book reviews, sketches, and other items they developed during the unit study. The individual reports, committee work and reports, book reviews, and unit examination will provide for assessment of the unit goals as follows:

Students' individual written reports will provide evidence of their progress in researching and writing clear and organized reports of their research. The written reports will also permit assessment of individual students' responses to one of the unit essential questions. Rubrics will be used to assess the book reviews.

The oral presentations of the findings of the four student research committees will provide a method of assessing students' progress in working cooperatively to summarize their individual findings and to present a coherent, organized report that addresses the required information (listed above). The presentations will also assist in assessing the students' speaking skills; their ability to locate information in order to prepare charts, graphs and displays; design and construct models; and to make use of art media—drawings, illustrations, and murals—to present visual information to indicate what they have gleaned from their research. Rubrics will be used in the assessment of the committee reports. The students' individual book reviews will demonstrate their ability to locate, read, and critically review a topical book. Rubrics will be used to assess the book reviews.

Students will take a unit examination at the conclusion of the study that includes questions on the information presented by the committees in their oral reports and their understanding of important terms and vocabulary. It will also require writing an essay from the viewpoint of a Native American living on a desert during the period of discovery by new settlers. The essay should include reactions to what students have learned about the loss of land and exposure to unfamiliar people and the new ideas the newcomers had for use of the land. Rubrics will be used to the assess essay section of the examination. The examination will provide information demonstrating the extent to which the students have gained knowledge and understanding of the four principal desert regions they have studied.

Exhibit 4.3 Complete Unit Chart for a Multidisciplinary Unit Plan.

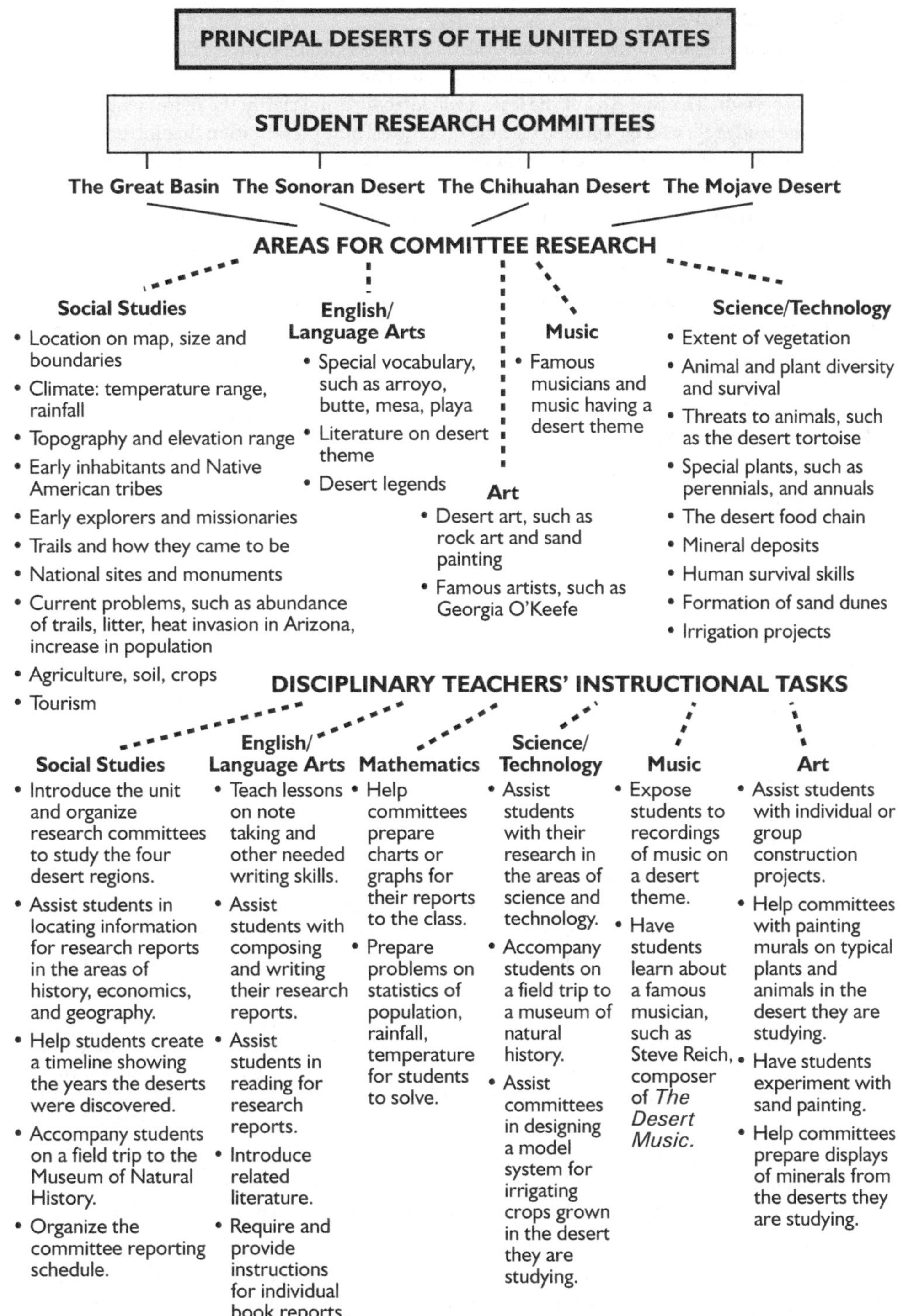

PRINCIPAL DESERTS OF THE UNITED STATES
STUDENT RESEARCH COMMITTEES
The Great Basin
The Sonoran Desert
The Chihuahan Desert
The Mojave Desert
AREAS FOR COMMITTEE RESEARCH
Social Studies
• Location on map, size and boundaries
• Climate: temperature range, rainfall
• Topography and elevation range
• Early inhabitants and Native American tribes
• Early explorers and missionaries
• Trails and how they came to be
• National sites and monuments
• Current problems, such as abundance of trails, litter, heat invasion in Arizona, increase in population
• Agriculture, soil, crops
• Tourism
English/ Language Arts
• Special vocabulary, such as arroyo, butte, mesa, playa
• Literature on desert theme
• Desert legends
Music
• Famous musicians and music having a desert theme
Art
• Desert art, such as rock art and sand painting
• Famous artists, such as Georgia O'Keefe
Science/Technology
• Extent of vegetation
• Animal and plant diversity and survival
• Threats to animals, such as the desert tortoise
• Special plants, such as perennials, and annuals
• The desert food chain
• Mineral deposits
• Human survival skills
• Formation of sand dunes
• Irrigation projects
DISCIPLINARY TEACHERS' INSTRUCTIONAL TASKS
Social Studies
• Introduce the unit and organize research committees to study the four desert regions.
• Assist students in locating information for research reports in the areas of history, economics, and geography.
• Help students create a timeline showing the years the deserts were discovered.
• Accompany students on a field trip to the Museum of Natural History.
• Organize the committee reporting schedule.
English/ Language Arts
• Teach lessons on note taking and other needed writing skills.
• Assist students with composing and writing their research reports.
• Assist students in reading for research reports.
• Introduce related literature.
• Require and provide instructions for individual book reports.
Mathematics
• Help committees prepare charts or graphs for their reports to the class.
• Prepare problems on statistics of population, rainfall, temperature for students to solve.
Science/ Technology
• Assist students with their research in the areas of science and technology.
• Accompany students on a field trip to a museum of natural history.
• Assist committees in designing a model system for irrigating crops grown in the desert they are studying.
Music
• Expose students to recordings of music on a desert theme.
• Have students learn about a famous musician, such as Steve Reich, composer of *The Desert Music*.
Art
• Assist students with individual or group construction projects.
• Help committees with painting murals on typical plants and animals in the desert they are studying.
• Have students experiment with sand painting.
• Help committees prepare displays of minerals from the deserts they are studying.

Disciplinary Teachers' Instructional Tasks

Social Studies Teacher

The social studies teacher will introduce the unit and essential questions and organize four student committees—one to research each of the four deserts in the study. This task will require three class periods. The first part of the lesson will introduce and clarify the five essential questions of the study followed by a guided viewing of a PowerPoint presentation that introduces the students to the four largest desert regions in the United States—the Great Basin, Chihuahua Desert, Mojave Desert, and Sonoran Desert. (The guided viewing protocol is explained in chapter 5 along with an sample lesson plan.) Following the presentation, students will be told that the class will be divided into committees to study each of the four desert regions. The students will be given an opportunity to consider which of the deserts they have seen in the presentation that they would like to investigate and then be asked to list the four regions in order of preference. Using the students' lists, committees will be formed by the social studies teacher—in consultation with other members of the team of teachers involved in the unit study.

Composition of the committees will be announced at the next class session, students will be reminded of the essential questions, and they will determine any additional questions that they would also like to include in their research. Although students may suggest other general areas, the list may include:

- Discovery
- Geography
- Climate
- Plant and animal life
- Early inhabitants
- Art
- Agriculture
- Natural resources
- Historic sites and national parks
- Famous residents
- Current problems

The committee assignments will then be given to students, and the four committees will meet to accomplish three tasks: (1) to select a committee chair and recorder, and (2) to divide the research responsibilities for the unit questions among their committee members. While the students are meeting, the teacher will circulate to assist where needed. The recorder for each committee will be responsible for submitting a record of the committee's decisions to the teacher at the end of the period.

After the committees have had time to begin investigating their deserts—approximately two weeks—conduct a lesson on timelines to show historical information. For most students at this level, only a review of timelines will be needed. Ask the four student committees to provide any information they have gleaned about the times of the initial discovery of each desert by European settlers. If any committee has not yet found such information, they will need to have some time to research it before continuing with the preparation of a timeline. Once all committees have the dates needed for the timeline, have the students prepare and post the timeline in the classroom.

Science Teacher

The science teacher will assume responsibility for an overview of the diversity of life forms in deserts, vegetation, the food chain, unique plants—sagebrush, Joshua trees, salt bush, agave, wildflowers—an ecological study exploring major threats to desert plant and animal life. Science classes will also review special mineral deposits found in deserts and the formation of sand dunes. The science teacher will assign a project related to irrigation in desert areas; the assignment will involve asking each committee to design an irrigation project for the desert it is researching. The irrigation project will become part of each committee report.

Social Studies and Science Teachers

Prepare students for a field trip to a local museum of natural history if available. The social studies teacher will help students to prepare a list of important questions to guide their time and research at the field site. On the day of the trip, both the social studies and science teachers will accompany the students. Students should have the list of the questions with them for reference as they try to gain answers at the museum. After returning to the school, the teachers will conduct a discussion using students' questions to elicit any answers they have gained from the trip. Students should record any new information from their trip in their notebooks for reference.

English/Language Arts Teacher

Select and introduce related literature on the desert theme to the students, such as *The desert: Land of lost borders* by M. Welland (2015).

The most current literature will need to be researched for this purpose. The teacher will make one or more selections to read and discuss with students in class. Students will be responsible for selecting a book and preparing a book review according to instructions to be outlined by the English/language arts teacher.

Other English/language arts classes will provide students with a review of note taking, recording, and documentation for reports; letter and e-mail messages for requesting information from outside sources; and an introduction of new vocabulary, such as *mesa, butte, playa,* and *arroyo.* Some time may be reserved to help the students locate information for their research. Some formal locational-skills lessons may need to be taught. It may be possible to ask the school librarian (or media specialist) to assist in teaching a series of lessons on locating reference materials in the library or media center. Time will also be reserved during English/language arts classes to explore legends of the desert and films portraying stories that take place in deserts.

Art Teacher

The art teacher will assist students in the preparation of the irrigation projects designed in science. They will study the work of famous artists associated with desert art, such as Georgia O'Keefe. During art classes, the committees will work on painting murals depicting typical plants and animals in the desert and prepare displays of minerals from the deserts they are studying.

Help students experiment with sand painting. Show Internet sites, such as the Penfield Gallery of Indian Arts at penfieldgallery.com/sand.shtml, and help the students to learn the original purpose and significance of the paintings. Students can then design their own sand paintings, using colored sand to create a design. Committees may include the examples they design in their final reports.

Activities Included in the Study

Committee Research and Reports

Student research committees will be formed to investigate each of the four desert regions of the unit study. Each committee will have six to eight student members. Composition of the group should be planned carefully, considering factors such as leadership, learning styles, social factors, the students' ability to share responsibilities, and their individual talents, interests, and academic capabilities. It will be important to ensure that all members of each committee share in both the research and reporting responsibilities. Develop a "buddy" system in committees that include special-needs students, who often leave the classroom during regular times devoted to research or project activities. Those who leave for special assistance programs can be paired with others in their committee groups who will review with them the committee's work during their absence.

The committees will be informed of the essential questions of the unit as the basis for their research, and unit-specific questions will be developed to guide the students' committee work. After they have completed their research, the committees will be responsible for reporting their findings to the class at the end of the unit. These reports will provide the culminating activity for the unit. The reports will be scheduled for each committee when research activity is nearing completion. The committees will be encouraged to report in different ways. Among others, possible reporting methods include:

- Panel discussions
- Demonstrations
- Dramatizations
- PowerPoint presentations
- Explanations of displays, constructions, and murals

Following each report, all students will participate in a discussion to summarize the information presented by the committee. The information will then be recorded in their notebooks. (Note that at the end of the study, a unit examination will be given that is based partly on the committee reports.)

The social studies teacher will provide students with guidelines for the content of the committee reports. Each report should include information about the discovery of the desert; its early inhabitants, geography, climate, predominant plant and animal species, agriculture, natural resources, historical sites and national parks, famous residents, and current problems. Each committee should also include the following for their reports:

- An explanation of items needed for survival in the desert it is studying. Encourage students to use the Internet for this kind of information because it is readily available at sites, such as DesertUSA.com.
- Charts or graphs of data such as the extent of vegetation, rainfall, and temperature variations in each of the four deserts.
- A model showing how an irrigation works to supply water for desert farming. The committees can opt to create a three-dimensional model with materials, a mural showing its design, and so on.
- A collection of photographs or drawings of plant and animal species in the region.
- A display of minerals found in the region it is investigating. The display can be a simple collection of photographs of the minerals, or if available, samples of the actual minerals.
- Samples of sand paintings.

Student Portfolios

Each student will maintain a portfolio during the study. Among other possible items, it should minimally include reports of the research they assumed responsibility for in their committees, book reviews, individual sketches for murals, the unit examination, and other individual contributions to committee research. Students should prepare their reports in writing. (Note that students who have difficulty preparing written reports may be given alternatives, such as designing a construction or project, preparing a PowerPoint presentation or a demonstration.) Encourage each student to use art media for a project that reflects understandings gained from their individual research.

Provide a form to guide the reporting process. The form should include information about the questions that the student was researching, answers to these questions, and the sources consulted for their research. Ask students to include the following information:

- The committee topic and the subtopic for which the student was responsible.
- The question(s) the student used to guide his or her research.

Findings

This section will vary in complexity according to each student's abilities. A simple list of findings, written in the student's own words, may be adequate for some. Others will be able to write several paragraphs or pages. Students using alternate reporting methods will need to give verbal explanations to communicate what they have learned.

References

Depending on each student's abilities, the documentation format can vary from a simple list of the books and other materials used to a more sophisticated and complete documentation format.

Individual Book Reports

Each student will read and prepare a review of a book from the library (either fiction or nonfiction) related to desert life. The book can be either prose or poetry. Students will need to write a review that encourages other students to read the book, or they can prepare a story map or plot profile for a work of fiction. The book reviews will help to indicate students' ability to read, analyze, and critically review a book on the desert theme. Students will also be demonstrating their ability to organize their ideas and write clearly. Rubrics will be used to assess individual book reports.

Unit Examination

At the end of the unit, students will take a unit examination designed by the teaching team and that is comprised partly of questions on the information presented in the four committee reports.

Materials

- Art materials for projects and report covers
- Computers with Internet access
- DVD and Internet video presentations on deserts in the United States
- Travel agency brochures that highlight desert vacation areas
- Sufficient quantities of social studies and science textbooks from a variety of publishers (four to six copies of each)
- Trade books from the school and public libraries on U.S. desert regions

Resources

New resources on national deserts may be published, and there are often new websites each time a unit is taught. The list of materials below provides only a sample of those available.

Butcher, R. D. (1976). *The desert*. New York: Viking Press.

Chihuahuan Desert. Retrieved from http://mbreiding.us/ert/Arizona/desertecology/chihua.htm

Chihuahuan Desert home page of the University of Texas. Retrieved from http://museum2.utep.edu/chih/chihdes.htm

Clapp, N. (2015). *Old magic: Lives of the desert shamans*. El Cajon, CA: Sunbelt Publications.

Desert Biome. (2013). The Encyclopedia of Earth. Retrieved from http://www.eoearth.org/view/article/151704/

Desert USA. (n.d.). Retrieved from http://www.desertusa.com

Deserts: Arid but full of life. (National Geographic). Retrieved from http://environment.nationalgeographic.com/environment/habitats/desert-profile/

Deserts: Geology and resources. United States Geological Survey. Retrieved from www.usgs.gov/science/

Digital desert. (n.d.). Retrieved from http://aeve.com/digitaldesertt/ddpi/lalol.html

Fowler, C. S., & Fowler, D. D. (2008). *The Great Basin: People and place in ancient times* (Popular Southwest Archaeology). Santa Fe, NM: School for Advanced Research Press.

Great Basin. Retrieved from http://www.encyclopedia.com/topic/Great_Basin.aspx

Great Basin Desert. Retrieved from http://www.desertusa.com/great-basin-desert.html

Images of the Great Basin. Retrieved from http://www.bing.com/images/search?q=the+great+basin&qpvt=the+great+basin&FORM=IGRE

Images of the Mojave Desert. Retrieved from http://www.bing.com/images/search?q=Mojave+Desert&qpvt=Mojave+Desert&FORM=IGRE

Images of the Sonoran Desert. Retrieved from http://www.bing.com/images/search?q=sonoran+desert&qpvt=sonoran+desert&FORM=IGRE

Jablonsky, A. (1994). *One hundred questions about desert life*. Oro Valley, AZ: Western National Parks Association.

Kane, C. W. (2011). *Sonoran Desert food plants: Edible uses for the desert's wild bounty*. Oracle, AZ: Lincoln Town Press.

Mails, T. E. (1998). *The Pueblo children of the earth mother*. New York: Marlowe.

Martinez, R. (2013). *Desert America: A journey through our most divided landscape*. New York: Metropolitan Books.

McMahon, J. A. (1997). *Deserts*. New York: Knopf.

Mojave Desert. Retrieved from http://digital-desert.com/wildlife/

Mojave Desert. Retrieved from http://mojavedesert.net/

Mojave Desert land trust. Retrieved from http://www.mojavedesertlandtrust.org/linkcampaign.php

Phillips, S. J., & Cornus, P. W. (1999). *A natural history of the Sonoran Desert*. Oakland: University of California Press.

Social and environmental aspects of desertification. Retrieved from www.usgs.gov/science/

Welland, M. (2015). *The Desert: Lands of Lost Borders*. London: Reaktion Books.

ACTIVITY

Study the web design in the Appendix, Exhibit A.5, from an interdisciplinary unit plan on the American Revolution, an intermediate topic also taught at the middle school level.

The design is prepared for an interdisciplinary unit; therefore, it does not indicate how it could be taught as a multidisciplinary study by a team of middle school teachers. Convert the many ideas for lessons and activities into a multidisciplinary unit chart that assigns responsibility for the different lessons and activities to individual team members. Plan your chart according to the information outlined in this chapter. You will need to work in a small group to complete this activity. Each member of the group should assume the role of one of the team members—social studies, English/language arts (literacy), mathematics, science, art, and so on. Work together to develop the chart.

Lesson Planning Strategies and Protocols

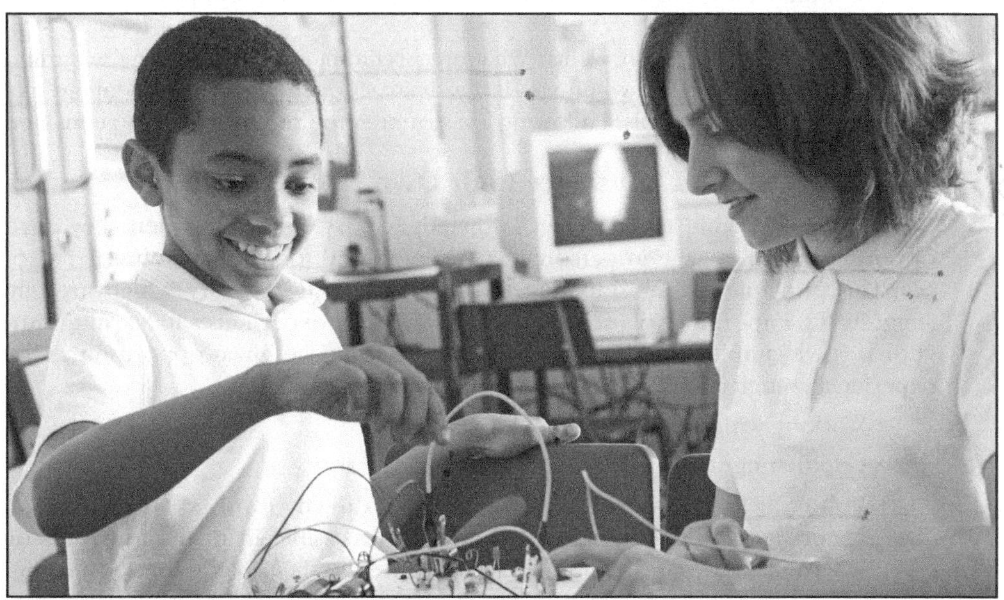

Overview

Chapter 5 is designed for teachers who plan lessons and activities involved in both interdisciplinary and multidisciplinary studies. The discussions of lesson-planning processes, protocols, and examples can also be useful for teachers who use other approaches to education at the elementary and middle school levels. The chapter addresses the following questions:

- What important aspects of learning and development are important to consider when planning lessons?
- How can Bloom's Taxonomy be useful in lesson planning?
- What are the essential components of a lesson-plan format?
- What critical elements need to be included in the procedure section of any lesson plan?
- How can protocols be helpful when planning some types of lessons, what are they, and how can they be applied?

Learning, Development, and Lesson Planning: What Needs to Be Considered?

Successful teachers have always attended to the literature and research regarding the psychology of learning and development. In discussions of developmentally appropriate teaching practices, Mayer (2008), Ryan, Cooper, and Tauer (2008), and Wakefield (1993) offer strong arguments for attending to child development and learning theory when planning for instruction. Others emphasize the need to understand the major principles of learning and their implications for the instructional processes.

The important question is this: What are preliminary considerations regarding learning and development when we design instructional plans for students in elementary and middle schools? Following are several important principles to consider.

Principle: Learners Construct Their Own Knowledge

Learners are able to construct knowledge most efficiently when they have opportunities to engage in personal experiences and to interact with other people. This principle is central to Piaget's (1973) adaptation theory, which strongly suggests the importance of including concrete, direct experiences in learning situations. For example, when possible, students should be given opportunities for experiences, such as:

- Working with manipulative materials
- Conducting their own experiments
- Visiting field sites where they can become directly involved with authentic materials and environments that are not accessible in their classrooms or where they can study genuine artifacts related to the topics they are studying.

Activities that encourage students to listen to others' viewpoints and to reflect on their own include:

- Cooperative learning projects and other group activities
- Debates and panel discussions
- Simulations
- Instructional games
- Whole-class discussions
- Learning centers that involve activities that require working with other students

Principle: New Knowledge Builds upon Existing Knowledge

In 1973, Kamii offered a detailed discussion of the relevance of the constructivist principle that new knowledge can only be built on a learner's existing knowledge base. This pedagogical principle is also based on Piagetian theory. When beginning to plan, we must know whether students have sufficient background knowledge for the concepts to be developed in a lesson. This determination can often be made near the beginning of the lesson by:

- Raising questions that help to determine what the students already know, and
- Providing a brief review of what students have learned about an ongoing study to help bridge the way to the new concepts to be taught in the new lesson.

These practices will also provide us with information about what our students know or believe they know about a topic before the lesson continues. Occasionally, we may discover that the new lesson needs to be delayed until sufficient background knowledge is developed.

Principle: Intrinsic Interest Is More Effective than Extrinsic Motivation

We know that when students are interested, learning is easier for them. Observation of students and conversations with them over time can provide information about their individual and group interests. Sometimes we can capitalize on specific interests of individual students during an interdisciplinary study. For example, we can suggest that an individual student conduct research on a subtopic of special interest that is related to a study the class is pursuing. Individuals can be invited to lead others in small-group studies and to present the results of their research to the class. Learning centers can be designed with activities that appeal to students' interests.

Principle: Concept Development Is Facilitated by Holistic Studies

In chapter 1, it was explained that research on the human brain suggests that concept development is facilitated by holistic, unified, interdisciplinary studies. This is a primary factor on which interdisciplinary instruction is based and on which the planning of lessons and units are structured. Although integration of the disciplines is appropriate for students at all levels, Jensen (2005) suggests that a holistic study may be "more useful for older students than younger ones" (p. 96). Jensen bases this statement on his belief that older students will have developed a greater fund of knowledge to help them form associations among the disciplines more easily. However, holistic studies are also appropriate for younger children as long as they study topics appropriate for their developmental level and have adequate concrete experiences to help them detect the interrelatedness of the disciplines.

Principle: The Learning Processes Are Important for Learning How to Learn

The idea that learning processes are important in all academic pursuits clearly suggests that to help students master the various processes needed for learning throughout life, we need to provide them with opportunities such as these:

- Experiencing the steps in the inquiry process as they conduct their own research on topics that are appropriate for their developmental levels
- Applying the scientific method of investigation and conducting their own experiments in science
- Practicing the various learning processes through activities provided in a learning center

Students who become skilled at the processes of learning are likely to be better equipped to become independent learners in the future.

Principle: Differentiated Instruction Is Essential for Promoting Learning in All Students

Today, any list of important teaching concerns must include attention to the many different ways students learn. Hall (2002) and Tomlinson and Moon (2013) provide exceptionally clear and comprehensive discussions of a *differentiated* instructional approach and assessment in such an environment. The authors not only promote this idea but also give us practical ways to manage it in our classrooms. In chapter 1, Sternberg's (1997) and Gardner's (1993b, 1999) theories regarding students' differing intelligences suggest that attention to individual cognitive strengths and working styles can enable more students to succeed in school.

However, Gardner has expressed his desire that his theory not be misinterpreted and that teachers seek appropriate applications of his theory in their practices (Viadero, 1995). For example, even though students have differing strengths in the nine multiple intelligence areas, certainly not all intelligences can or need to be addressed in a single lesson. Instead, lesson plans constructed over time should attempt to include opportunities for students to use their strongest intelligence areas to learn and show what they have learned.

Although the theories are similar, Gardner does not equate his MI theory with *learning styles* theory. Definitions of learning styles tend to vary; however, most suggest that they are the unique, individual strengths, preferences, and approaches students use as they attempt to acquire knowledge. Implications of learning styles theory suggest that when planning for instruction, we should consider practices that will help our students gain knowledge in different ways. For example, students can sometimes be offered choices, such as the following:

- Students who are researching a topic might be given a choice of writing a conventional paper or reporting in some other way—a computer presentation, a demonstration, a performance, a panel discussion, and so on.
- In the lower elementary grades, students might paint a mural or construct a diorama to show what they have learned.
- Learning-center activities can also offer opportunities for students to apply their individual learning styles and multiple intelligences by engaging in independent, hands-on activities, particularly in mathematics, science, and art.

In summary, organizing instructional plans that generate student interest and foster their participation is an important concern in the teaching and learning processes. Attention to students' developmental and individual learning preferences can help to ensure that students become more involved in the lessons and activities that are designed for them.

Bloom's Taxonomy: How Can It Assist the Lesson-Planning Process?

Teachers determine the questions, standards, and instructional objectives of their lessons, units, and learning-center activities. When planning the procedure of a lesson, we often find that we need to raise questions and give directions that range in level of difficulty. Questions may vary considerably from those that elicit fundamental, factual information to those that involve higher levels of thought.

How can we estimate the difficulty levels of our objectives, questions, and directions? Perhaps the most widely recognized classification system designed to help teachers determine the cognitive levels of the lessons they plan is Bloom's Taxonomy. Bloom (1956) outlined a six-level taxonomy to help determine the relative difficulty of instructional objectives. The taxonomy is also helpful for classifying questions, directions, and test items. A brief outline of Bloom's Taxonomy in the cognitive domain follows.

Level 1: Knowledge

Objectives and questions at level 1 require students to provide limited, memorized, factual responses. Genuine understanding may or may not be demonstrated in students' responses. Questions at this level usually require simple, convergent responses.

EXAMPLES

- What is the name of the largest city on the West Coast of the United States?
- What is the meaning of the word *irrigation*?
- Who is the author of *The Deerslayer*?

Level 2: Comprehension

Understanding is required at the comprehension level. When responding to questions at this level, students may need to explain, summarize, translate, and give examples to demonstrate their understanding.

EXAMPLES

- Write a summary of the main points in this article.
- Explain how an irrigation system works in a desert area.
- Give an example of a crustacean.

Level 3: Application

Students must use processes, problem solving, and research skills to determine their responses at the application level of the taxonomy. This level is exceptionally important because it is in applying what they know and understand that we are able to assess students' *real* understandings.

EXAMPLES

- Now that you have recorded the daily temperature on this graph for the past three weeks, what does the record appear to indicate?
- Sort these rocks into the three classifications we just studied.
- Solve these new mathematics problems using the process you have just studied.

Level 4: Analysis

Analysis requires interpreting, noting inferences, thinking beyond the literal level when reading, detecting cause-and-effect relationships, and drawing conclusions. Analytical questions usually invite more divergent responses.

EXAMPLES

- What are some reasons why our experiment with plants failed?
- What reasons can you give for the boy's actions in this story?
- Why do you think it is important to exercise our right to vote?

Level 5: Synthesis

Questions and directions for students at level 5 often ask for creative and divergent responses. New, or original, thinking is required to produce plans, raise hypotheses, predict, or produce original proposals, designs, art, or music.

EXAMPLES

- Devise a plan that will help to minimize the environmental problems caused by the increasing number of people settling in desert areas today.
- Write a poem that shows how you feel in the spring.
- Construct a diorama that demonstrates some aspect of what you have learned about your study of ancient Greece.

Level 6: Evaluation

Students make judgments at level 6. They decide ratings and express opinions based on standard or personal criteria.

EXAMPLES

- Does this essay on desert life include accurate information about current problems experienced by the people who live there?
- Which of these two plans to save endangered animals is better, or more likely to be effective?

Lesson-Plan Formats: What Are the Essential Components of a Lesson Plan?

Designing the plans for lessons and activities included in an interdisciplinary study is one of our most serious concerns. In addition to planning lessons that involve literacy, science, and social studies concepts, we also plan for a variety of activities, such as group discussions, cooperative group and committee work, panel discussions, dramatizations, simulations, and role-playing.

Each lesson or activity in a unit needs to contribute to the development of its standards and unit goals. Teachers who are new to the interdisciplinary approach usually find that, at first, it is helpful to include considerable detail in their lesson plans, especially when developing the steps they plan to follow in the lesson procedure.

Most lesson-planning formats are similar; all include sections for listing learning standards, goals or objectives, materials, assessments, the procedure, and materials. Some also include other sections, such as key—or focus—questions. The lesson procedure—the sequential, step-by-step outline for teaching the plan—is often considered the heart of any lesson plan. However, a procedure cannot be developed until decisions have been made about the learning standards, goal(s), and key questions, and until the methods of assessment are clear. These are essential in order to know what must be accomplished in the lesson procedure and how the students will be assessed in meeting the goals. The procedure then provides a detailed outline of how the lesson is expected to proceed. It includes information about the role of the teacher and may also provide notes about the anticipated actions and reactions of students during the lesson.

In some lesson plans, the procedure section is divided into distinct sub-sections, including motivation, development, and closure. Cooper (2006), Ornstein and Lasley (2004), Reiser and Dick (1996), and Roberts and Kellough (2008) use subdivisions for the procedure section in their lesson-plan formats. Segmenting the procedure section in this way can help to highlight important groups of steps in a lesson plan. For example, in the *Five-Step Lesson Plan* (Hunter, 2004), the procedure is subdivided into six parts: *anticipatory set, motivation, application, guided practice, closure,* and *follow-up activities*. Many find that the Five-Step Lesson Plan, which is explained later in this chapter, is particularly well suited for planning skills-oriented lessons. Other formats that do not segment the procedure section may be easier to adapt for lessons in history, literature, science, and for planning committee work or conducting field trips. Borich (2014), Post, Ellis, Humphreys, and Buggey (1997), and the backward design lesson plan format outlined by Moore (2009) tend not to segment the procedure section of the lessons they describe.

The procedure section for lessons in this text is not segmented; instead, it should be found flexible enough to accommodate planning most kinds of lessons and activities, including those needed for interdisciplinary and multidisciplinary units. Although *essential questions* are appropriate for the larger units of study, "lessons are simply too short to allow for in-depth exploration of essential questions" (Wiggins & McTighe, 2012, p. 8). Instead of listing essential questions, the lesson-plan format in this text includes a place for ***key questions*** or *focus questions*. Key questions are short-term, lesson-specific questions that indicate the intent of the lesson. Those questions are aligned with its goals and assessments. See Exhibit 5.1 on the following page for the lesson-plan outline that is followed in the sample lessons developed in this chapter.

The sequence in listing the various components of the lesson plan can differ from the outline shown here in order to accommodate individual preferences. For example, some teachers prefer to list the materials section before the procedure. The lesson plan topic, grade level, estimated time, and materials need little explanation. Unit and lesson plans both need to include lists of *learning standards* and *goals*. Most lesson plans also include at least one key question, one or more spe-

cific, short-term, ***behavioral objective(s)***, and an assessment plan.

Although a unit can address a number of learning standards and goals, a single lesson can address relatively few, often only one. The obvious reason for this is that a lesson is much narrower in scope than a unit and is usually taught over a short period of time. A lesson plan must include only the learning standards and goals that are specifically addressed in the lesson and aligned with its assessment plan and procedure. More information follows regarding learning standards, lesson goals, key questions, behavioral objectives, assessment plans, and lesson procedures.

Exhibit 5.1 Lesson Plan Outline.

Topic:
Level:
Estimated Length:
Learning Standards:
Goals:
Understandings
Knowledge
Skills
Dispositions
Key Questions:
Behavioral Objectives
Procedure:
Assessment Plan:
Summary/Evidence
Learning Plan:
Materials:
Resources:
Reflections:

Learning Standards

Learning standards are the comprehensive, long-term requirement in English/language arts and literature, social studies, science, and technical areas toward which a lesson contributes. The Common Core State Standards (CCSS), which are used in this text, were developed at the national level with contributions from professional education organizations. Individual state departments of education as well as committees of teachers and administrators in a school district may also add other standards for local use.

Learning standards communicate clearly and provide for a degree of uniformity from teacher to teacher and school to school. By using learning standards, we can help to ensure that our students are introduced to similar content regardless of where they attend school. In addition to the CCSS Learning Standards, states also have sets of standards for disciplines, such as social studies, that should be cited in lesson plans.

Goals

Lesson goals differ from learning standards in that they are written by individual teachers for a particular group of students. Goals specify the outcomes that are desired as a result of teaching a lesson. They indicate those understandings, knowledge, academic skills, and dispositions the lesson intends to foster. A lesson may only include an understanding goal, or a knowledge goal, or a skills goal, or even a disposition goal. Usually only one or possibly two of these areas will be the intended purpose of a particular lesson. For example, many lesson plans will only have as a goal the development of an understanding or a skill.

Goals for any lesson usually will vary considerably from one teacher to another. Even when the same topic is studied using the same materials, teachers may emphasize different goals for a particular lesson. Examples of learning standards and other goals follow.

EXAMPLES OF A LEARNING STANDARD AND FOUR GOAL TYPES

Students will:

Determine two or more main ideas of a text and explain how they are supported by key details; summarize the text (*CCSS, RI.5. 2*).

Understanding

Students will understand that all living things need food, air, and water to survive.

Knowledge

Students will know basic parts of plants.

Skill

Students will improve their ability to use a microscope to examine specimens.

Disposition

Students will share in the use of materials.

Key Questions

Key or focus questions have an important role to play in a lesson plan. Key questions "define tasks, express problems, and delineate issues" (Elder & Paul, 2002, p. 3). They reflect the process of inquiry, which always begins with questioning. A key question can be prepared that requires thought and responses at any level of Bloom's Taxonomy. To maintain the focus of a lesson, key questions must be aligned with the lesson's goals and assessment plan. The best key questions are those that are stimulating, require use of background knowledge and personal experiences, involve students, and infer the assessments that will be used to gain evidence of students' mastery of the lesson goals.

EXAMPLES

- How can we show support for the answers we give when questioned about information in a reading selection?
- How can the painting of a mural inform others of our findings from research?
- What can we do to show support for a friend?
- Why should a citizen exercise his/her right to vote?
- What is an appropriate form for a business letter?
- What factors should we consider before constructing a birdhouse for a specific kind of bird?

Note that each key question is short-term, specific, and comparatively narrow in scope. In order to assess students' ability to respond to the questions, students will most likely need to provide oral or written responses or produce a product. Consider the last example above: After teaching the lesson on wrens, we could simply ask students to explain verbally how to construct the birdhouse for wrens. (This would require the kind of thinking involved at the comprehension level of Bloom's Taxonomy.)

However, the key question may suggest that we want to know if students would actually be able to construct a birdhouse suitable for a wren (an *application-level* task). If so, we need to see if the students can do just that, possibly by having them draw plans for the birdhouse or, even better, actually construct one.

Behavioral Objectives

Every lesson plan includes at least one short-term objective. Lesson objectives usually conform to the format and terminology associated with *behavioral objectives*, which indicate specifically what students must do to demonstrate mastery of the lesson goals and that they are capable of responding to its key questions. Behavioral objectives are always student-focused to provide measures of assessment for the lesson. Following are three questions to consider when writing a behavioral objective statement:

1. What standards, goals, and key questions are being addressed in the lesson?
2. How will the students demonstrate that they have met them? What specific performances will students be expected to demonstrate? Performances are indicated by verbs describing observable student behaviors. Several examples of verbs that are acceptable for writing behavioral objectives are: list, define, label, describe, translate, explain, demonstrate, perform, compare, classify, design, summarize, select, and compare. All of these behaviors can be observed. Examples of verbs that are not acceptable are: know, understand, learn, and apply. These verbs do not clearly indicate an observable behavior.
3. How well are the students expected to demonstrate the behavior? How well will they need to perform what they are required to do? What is the standard that needs to be reached in order to meet the objective?

Behavioral objective statements can be written in a single sentence that includes (a) for whom the lesson is planned, (b) the behavior indicating that students have met the standards and key questions addressed in the lesson, (c) the special conditions (if any) under which these behaviors should be performed, and (d) how well the students must perform to meet the standards successfully.

EXAMPLES

- After a trip to the zoo (*describes a condition*), each student (*tells for whom the objective is intended*) will complete a drawing of one animal observed at the zoo and compose a sentence for each picture that includes at least one fact learned about the animal as a result of the field trip (*explains the specific behaviors to be demonstrated by the students*). *Note that the degree of acceptable performance for this objective for kindergarten or early first-grade level is implied to be 100 percent.*
- Given a compass and five written directions to follow (*the conditions*), each student (*for whom the objective is intended*) will accurately follow four of the five directions (*the behavior to be demonstrated and degree of acceptable performance; upper elementary grade level*).
- After completion of a unit on the theme Emerging African Nations (*the condition*), the students (*for whom the objective is intended*) will pass a comprehensive unit test on major concepts developed in the unit (*the behavior to be demonstrated*) with at least 75 percent accuracy (*the degree of acceptable performance; middle school level*).

Assessment Plan

The next section of a lesson plan includes two parts:

- A *summary* of the procedure to be planned and the technique(s) the procedure will use to assess the students' progress in meeting the lesson goals and ability to respond to the key questions.
- *Evidence*, a clear statement that is added after the complete procedure has been planned, specifying the number of the step—or steps—in the procedure where it will be possible to determine the students' ability to perform the tasks stated in the behavioral objectives.

Summary. In this part of the assessment plan, decisions need to be made before planning the lesson procedure about the best methods that will be used to determine the students' progress in meeting the goals of the lesson after it has been taught. Methods can include a wide variety of ways to accomplish this, such as holding a discussion with the class for general types of information and where it is not absolutely necessary to know if every student has mastered the goal. More often, we want to know how well each student has processed an understanding, knowledge, or skill. Written responses may be needed for interpretations of a literary passage or informational article. Constructions, performances, and examinations may be considered the most valuable methods for determining progress toward other goals.

EXAMPLE

Students will have a guided reading lesson of an informational section in their science text on plants. Each student will be required to write a summary of the information presented in the text.

Evidence. This part of the assessment plan can only be completed after the procedure of the lesson has been finalized. At that point, a statement can be added to the assessment plan that simply explains at which step or steps in the procedure the specific behaviors indicated in the behavioral objectives are performed by the students and can, therefore, be assessed. To determine if the evidence is clear, we need to be certain that the lesson is focused, that the procedure is aligned with the assessment plan and other components of the lesson—its standards, goals, and key questions.

EXAMPLE

The performance required by the behavioral objective of this lesson can be assessed at steps 4–6 in the lesson procedure.

The Lesson Procedure

As we gain experience in planning, we usually modify our planning strategies and tend to use shorter formats that fit our individual needs and teaching styles. Even so, it is important to consider, at least mentally, the steps that we will follow when teaching the lesson, and we need to ensure that several *critical elements* are always included in the lesson procedure.

Critical Elements in the Procedure Section

While designing the procedure section of a lesson plan, we should try to visualize what will occur at each step. One way to do this is to imagine recording the lesson with a video camera while trying to anticipate student responses and reactions as the lesson proceeds. Recognizing possible student behaviors—their reactions, interpretations, and potential misinterpretations—before teaching the lesson can help to allay some of our fears about what to do when the unexpected occurs during the lesson.

Regardless of how the procedure section is set up, it needs to include several elements which are critical to the potential success of the lesson. Others have stressed the importance of similar elements (Duplas, 2008; Ryan, Cooper, & Tauer, 2008). Following are critical elements that should be included in any lesson procedure.

- A clear *introduction* to the lesson and its purpose to help students to focus their thinking on the lesson topic
- A *connection* between students' current background knowledge and the concepts or skills to be developed by the new lesson
- Questions and/or other techniques that cause cognitive conflict in students' minds, that help them to realize they have something new to learn
- A step or steps at which the behavioral objective(s) of the lesson can be assessed
- Closure to the lesson

An Introduction. The lesson should be clearly introduced to help students focus their thinking on the lesson topic or problem and to inform them about what they should be able to do to show they have gained the desired results. This can often be accomplished informally. For example, a brief statement such as "Today, we are going to begin studying more about the planet Mars," or another explanation, can let students know what the lesson will be about or what the activity will involve. Students should then be told what they will be expected to do if they have understood the objective of the lesson.

A Connection with Students' Background Knowledge. Help students make connections between the new lesson and what they already know about the topic. This should happen early in the lesson procedure. Possible ways to accomplish this include:

- Reviewing what has been studied or learned previously about the topic,
- Reminding students about what they have been taught about the topic, and
- Asking students what they think they know about the new topic.

Occasionally, we may need to provide a preliminary experience or an entire lesson to help prepare students for new concepts and to develop adequate background for the information to be included in a new lesson.

Questions and Other Techniques that Produce Cognitive Conflict. Students construct their own knowledge, and the construction process cannot begin—nor will students become interested in learning anything new—until they first realize that there is something they do not know that is of importance to them. This constructivist viewpoint strongly suggests that motivation must develop from within. Therefore, instead of assuming the role of motivator, we need to help our students become aware of the need to develop some new knowledge or skill. In each lesson procedure, we must introduce *cognitive conflict* to help students realize that there is something they do not already know; then the process of acquiring new knowledge can begin. We can introduce cognitive conflict in a number of ways.

EXAMPLES

- Ask important questions during the lesson relating to the concept(s) to be developed.
- Have students observe a discrepant event—something they will have difficulty explaining immediately.
- Provide purposes for students or elicit purposes from the students before a reading, listening, or viewing experience or before they observe a demonstration.

Because questioning strategies are fundamental in presenting conflict, we need to become skilled at formulating both convergent and divergent question types. *Convergent questions* generally require a relatively narrow range of responses from students, whereas *divergent questions* are relatively open-ended and often encourage students to think critically and creatively. Models of the two question types are shown in Exhibits 5.2 and 5.3 (on the following page).

Exhibit 5.2 A Convergent Question-and-Response Pattern.

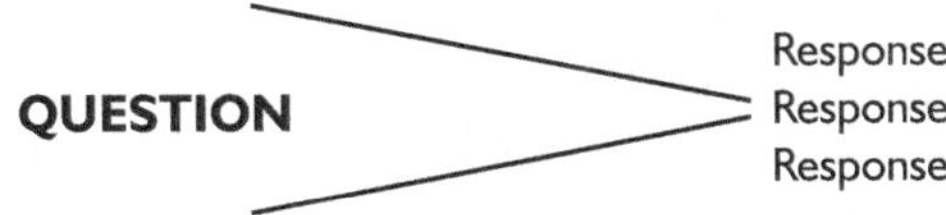

EXAMPLES (CONVERGENT QUESTIONS)

- Name two treaties that have involved European nations during the last two centuries.
- Please define *amphibian*.
- What is the second largest city in the world?
- In what country is the Congo River located?
- Which mathematics process is needed to solve these equations?

Exhibit 5.3 A Divergent Question and Response Pattern.

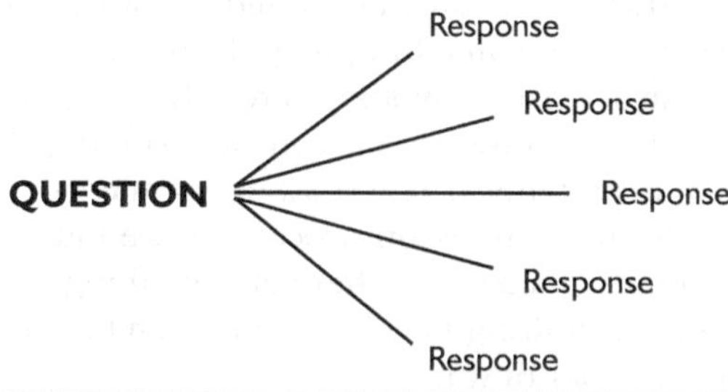

EXAMPLES (DIVERGENT QUESTIONS)

- Can you think of a way to improve our local system of mass transit?
- How did you feel when you listened to the recording of *Appalachian Spring*?
- What do you think this line in the poem means?
- What do you find especially interesting in this piece of art?

Holding a discussion during a lesson is often critical to helping students process the new concepts introduced in the lesson, particularly when stimulating, thoughtful questions are raised (Wiliam, 2014; Caram & Davis, 2005; Cooper & Kiger, 2008; DuPlass, 2008; Macbeth, 2003). Therefore, preparing for class discussions is an important step in the design of many lesson plans.

Some discussions arise spontaneously. Others we plan to include in a formal lesson in reading or another discipline. A discussion can even involve a lengthy debate about some specific issue or problem. To help students focus on the lesson topic and to ensure more productive discussions, the following suggestions may be helpful:

- Before beginning any discussion or raising a stimulating question, try to ensure that students have sufficient general background knowledge about the topic.
- Before the discussion, remind students of the rules that have been established for good discussions, such as raising one's hand before answering to allow more students opportunities to contribute. Interrupting a discussion to talk about rules distracts the group from the point of the discussion. If possible, ignore students who call out or who make unnecessary noise when raising their hands; instead, immediately call on another student.
- Maintain an emotional climate in the classroom that is conducive to a discussion. Students who feel safe from ridicule or sarcasm by other students or their teacher are likely to be more willing to contribute. They may also be more willing to risk making mistakes when answering questions.
- Decide in advance how to handle students who never volunteer to participate. Sometimes, a simple nod will invite a shy student to contribute. Make

decisions about whether or not to call on students by name if they do not volunteer. Some teachers believe that calling on students gives them an invitation to participate. Other teachers believe that calling on a student by name may be intimidating and even may increase the chance that these students will not volunteer in the future. In addition, other students in the group may believe that they do not need to offer to respond when a specific student is called upon for an answer.

- Raise only one question at a time. Silence after a question is raised does not necessarily indicate that students have failed to understand the question. They may need a few moments to consider a possible response. Wait at least four or five seconds before restating the question or raising another.
- Ask both convergent and divergent questions. Questions that require students to recall information are easy to prepare. However, it is also important to plan questions that require students to think critically and creatively.
- When a student responds with a vague answer to a question, ask for some clarification. Often, simply asking the student something like "Can you tell us more?" or "Can you give us an example?" will invite a clearer response.
- Summarize or ask students to summarize periodically during a discussion. Doing so will help to maintain focus on the main topic.

These general suggestions may help to make discussions during lessons more productive and interesting for students.

Assess the Lesson's Behavioral Objectives. At some step or steps in the procedure of a lesson, it should be clear that the behavior indicated in each behavioral objective is able to be assessed. For example, if in the behavioral objective students are required to underline all the verbs in a paragraph during a lesson on distinguishing verbs from other parts of speech, there should be a step in the procedure where students are asked to do so, thus ensuring that the objective is capable of being assessed.

Bring Closure to the Lesson. At the end of the lesson, the design of the procedure needs to include a way to bring the lesson or activity to closure. This important step helps students to summarize what they have gained during the lesson. "How a lesson ends can affect a learner's ability to organize, evaluate, and store information presented in class (Reese, 2014). Closure can be accomplished in a variety of ways, including those that appear below.

- Review with students what they have learned.
- Have one student or several students summarize what they believe they have learned.
- Hold a discussion about the students' different projects—drawing pictures, designing murals, preparing dioramas, constructing with papier-mâché or another art medium, presenting a drama or dance performance—that reflect the concepts they have gained from completion of the project.

Other Considerations for Planning the Lesson Procedure

In addition to the critical elements outlined above, other things are also important to consider when planning the lesson procedure.

Follow Appropriate Methods, Techniques, and Protocols. The method, approach, or technique used to structure the lesson procedure should be appropriate for the objectives of the lesson. For example, in the course of an interdisciplinary study, it may be helpful to have students read a selection from an article or other content material on the unit topic. It is appropriate to follow a *guided reading* protocol for this kind of lesson. (Guided reading is explained and illustrated with a sample lesson later in this chapter.) If a skill, such as letter writing or outlining, is being taught, following the *Five-Step Lesson* protocol is suitable. (The Five-Step protocol is also explained and illustrated with a sample lesson later in this chapter.)

Anticipate Possible Student Reactions and Responses. At various steps in the lesson procedure, students may be asked to respond in some way. For example, if a question is raised, students' possible responses can be noted in the lesson plan. Although students' anticipated responses and reactions are not typically included in lesson-plan procedures, doing so can help minimize problems that arise from unexpected reactions when the lesson is taught.

Attend to the Principles of Learning, and Consider Students' Learning and Working Styles. We should consider students' different learning and working styles when planning steps in the lesson procedure. Students' multiple intelligences, interests, and talents can often be addressed if they have been considered when preparing the lesson procedure.

All steps in the procedure should be well detailed and clear enough so that another teacher could follow the plan if necessary.

Sequence the Procedure Steps in a Logical Order. Check the sequence of the procedure to ensure it is clear, in logical order, and easy to follow.

In summary, attention to the preceding critical elements and other considerations for designing lesson procedures can help to promote a greater degree of success when the lesson is taught. Productive instructional sessions are more likely to occur when the procedure section of a lesson plan:

- provides a clear introduction to the lesson and helps students focus their thinking on the lesson theme,
- helps students make connections to what they already know about the lesson topic,
- stimulates thinking with questions and other techniques that cause conflict in students' minds,
- provides for assessment of the lesson objectives, and
- brings closure to the lesson.

Finally, lessons are more likely to be successful when their procedures follow appropriate methods, techniques, and protocols; attend to principles of learning and include notes about possible student reactions and responses; attend to students' different working and learning styles; provide enough detail; and are carefully sequenced.

Materials and Resources. It is only necessary to list the most essential materials and resources that will be needed to teach the lesson. Often, there are new materials each time the same lesson is taught, so the items in these sections of a lesson plan are never permanent.

Reflections. After a lesson has been taught to a group of students, we need to return to the plan to assess its success. Notes can be made in this section of the lesson plan to suggest modifications, such as changes in the sequence, steps where we need to proceed more slowly or more rapidly, steps that need to be added or deleted, rewording questions that were unclear, and so on—anything that needs to be changed to improve the way the lesson proceeds the next time it is taught.

Protocols for Planning Some Lesson Procedures

In most professions, there are protocols for some procedures. For example, in the medical profession, surgeons follow protocols for surgery; and in the legal profession, lawyers and judges have established procedural protocols for many deliberations. Many of the lessons and activities that are taught in elementary and middle schools can be planned by following established protocols that have evolved in the teaching profession. In teaching, a lesson *protocol* is a specific procedure that has been found to work well in practice over time and includes all of the critical elements discussed above.

We have learned that some specific instructional procedures—or protocols—work better than others for different types of lessons. There are activities, such as simulations and role playing, that have well-established procedures. Following are protocols that can be used when planning the kinds of lessons that are used frequently.

1. *Guided reading*: For many lessons in reading (Related to guided reading is the survey, question, read, recite, review—or SQ3R—technique; however, it is taught to students to apply independently.)
2. *Guided listening*: To help students attend and gain more from a listening activity
3. *Guided viewing*: To help students attend and gain more from viewing visual materials
4. *The know, want to know, learned (K-W-L) technique*: For establishing purposes and organizing for any kind of study
5. *The Five-Step Lesson*: A protocol especially useful for skills instruction
6. *The scientific method*: For lessons in which students undertake authentic science experiments

Each of the protocols is explained and illustrated with examples below. Note that steps in each of the sample lesson plan procedures that follow in this chapter are annotated to explain the purposes of the various steps and indicate inclusion of the critical elements in each of the lessons. The annotations are not typically included in a lesson plan.

Protocol: Guided (Directed) Reading Instruction

Guided reading is also known as directed reading, the directed reading activity (DRA), and the directed reading–thinking activity (DRTA) (Stauffer, 1969). Teachers have used guided reading successfully in teaching reading for many years (Cooper & Kiger, 2008). According to Heilman, Blair, and Rupley (2002), this protocol is generally followed in reading most commercial textbook series. It is a logical approach to use for many instructional reading activities and is especially suitable for reading content material in connection with interdisciplinary studies. The four steps in the protocol are:

1. *Pre-reading and introduction to the selection to be read.* Students are helped to make a connection between what they will be reading and their current background knowledge. Important new vocabulary and concepts are introduced. It is usually best to include only the essential new vocabulary and concepts that we believe students will not be able to decode or comprehend successfully on their own. Students may lose interest if too much time is spent at this step in the protocol. Also, we want to encourage students to use the word-analysis skills they have developed to attack new words they meet and to use context and other comprehension clues to understand new concepts that are included in new reading materials.
2. *Guided silent reading of the selection.* We need to set specific purposes for reading the new selection; this is especially important when students are being helped to read difficult material at their instructional reading level (Tovani, 2005). If the selection is long, it can be subdivided into shorter sections for silent reading. Vacca and Vacca (2014) suggest that students in the middle elementary grades can usually read passages of approximately 500–900 words. Younger students should be assigned somewhat shorter passages at a time. To set a purpose, the teacher can raise a specific question that can be answered only after the passage is carefully read. Students can often set their own purposes by deciding what they would expect to find in the reading, or they may be asked to predict what they believe will occur in the selection before they read silently to determine if their predictions are accurate.
3. *Discussion following silent reading and oral rereading to support responses to questions.* After students have finished reading the selection (or part) silently, questions are raised relating to the main purpose set for reading. If students have made predictions, they can be asked about the accuracy of their predictions. During the discussion, students should be asked to read a sentence or short part of the selection orally that provides supporting evidence for their answers, or to read orally a part of the text that confirms their predictions. In the primary grades, it may be necessary to have students reread more of the selection orally to determine their use

of the word-analysis skills they have been taught. However, asking students to read an entire selection orally after they have read it silently is not usually necessary beyond beginning reading levels. Doing so not only prolongs the activity, but it can also interrupt the flow of information or narrative, reduce overall understanding of the reading material, and even destroy students' interest. Students generally read silently when reading on their own and when taking examinations; therefore, it seems logical to encourage them to read silently and be prepared to support their answers during instructional sessions. If we do not encourage the practice of reading silently for comprehension, students may be at some disadvantage when they must do so in test situations. The guided reading protocol may, in fact, be of considerable help to students who need to improve their scores on such tests.

4. *Follow-up skills and enrichment activities.* Practice with skills on worksheets or in workbooks may be helpful for some students after reading a selection. However, other activities, such as creative writing, outlining a selection, preparing a dramatization based on a narrative selection, or writing a short report of content material, may be more beneficial and engender greater student interest.

Guided reading encourages students to read the way most of us read through life—silently, as we follow a narrative or search for information in reference books and other content materials. Following is a sample lesson plan using the guided reading protocol. It assists students with reading a selection on the Boston Tea Party during their study of the American Revolution. This unit develops an understanding of the reasons for discontent among the American colonists prior to the outbreak of war.

Sample Lesson Plan Following the Guided Reading Protocol

Topic: The Boston Tea Party

Level: Grade 5

Estimated Time: 35–40 minutes

Learning Standards

Students will:

- Determine two or more main ideas of a text and explain how they are supported by key details; summarize the text. (*CCSS R.5.2*)
- Use a variety of intellectual skills to demonstrate their understanding of major ideas, eras, themes, developments, and turning points in the history of the United States and New York. (*New York State Learning Standard for Social Studies 1*)

Goals

Students will understand that:

- Serious disagreements about political issues can cause anger and frustration among people, which can result in national rebellion and revolution.

- The historical event, the Boston Tea Party, was an outward expression of American colonists' anger about taxation without representation.

Students will improve their skills:

- In comprehending information when reading in academic content areas.

Key Questions

- What can result when people have serious disagreements about political issues?
- Why did the American colonists carry out the Boston Tea Party?

Behavioral Objective

After reading a selection on the Boston Tea Party, students will respond accurately to five of the six questions raised about the reading and support their responses by orally reading appropriate sections in the text.

Procedure

Pre-Reading

Steps 1–4: *Students are helped to make a connection between what they will be learning and their previous study of colonial history. They are introduced to the topic of the new selection to be read.*

1. Remind the students that they have been studying colonial history prior to the American Revolution. Explain that they are now ready to learn more about the specific activities that eventually led to war.
2. Ask the students if they can recall the names of some of the colonial leaders. *Students may recall those who played significant roles, including John Hancock, Samuel Adams, John Adams, and others.*
3. Tell the students that, today, a short selection from the Internet about the Boston Tea Party has been duplicated for them to read; it is a significant event that occurred before the revolution.
4. Explain that the selection will help them to know more about the causes of the American Revolution.

Steps 5–7: *New vocabulary and concepts are introduced.*

5. Ask students if they know the meaning of the word *representation*. Write the word on the board. *Students may respond that it means to have a part or role in something. Explain further if necessary by writing the word in a sentence, such as: "We have representation in our school through our Student Council."*
6. Ask the meaning of donning a disguise. Write the phrase on the board. *Students are likely to know that it is something you wear to keep people from knowing who you are. If they are unsure, explain further.*
7. Write the word *intolerable* in a sentence on the chalkboard: "The weather was miserable; it was intolerable." Ask students what intolerable must mean. *Students will probably equate it with miserable, hard to take.*

Guided Silent Reading

Steps 8–9: *Students are given an overall purpose for reading the selection silently, and they receive the selection.*

8. Say, "Now, I would like you to read the selection silently. As you read, try to determine the main reason why the Boston Tea Party took place." Tell students they may take

notes and to turn the selection over on their desks when finished reading, so that we will know when everyone is ready to discuss what they have learned.

9. Distribute the reading selection to each student. Explain that if they have any difficulty while reading they should ask for help.

Discussion

Steps 10–11: *Discussion follows silent reading. Questions are raised that are related to the purpose established in step 8. The behavioral objective is checked.*

10. When most students have completed the reading, ask the class for the main reasons for the occurrence of the Boston Tea Party. Note their answers on the board. As students contribute responses, ask them to locate and read a sentence or two that supports what they contribute orally to the class. *Students should include the idea that the British had imposed taxes on the colonists without their having a voice. The colonists had no representation in the British Parliament, the body that imposed taxes on the colonists. Students may also cite the Tea Act and Stamp Act.*
11. Raise other related questions, and ask for supporting evidence in the text:
    - What did the Tea Act do in addition to lowering the price of the East India Company tea? *Students should respond with the idea that it made it impossible for the colonists to buy tea from any other place.*
    - Why were the British concerned about the East India Company? *Students should reply that the company wasn't selling enough tea.*
    - Why couldn't the colonists do anything about the tax? *Students should suggest that they hadn't decided on the tax, that it was decided by the British Parliament, in which they had no voice.*
    - Why do you think the colonists who emptied the tea into Boston Harbor disguised themselves as Native Americans? *Students should say that it was so that no one would be able to tell who they were.*
    - How did this make the British feel? *Students should reply that the British became angry.*

Closure

Steps 12–13: *The lesson is brought to closure with a summary of what students have gained from the selection, and the key questions are assessed.*

12. Bring the lesson to closure by asking the students what they believe was the colonists' main purpose in the Boston Tea Party affair. Finally, ask what this lesson suggests can happen when there are serious disagreements between nations about political issues. *Students should suggest that the colonists hoped to make the British end the taxes they had imposed. They should also suggest that when there are such disagreements, the people may try unusual methods to resolve them.*
13. Ask students to copy the reasons listed on the board into their notebooks for future reference.

Assessment Plan

Summary and Evidence

The behavioral objective and the key question of this lesson require students to correctly answer at least five of six questions raised during the discussion and to support their reasons by selecting and reading orally an appropriate passage in the text. Assessment of the behavioral objective can be assessed in steps 10 and 11 in the lesson procedure. The key questions are assessed at step 12. Students' comprehension will be determined by observation as well as their responses to the questions.

Materials

Social Studies for kids: The Boston Tea Party. Retrieved from http://www.socialstudiesforkids.com/articles/ushistory/bostonteaparty.htm

(Assemble a collection of reference items from the school media center and local public library for student use. Examples appear below.)

Resources

Antram, D. (2013). *You wouldn't want to be at the Boston Tea Party: Wharf water tea you'd rather not drink*. London: Franklin Watts.

Krull, K., & Mortimer, L. (2013). *What was the Boston Tea Party?* New York: Grosset & Dunlap.

Madden, J. (2011). *History of the Boston Tea Party for kids*. San Francisco: Shamrock Eden Publishing.

Sons of Liberty (a History Channel mini-series on the events that precipitated the Revolutionary War). http://www.history.com/shows/sons-of-liberty/about

Unger, H. G. (2011). *American tempest: How the Boston Tea Party sparked a revolution*. Philadelphia, PA: Da Capo Press.

Reflections

After this lesson has been taught for the first time, notations will be made about its success with students, any problems that arose during the lesson, and any steps in the procedure that need to be changed if the plan is used for another group of students. For example, some questions may have stimulated student interest and participation; others may need rephrasing to be clear; there may be a need to raise additional questions; others may need to be deleted because of their failure to elicit responses from the students.

Protocol: SQ3R: Survey, Question, Read, Recite, Review for Independent Reading

A technique related to guided reading is SQ3R. Students learn to apply the steps in the protocol independently because the teacher is not present. SQ3R is self-guided reading. The five steps in SQ3R are as follows:

1. *Survey.* Students learn to look over the selection they will be reading and try to recall what they know about the topic. Titles, headings, subheadings, illustrations, photographs, captions, and introductory paragraphs are examined.
2. *Question.* The teacher is absent, so students raise specific questions to guide their reading. They can learn to turn boldface headings into questions to help with this step.
3. *Read.* Students read the selection, keeping in mind the questions they raised.
4. *Recite.* Students try to answer their questions after reading. They prepare notes for later review.
5. *Review.* Students check their notes to review what they gained from the reading material.

Protocol: Guided Listening

A guided listening protocol is similar to guided reading. It provides direction for students when material is read to them or when they are listening to a speaker or some recorded material. These are lessons that are frequently found in interdisciplinary studies. To follow this protocol, we need to:

- Help students make the necessary cognitive connection with the topic of the material they will hear.
- Clarify new concepts or vocabulary included in the listening activity.
- Help students attend to the material they will be hearing by providing or eliciting from students a purpose or purposes for listening.
- Hold a discussion following the listening session to determine what students have gained from listening.

The sample lesson plan below follows the guided listening protocol and is designed to introduce students in a fourth grade to their new interdisciplinary study of Alaska. Important understandings addressed in this lesson are that lifestyles in world communities are influenced by environmental and geographic factors and that culture and experience influence perceptions of places and regions in the United States, Canada, and Latin America.

Two Lesson Plans Following a Guided Listening Protocol

Example 1: An Introduction to a Unit on Alaska

Topic: Eskimos of Alaska

(This lesson is a guided listening activity designed by teachers Audrey Asaro and Smithe Jean-Baptiste that introduces students to an interdisciplinary unit on the study of Alaska.)

Level: Grades 4–5

Estimated Time: 30–45 minutes

Learning Standards

Students will:

- Paraphrase portions of a text read aloud or information presented in diverse media and formats, including visually, quantitatively, and orally. (*CCSS SL.4.2*)
- Use a variety of intellectual skills to demonstrate their understanding of the geography of the interdependent world in which we live—local, national, and global—including the distribution of people, places, and environments over the Earth's surface. (*New York State Learning Standard for Social Studies 1*)

Goals

Students will understand that:

- Physical environment influences life and culture in diverse world regions.
- Cultural differences exist among people living in different regions of the United States.

Students will improve their skills:

- For listening to information read aloud to them.

Key Questions

- How does geography influence the lives of the Alaskan Eskimo people?
- Are there cultural differences between the Alaskan Eskimo people and our own culture? If so, how do we differ? In what ways are we alike?

Behavioral Objective

After listening to a reading of the book, *The Seasons and Someone*, each student will suggest in writing that geographic location and environment influences differences in lifestyle between Alaskan Eskimo people and our own, and state at least one way they differ and one way they are similar.

Procedure

In preparation for this lesson, a map of the Western Hemisphere should be displayed, and a small collection of materials on this topic should be available in the classroom. Have the students meet in a section of the classroom conducive to listening, where they will listen to a reading of *The Seasons and Someone*, by Virginia Kroll. This book is about a young Eskimo girl and her family. Indented notes indicate the purposes of specific steps in the procedure.

Pre-Listening

Steps 1–4: *Students are helped to recall what they already know or believe they know about the topic. This establishes the needed connection to the reading material they will hear.*

1. When ready for the lesson, ask students what they know about the Eskimo people. *Students will probably reply that Eskimos are people who live in the cold weather of the North, that they live in igloos, and that they are people of the snow.*
2. Ask if students know the part of the United States where Eskimos are living. *Some students may know that Eskimos live in the state of Alaska or in the north.*
3. Ask if students know any other parts of the world where Eskimos are living. *Some students may cite the North Pole and Canada. Some may not know.*
4. Ask for volunteers to point out Alaska, Greenland, Canada, and the parts of Asia where Eskimos live. Assist students as needed in finding these locations.

Steps 5–7: *Students are given specific purposes for listening to the selection.*

5. Before beginning to read the story, ask students to listen carefully to learn about the family's living environment, how it is similar and different from ours, what their homes are like, the kinds of clothing they wear, and the kinds of animals they have. List these purposes on the board or on a chart for student reference during the reading.
6. Begin the oral reading with the author's note. The note explains that Eskimos inhabit the northernmost areas of the world, areas that have the coldest and most bitter weather. The note also gives some information about Eskimo beliefs, customs, and homes. Ask students if they have any questions. Respond as needed; then continue.
7. During the reading, stop occasionally to show students the beautiful illustrations of Eskimo life and the Eskimo environment. Also, ask for any questions, and remind students about the list of purposes for listening.

Discussion Following Listening

Steps 8–9: *Students' written responses at step 8 and the discussion in step 9 will provide for assessment of the lesson objective.*

8. After the story has been read aloud, begin assessing what students have gained from the listening activity by asking each student to take a few minutes to write (1) what he or she learned about how geographic location influences Eskimo life in Alaska when compared with our own and (2) to state one way our lifestyles are alike and one way they differ. Refer to the list on the board as an outline.
9. After students have finished writing their answers, collect the written lists to assess later, and then bring closure to the lesson by asking each student to tell one thing he or she learned from listening to the story about this Eskimo family that is either alike or different from our lifestyle or how the geography influences their lives. *Students should include references to the cold geographical climate which influences the kinds of homes they live in, the clothing they wear, and the foods they eat. It is expected that students will mention animals that live in the environment, such as oxen, seals, birds, and polar bears. They may suggest that we all live in families, that we have pets, and so on.*

Closure

Step 10: *The lesson is brought to closure.*

10. To conclude the lesson:
    - Tell the students to keep in mind all they learned from this story about one Eskimo family, and explain that this lesson begins a new study during which they will be working in committees to complete research on Alaska for the next several weeks.
    - Direct students' attention to the materials that have been collected in the classroom on Alaska for their use. Explain that they may look at these materials to get some ideas about what they may be able to learn about Alaska.
    - Ask students to begin thinking about what they would like to learn about Alaska as they begin the study. Explain that after they have had a few days to look over the materials and to think about what they would like to learn, the class will prepare an outline and list of their questions to help guide their research. *Note that the essential questions of the unit will be compared with the students' questions. Essential questions that are not included in the students' questions will be added.*

Assessment Plan

Summary and Evidence

A book will be read to students, who will then be asked to suggest how the geography of the areas where Eskimos live affects their lifestyle. Students will also be required to contrast the geographical differences between the lands of Eskimos and their own area. Assessment of the behavioral objective and key questions can be accomplished at steps 8 and 9 of the lesson procedure. Students' listening skills will be assessed by observation of their attention during the reading and their written responses.

Materials

Assemble a collection of materials on Alaska and Eskimos, including large maps of the United States and the world.

Resources

Brown, T. (2006). *Children of the midnight sun: Young native voices of Alaska*. Portland, OR: Alaska Northwest Books.

Kroll, V. L. (1994). *The seasons and someone*. San Diego, CA: Harcourt Brace.

Spilsbury, L. ((2011). *Igloos and Inuit life* (The big picture: Homes). North Mankato, MN: Capstone Press.

Stankovich, G. (2013). *The story of Owinga: A little Eskimo girl*. Bloomington, IN: Xlibris.

Yacowitz, C. (2003). *Inuit Indians* (Native Americans). Portsmouth, NH: Heinemann.

Reflections

After this lesson has been taught for the first time, notations will be made about its success with students, any problems that arose during the lesson, and any steps in the procedure that may need to be changed if the plan is used for another group of students. For example, some questions may have stimulated student interest and participation; others may need rephrasing to be clear; there may be a need to raise additional questions; others may need to be deleted because of their failure to elicit responses from the students. It may be found necessary to divide the reading into several sections with only one reason given for each section read aloud.

The second example of a guided-listening lesson plan is an alternative to the guided-reading lesson above on the Boston Tea Party during a unit of study on the American Revolution. This guided-listening lesson reviews a firsthand account of the sequence of events surrounding the Boston Tea Party. It also assists students in understanding the events that led to war with the British.

Example 2: The Boston Tea Party

Topic: The Boston Tea Party

Level: Grades 5–6

Estimated Time: 30–45 minutes

Learning Standards

Students will:

- Summarize a written text read aloud or information presented in diverse media and formats, including visually, quantitatively, and orally. (*CCSS SL.5.2*)
- Use a variety of intellectual skills to demonstrate their understanding of major ideas, eras, themes, developments, and turning points in the history of the United States and New York. (*New York State Learning Standard for Social Studies 1*)

Goals

Students will:

- Understand that the Boston Tea Party was caused by anger of the colonists about a British plan to force the colonies to allow them to deliver their tea to the colonies in Boston.
- Know that the Boston Tea Party involved several major events, including:
  - — A meeting of citizens at a church in Boston with their governor to decide if any action would be taken to prevent the tea from being delivered by the British.

— The lack of any resistance from the British as the tea was dumped.

— The attempt of some Bostonians to rescue the tea from the water after it had been dumped.

— A number of colonists dressed as Native Americans who boarded a British cargo ship to dump its tea into Boston Harbor and prevent the tea from being unloaded onshore.

- Improve their comprehension skills in listening to informational text read aloud.

Key Questions

- Why did the colonists plan the Boston Tea Party?
- What events took place on the day of the Boston Tea Party?

Behavioral Objective

After listening to a reading of an eyewitness account of the Boston Tea Party, students will respond accurately to at least 12 of the 14 questions raised during discussion.

Procedure

In preparation for this lesson, a period map of Boston Harbor in the pre-revolution era should be projected from the Internet or otherwise displayed. Students have been studying events leading to the American Revolutionary War. This lesson will involve a reading by the teacher of a firsthand account of the events of the 17th of December, 1773, when the Boston Tea Party occurred. Indented notes indicate the purposes of specific steps in the procedure.

Pre-Listening

Steps 1–4: *Students are helped to recall what they already know about the topic. This establishes the needed connection to the reading material they will hear. They are also introduced to vocabulary that may be unfamiliar to some.*

1. When ready for the lesson, ask students if they can recall some of the events leading to the American Revolutionary War that they have been studying. *Students should recall the formation of the Stamp Act, Sons of Liberty, the Townshend Acts, the Boston Massacre, and the Tea Act.*
2. Ask if students know what a *rebel* is. *Some students may suggest that a rebel is a person who objects to something.* Clarify the meaning as needed.
3. Read the sentence: "Jim thought it would be expedient to help his mother with the dishes so they could get to the movies on time." Ask students if they can tell what *expedient* means in the sentence. *Students will probably suggest that his helping would make it possible to get to the movies on time. Clarify if needed.*
4. Say: On Halloween, many people go to parties in a disguise. Ask: What does *disguise* mean? *Students are likely to say, "dress so that people can't recognize you." Again, clarify if needed.*

Step 5: *Students are given an overall purpose for listening to the selection.*

5. Explain that the students will be listening to a reading of an account of another historical event leading to the American Revolution by George Hewes, an eyewitness, a colonist who was present at the event. It is his personal record of the events of December 17, 1773, the day of the Boston Tea Party. Before beginning the reading, ask students to listen carefully to learn about the various events of that historical day and evening. Also explain that because the account includes so much information, it will be read aloud in several sections.

Listening and Discussion

Steps 6–13: *Students' responses at steps 7, 9, 11, and 13 in the discussion will provide for assessment of the behavioral objective.*

6. Before reading the first paragraph, ask students to listen in order to learn what the British were planning to do to make sure that the tea that had arrived from England in Boston Harbor would be delivered on shore.
7. After reading the paragraph, ask if anyone can tell what the British planned to do. *Students should suggest that the British had cannons with them that they would use if needed to unload the cargo. If students need help, read part of the last sentence aloud, "... they should on that day force it on shore, under the cover of their cannon's mouth," and ask students if they can tell from that sentence what the British had planned.*
8. Before reading the next three paragraphs, explain that they will learn that people attended an important meeting. Ask the students to listen in order to learn the result of that meeting.
9. After reading the three paragraphs, ask students the following questions:
   - What was the purpose of the meeting? *Students should respond that it was to decide if the colonists would do anything to prevent British tea from being unloaded in Boston.*
   - When Governor Hutchinson was asked if he would take some measures to prevent the tea from being unloaded, how did he respond? *Students should say that he told them he would let them know his answer later that day, but then, he left the city.*
   - What was the result of the meeting? *Students should respond that the meeting broke, and the people hurried off to Griffin's Wharf.*
10. Before reading the next five paragraphs, ask students to listen in order to learn about the events that occurred at the wharf and on the ships.
11. After reading the five paragraphs, ask the following questions:
    - What did George Hewes see when he went out into the street leading to the wharf? *Students should note that like Hewes, other people were all dressed in disguise.*
    - At the wharf, after the participants were divided up to board the three ships carrying the tea and boarding the ship to which Hewes was assigned, what did he have to do? *Students should say that he was responsible for demanding the keys to the cargo hatches and some candles.*
    - How did the men go about emptying the tea? *Students should include the idea that they used tomahawks to open the chests, and that they then poured the contents into Boston Harbor.*
    - Why do you think they wanted to make sure the tea was exposed to the sea water? *Students should reply that doing so would make the tea unusable.*
    - How did the British ships near them respond? *Students should say that they did not do anything to stop them.*
    - How long did it take to dump all the tea? *Students should recall that it was only about three hours.*
12. Before reading the remaining paragraphs, ask students to listen in order to learn what some people on the shore tried to do after the tea was in the water.

13. After completing the selection, ask the following questions:
    - What were some people on the shore trying to do and why? *Students should recall that some people were trying to save the tea from the water to use for themselves.*
    - How did the men react to one person taking tea? *Students should recall that they seized him, tore off his coat, and chased him through the crowd.*
    - How did they keep others from trying to take the tea that remained in the water the next day? *Students should explain that some sailors and other men rowed small boats in any area where there was still tea and beat the tea to make it sink.*
    - How did the men who were on the ships ensure that no one in the group or onshore could ever tell who they were? *Students should mention the disguises.*
    - Can you suggest the main cause of The Boston Tea Party? *Students should include the idea that the colonists wanted to prevent the British from delivering their tea in the colonies. They may also recall that colonists were angry about a duty or tax on the tea that they did not want to have to pay.* (Note that this account doesn't include information about the British East India Company's financial problems and the drastic lowering of the price of its tea, which would interfere with tea purchases from colonial companies.)

Closure

Step 14: *The lesson is brought to closure.*

14. Ask students to participate in reviewing the major events of the day of the Boston Tea Party, and write their summary on the board. Finally, ask students to copy the summary in their notebooks.

Assessment Plan

Summary and Evidence

Students can be assessed on their listening comprehension of the events of the Boston Tea Party affair by their responses to a number of questions during a guided listening experience. The behavioral objective of this lesson asks students to respond accurately to at least 12 of the 13 questions raised during the lesson discussion. The learning standards, understanding goal, and first key question may be assessed in part with the reasons students' suggest for the final question of step 13. The knowledge goals and second key question can be assessed by students' responses to the questions at steps 7, 9, 11, and 13. Students' skills in listening for informational text can be assessed by observation of their participation throughout the questioning steps in the lesson.

Materials

Locate for projection a pre-revolution map of the Boston Harbor area.

American Revolution Organization: *The Boston Tea Party.* Retrieved from http://www.theamericanrevolution.org/EventDetail.aspx?event=3

Resources

Antram, D. (2013). *You wouldn't want to be at the Boston Tea Party: Wharf water tea you'd rather not drink.* London: Franklin Watts.

Krull, K., & Mortimer, L. (2013). *What was the Boston Tea Party?* New York: Grosset & Dunlap.

Madden, J. (2011). *History of the Boston Tea Party for kids.* San Francisco: Shamrock Eden Publishing.

Sons of Liberty (a History Channel mini-series on the events that precipitated the Revolutionary War). http://www.history.com/shows/sons-of-liberty/about

Unger, H. G. (2011). *American tempest: How the Boston Tea Party sparked a revolution.* Cambridge, MA: Da Capo Press.

Reflections

After this lesson has been taught for the first time, notations will be made about its success with students, any problems that arose during the lesson, and any steps in the procedure that need to be changed if the plan is used for another group of students. For example, some questions may have stimulated student interest and participation; others may need rephrasing to be clear; there may be a need to raise additional questions; others may need to be deleted because of their failure to elicit responses from the students. Students' comprehension skills will be assessed by observing their attention to the reading and their answers to questions raised during the discussion.

Protocol: Guided Viewing

A guided viewing protocol is also similar to guided reading, but it provides direction for students when they are watching a video, a computer presentation such as PowerPoint, or a filmstrip for some specific information. The following steps are included in the guided viewing protocol:

- Students are helped to make the necessary cognitive connection with the topic of the material they will be viewing.
- New concepts or vocabulary that will be included in the visual material are introduced.
- Specific purposes for viewing are given to direct students' attention and help them focus on the visual presentation.
- Discussion is held with the students to determine what they have gained from the viewing activity.

Guided viewing encourages students to watch attentively as they follow a narrative or search for information in visual materials. See the sample lesson plan below which follows the guided viewing protocol. It is a lesson that introduces students to a new interdisciplinary study on the exploration of outer space and addresses important understandings that scientific investigation often involves considerable failure before success and that new scientific discoveries can stimulate important turning points in history.

Lesson Plan Following a Guided Viewing Protocol

Topic: Exploring Space, a Lesson that Introduces a Multidisciplinary Unit on the Exploration of Outer Space

Level: Adaptable for grades 5–6

Estimated Time: 30–40 minutes

Learning Standards

Students will:

- Integrate information presented in different media or formats (e.g., visually, quantitatively) as well as in words to develop a coherent understanding of a topic or issue. (*CCSS RI.6.7*)

- Investigate key events, developments, and major turning points in world history to identify the factors that brought about change and the long-term effects of these changes (*New York State Learning Standard for Social Studies 2*)

Goals

Students will understand that:

- Trial and failure often precedes successful outcomes in scientific exploration; the Space Age in the United States included many failures before success.

Students will know:

- The main events that occurred during the Space Age (1947–1961).

Students will improve their skills:

- In extracting information from visual presentations.

Key Questions

- Why did the successful exploration of space take such a long time?
- What critical events occurred during the Space Age (1947–1961) that brought about advances in the exploration of outer space?

Behavioral Objective

After viewing a documentary on the Space Age (from 1947 to 1961), students will list in a class discussion at least three significant events in the history of space exploration and infer that considerable failure occurred before success.

In preparation for this lesson, have all equipment ready in advance—a computer with a DVD-ROM drive, an LCD projector, and a chart on which to record students' contributions following the presentation. Indented notes indicate the purposes of specific steps in the procedure.

Pre-Viewing

Steps 1–2: *Students are helped to establish a connection to the information presented in the material to be viewed.*

1. Say, "You know that U.S. scientists have been exploring outer space." Ask if students know some of the accomplishments of the twentieth-century U.S. space program. *Students are likely to recall that U.S. astronauts landed on the moon, that satellites were launched, and that we had a space shuttle program.*
2. Ask students if they know when the first satellite was launched. *Some students may know that it was* Sputnik *in 1957. Others may not know.*

Steps 3–4: *Students are introduced to the lesson topic and the presentation.*

3. Explain that we are beginning a new study about the exploration of outer space and that, today, students will view a presentation that includes information about the Space Age in the twentieth century.
4. Explain that in the presentation, they will see film clips of significant events that occurred during the Space Age.

Guided Viewing

Steps 5–7: *Students are given specific purposes for viewing the documentary.*

5. Introduce the video. Say, "As you view the presentation, look for some of the most significant events—the turning points—that took place during the Space Age."
6. Explain that the presentation has a great deal of information and that students may ask to have it paused at times so that they can take notes.

7. Show the presentation. Remind students to watch carefully and to take notes about the events they see. *Pause the presentation when students need more time to take notes.*

Discussion Following Viewing

Step 8: *Discussion includes questions designed to assess the behavioral objective of the lesson.*

8. After the presentation, hold a discussion about information the students have gained from viewing the documentary, and list contributions on a chart such as the one shown below in Exhibit 5.4.

Exhibit 5.4 Chart on which to Record Contributions after Viewing a Documentary on the Space Age.

Space Age Exploration **1947–1961**
Important events:
First living things in space:
Why launching the first satellite took so long:
Other information:

Ask the following questions:

- What were some of the most important events that occurred during the Space Age? *Students will suggest most of the events given in the presentation, including* Sputnik *in 1957 and the first U.S. satellite in 1958. They may also recall that Gargarin was the first human to travel in space in 1959.*
- What living things were sent into outer space before any humans rocketed into orbit? *Students should mention rats, dogs, and monkeys.*
- Why do you think it took such a long time for the first U.S. satellite to be launched? *Students should have noticed that failures occurred in the space program before the first successful satellite was launched.*

- Do you recall any other information that was included in the presentation? *Students may have noted that outer space begins at 250 kilometers above the earth and that the temperature in outer space is −273°C.*

Closure

Steps 9–11: *The lesson is brought to closure with a summary of the information gained by viewing the documentary.*

9. Summarize the lesson by reviewing the students' contributions recorded on the chart.
10. Remind students that their new study will include conducting research on space exploration, and ask what the first step will be in conducting their research. *Responses should indicate the need for questions to guide their research.*
11. Conclude the lesson by asking students to prepare at least two questions to guide their research before the next session.

Assessment Plan

Summary and Evidence

This lesson requires students to learn about significant events in the history of space exploration. After viewing a documentary on early exploration of space, they will be asked questions during a class discussion of the program in order to determine if they have gained the understandings expected. They will also be asked to suggest the cause of delays in the program's success. It will be possible to assess the behavioral objective and key questions at step 8 in the lesson procedure. Students' skills in viewing visual presentations will be assessed by observation and their responses to the questions raised during the discussion.

Materials

Have an LCD projector and chart paper available.

A century to remember: The great events of the 20th century [DVD] (1999). St. Laurent, Quebec, Canada: Mendacy Entertainment Group.

Resources

Dusek, J., & Pisala, J. (2014). *Space atlas: A voyage of discovery for young astronauts.* New York: Sterling Children's Books.

Gibbs, S. (2014). *Space case (Moon base alpha).* New York: Simon & Schuster Books for Young Readers.

Sparrow, G. (2006). *Exploring the universe (Secrets of the universe).* Milwaukee, WI: World Almanac Library.

Waxman, L. H. (2013). *Exploring the international space station.* Minneapolis, MN: Lerner Publications.

Wilkinson, P. (2012). *Spacebusters: The race to the moon.* New York: DK Publishing.

Reflections

Reflections on the success of the plan and needed modifications will be added after the lesson is taught for the first time. There may be a need to modify some of the questions, raise others, show shorter portions of the presentation at a time with one question for each segment.

Protocol: K-W-L

The know, want to know, learned (K-W-L) technique was initially designed to assist students with reading comprehension (Ogle, 1986). Today, it is also commonly used to help students organize for research or to prepare plans for a field trip. Before the lesson, the teacher prepares three large charts or sections of chalkboard, each of which has one of the letters *K, W,* and *L* at the top. Students' responses will be recorded under each letter. The charts form the three columns needed for the protocol. The charts or board sections must be large enough to be easily read and to accommodate all student responses. The K-W-L protocol includes the following five steps:

1. Students are asked to list what they know about a topic, and their ideas are written in the *K* column. Ogle (1986) suggests that two steps be included in the *K* section. First, students are given an opportunity to suggest all that they know or think they know about a topic. To stimulate student thinking during this initial brainstorming,

   > . . . ask volunteers after they have made their contributions, "Where did you learn that?" or "How could you prove that?" By not simply accepting the statements that students offer but probing to make them think about the sources and substantiveness of their suggestions, you challenge both contributors and the rest of the class to a higher level of thinking. (p. 566)

   Second, students are helped to find common categories among the information they have suggested. For example, if several students have mentioned several different foods that an animal eats, "foods" can become be one of the common categories; similarly, other categories can include those in which students have suggested more than one item.
2. In the *W* section, students are asked to list what they would like to learn as they research the topic. The students set the main purposes of their study. As students contribute to the *K* and *W* sections during the initial lesson, their contributions are written on the chart in complete sentences.
3. Students copy the first two sections for reference as they conduct research to determine whether what they thought they knew about the topic in the *K* section is accurate and to find answers to questions in the *W* section of the chart. The *W* and *L* sections will often require considerable time to complete.
4. Time is provided for the students to gather information, to find answers to their questions, and to locate support for the information recorded in the *K* column. This step will require a number of active research periods.
5. As the students gain information, they enter it in the third—what was learned, or *L*—section. The information included in this section helps students to confirm or modify the information they have included in the *K* section of the chart, to realize what they have learned about a topic, and what they have been unable to learn relative to the questions they raised initially. The students can then try to determine where to search for additional information.

Following is a sample lesson plan on the season of spring which follows the K-W-L protocol. This lesson is designed to introduce the interdisciplinary unit of study that is prepared in chapter 3. This lesson engages students' thinking about the changes brought about during the spring season, and the students are involved in helping to raise the questions to be investigated.

Two Sample Lesson Plans Following a Know, Want to Know, Learned (K-W-L) Protocol

Example 1: A K-W-L Lesson Plan on Spring

Topic: Spring

Level: Grade 2

Estimated Time: 20–25 minutes

Learning Standards

Students will:

- Participate in collaborative conversations with diverse partners about second-grade topics and texts with peers and adults in small and larger groups. (*CCSS SL.2.1*)
- Understand that seasons of the year, weather, and climate are determined by physical changes in the environment. (*generic standard*)
- Raise questions and issues to generate inquiries and conduct investigations. (*generic standard*)

Goals

Students will:

- Understand that research can begin with raising a question or questions.
- Gain experience with using the know, want to know (or learn), learned (K-W-L) technique to guide the study of a topic.
- Be respectful of others while participating in discussions.

Key Question

What do we already know about spring, and what do we want to learn about it?

Behavioral Objective

After contributing what they already know about the season of spring, students will generate at least five questions that will be used to help guide their study of their new unit on spring.

Procedure

In preparation for the lesson, three sections of the chalkboard, dry-erase board, or large charts (e.g., on a smart board) will be needed for the three columns. Use vertical lines to separate the columns, and leave a space at the top on which to write headings for the K-W-L areas, as shown in Exhibit 5.5 on the next page. Indented notes indicate the purposes of specific steps in the procedure.

Select a day for the field trip in advance, and secure the necessary permissions. Invite two adults from the list of parent volunteers to assist with supervision on the walk. (Refer to chapter 3, Exhibit 3.10, for more specific details on planning a field trip.) The field trip will be taken after this introductory lesson, which is designed to prepare the students for their walk. The first lesson begins with a class meeting in the early afternoon during the time regularly devoted to unit studies. Because this lesson will involve discussion, before beginning the lesson remind students about rules for participation.

Exhibit 5.5 A K-W-L Chart.

What We Know	What We Want to Know	What We Learned

Introduction

Steps 1–4: *To help students make a connection to the new unit topic, they are asked to recall previous studies involving their local neighborhood and their school. They are asked about the changes they have recently noticed in their neighborhood and are introduced to the topic of their new study.*

1. Begin the lesson by reminding the students that they have been studying their neighborhood this year and that their last unit was called *Our School.* Ask the children to recall some activities from that unit. *The students may say that they remember drawing a map of the school and visiting and interviewing several people who work in the school: the nurse, the school principal, and a custodian. They may also remember that they learned about these people's jobs, that they saw where the people do their work, and that they were given a chance to see some materials used in these jobs. The children may also recall drawing and labeling pictures of school helpers.*
2. Ask the students if they have noticed that the school custodians are beginning to do some work they have not been able to do all winter. *The students may have noticed that the school custodians are working outside on the grounds.*
3. Ask the students if they can think of any reasons why work is beginning outside at this time of year. *The students may say that it is because the grass is growing and it is warmer. They may also say it is now spring.*
4. Explain that they will be studying this new season and that "spring" is the topic of their new unit.

Discussion

Steps 5–7: *The K section of the K-W-L chart is completed. Students suggest signs of spring to look for on their field trip, and their contributions are listed in the K section of the K-W-L chart.*

5. Ask the students what they already know about the spring season. Use a concept web to record what the children say. (See Exhibit 5.6 for a concept web showing the children's initial concepts of spring.) Then write their responses in the K section of the

K-W-L chart. *Responses may include that it is a special time of the year, a time when the weather gets warmer and they no longer have to wear heavy clothing. They may say the grass and some flowers begin to grow in spring and that the trees have buds. Some children may remember that some important holidays occur during the spring season.*

Exhibit 5.6 A Students' Concept Web for Spring.

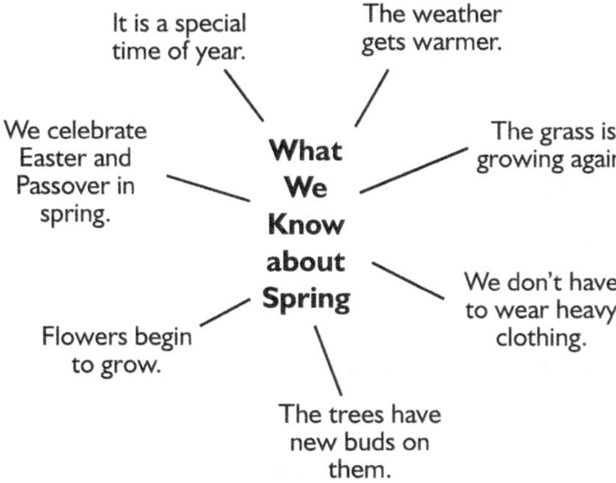

6. Suggest that all of the ideas they have noticed are important ones. Then ask the students if they know that their ideas are actually "signs" of the spring season. Write "sign" on the board, and ask if the children know what it means. *Children may probably say that a sign is a signal or idea of something. Other similar responses may be given.*
7. Tell the students that there may actually be other signs of spring they have not yet noticed, and explain that at the end of the week, the class will take a walk along several streets near the school to look for signs of spring in the neighborhood. Then ask, "What signs of spring do you think we will find when we take our walk in the neighborhood?" Write the signs that the students suggest in a list on a large sheet of paper separate from the K-W-L chart. *The students will be likely to suggest looking for different kinds of flowers and noticing where the grass has begun to turn green. They may also mention looking for birds that have returned after the winter and examining trees and shrubs for signs of new growth.*

Step 8: *Students contribute possible questions to the W section of the K-W-L chart.*

8. Next, ask the students what, in addition to signs of spring, they would like to learn about the spring season. Write any questions they contribute in the W section of the K-W-L chart. Possible questions include: What other changes occur during the season of spring? How does spring affect us? How can we grow some spring plants? How do spring flowers differ from one another? Do we have a lot of rain in the spring? What holidays do we have in the spring? What are some migratory birds that come back in the spring? (Note that the students' questions will be reviewed to ensure that they include the essential questions of the unit; essential questions that are not included will be added.)

Closure

Steps 9–10: *The lesson is brought to closure with a review of the contributions students have made to the K-W-L chart, and permission slips for their field trip are distributed.*

9. To conclude the lesson, summarize briefly by reviewing the *K* and *W* sections of the *K-W-L* chart, and ask the students to copy information on the chart in their notebooks for later reference.
10. Finally, distribute permission slips and explain that each child must take a permission slip home to be signed. Tell them that the slips must be returned in two days so the class can take the walk.

Assessment Plan

Summary and Evidence

In this lesson, students are required to complete the *K* and *W* sections of a *K-W-L* chart to record what they believe they already know about the season of spring and to raise at least five questions to help in the planning of their study. Steps 5–8 in the procedure of the lesson will make assessment of the behavioral objective and the key question possible.

Materials

Chart paper and a supply of parental permission slips to distribute to each child in the class.

Reflections

After this lesson has been taught for the first time, notations will be made of any steps in the procedure that need to be changed when the plan is reused. For example, there may be a need to raise further questions; others may need to be deleted or need changes in wording for clarity.

Example 2: Endangered Species

Topic: Introductory Lesson to Prepare for a Study of Endangered Animals and Birds

Level: 4th grade (adaptable for levels 3–6)

Estimated Time: 30–40 minutes

Learning Standards

Students will:

- Conduct short research projects that build knowledge through investigation of different aspects of a topic. (*CCSS W.4.7*)
- (a) Engage effectively in a range of collaborative discussions (one-on-one, in groups, and teacher-led) with diverse partners on *fourth-grade topics and texts,* building on others' ideas and expressing their own clearly.

  (b) Follow agreed-upon rules for discussions and carry out assigned roles.

  (c) Pose and respond to specific questions to clarify or follow up on information, and make comments that contribute to the discussion and link to the remarks of others. (*CCSS SL.4.1b.1c*)
- Understand that human decisions and activities have had a profound impact on the physical and living environment. (*New York State Learning Standard in Mathematics, Science, and Technology 4, Part 7*)

Goals

Students will:

- Prepare for research of endangered animals and birds.
- Know the meaning of the term *endangered species*.
- Further develop their research skills.
- Continue to develop their willingness to participate in class discussions.

Key Questions

- What do we mean by endangered animals and birds?
- What do we want to know about them?
- How can we learn about them?
- Why are questions important for studying a topic?

Behavioral Objective

In preparation for their study of endangered animals and birds, students will complete the first two sections of a K-W-L (Know, Want to Know, and Learned) chart by suggesting: (1) what they think they know about them, (2) at least five animals and/or birds they believe are endangered, and (3) at least three questions they have about endangered animals and birds.

Procedure

In preparation for the lesson, a K-W-L chart will be prepared with the headings "Know," Want to Learn," and "Learned." Indented notes indicate the purposes of specific steps in the procedure.

Introduction

Steps 1–4: *Review and help students connect with vocabulary that they already know and will be using extensively in the unit's work. (Not all essential vocabulary will be discussed at this point, however. For example,* extinct *and* extinction *will be introduced later.)*

1. Students will meet as a class and be asked to explain what the word *danger* means. *Students will probably suggest that there is possible harm in some situation.*
2. Next, ask students if they can suggest what *endanger* would mean. *It is likely that students will mention having the possibility of being in danger. If not, clarify the meaning.*
3. Explain to students that, in their new unit, they will study *endangered species*, the animals and birds that are currently endangered.
4. To be certain that the students understand the terms used, ask if anyone can explain what is meant by endangered species. *It is possible that some of the students will have heard the term; some may know they are animals and birds that are in danger of not being here in the future. Ensure that the students are clear about the meaning of the word* species, *and explain further if needed.*

Step 5: *Begin the development of the K-W-L chart by asking students to name any species they think they know may be endangered. This list will be checked as student research progresses.*

5. Ask students to tell what they think they know about endangered animals and birds and to name animal and bird species they think may be endangered. *(Write all responses under the K section of the K-W-L chart.)*

K-W-L Chart Development

Steps 6–7: *Elicit some of the questions the students will research.*

6. Next, ask students what they believe they should try to learn about endangered animals or birds. The questions students raise should be listed in the W section of the K-W-L chart using complete sentences for each student's question.) *Students may raise the following questions among others:*
   - What animals and birds are endangered?
   - What kind of danger are they in?
   - Why are they endangered?
   - How can we prevent them from being endangered?
7. After all student questions are listed, add any essential questions from the unit plan that are not included in the students' list.

Steps 8–9: *Encourage students to think about how they can gain answers to their questions and to consider ways to locate information.*

8. Next, ask the students what we will need to do to complete the Learned (L) section of the K-W-L chart. *Students will be likely to say that they will need to look up information, do some research.*
9. Ask the students to list some of the ways they believe they can research the answers to their questions. *Students may suggest reading, using the Internet, and asking people who study animals and birds.*

Steps 10–11: *Review for the students the procedure they will be following for their research activity for their study.*

10. Explain that tomorrow they will view a presentation that includes several endangered animals and birds. After the presentation, the students will form committees consisting of 3–4 students. The students in each committee will select a chair and recorder and then choose an animal or bird to research—either one seen in the presentation or one from an official list of endangered animals and birds. Explain that committees will research the questions listed in the W section of the K-W-L chart for their research, but that they can add other questions to research if they believe it they are needed. *(Note that the next day, while the committees are meeting, it will be important to check with each committee to learn the names of the chair and recorder, the specific endangered species the committee will investigate, and any additional questions the members have added.)*
11. Ask if anyone has questions about the procedure they will be following for the study, and respond as needed.

Closure

Step 12: *Brings the lesson to closure.*

12. (a) Review information students have generated in the K and W sections of the K-W-L chart.

    (b) Ask students if they can explain why the questions they have raised are important for their research. *Students should say that if they had no questions, they would not know where to begin to do their research.*

(c) Have students write their understanding of the term endangered species on a slip of paper with their names, and collect the papers.

(d) After collecting the papers, ask students to volunteer what they wrote for the meaning of endangered species.

Protocol: The Five-Step Lesson

Skills instruction can follow a fairly traditional outline. A five-step lesson plan (Hunter, 2004) is especially appropriate for teaching skills lessons. The protocol includes the following five elements:

1. An *anticipatory set,* during which the teacher sets the purpose for the lesson, introduces students to the concepts that the lesson will include, and helps students to make the needed connections between their present skills and the new skill to be developed.
2. The *presentation* of the lesson, in which the teacher uses various techniques to present a model of the skill to be developed. The teacher demonstrates the skill for the students.
3. *Guided practice,* in which students are assisted with practice applications of the new skill.
4. *Independent practice,* in which students practice the new skill they have just been taught. Following the lesson, additional practice is assigned.
5. *Closure,* in which students are helped to summarize what they learned about the new skill and its applications during the lesson.

See the sample lesson plan below on the skill of outlining. This is an important skill for all students. The lesson assists students in this skill which they will be using in their interdisciplinary units.

Two Sample Lesson Plans Following the Five-Step Protocol

Example 1: Creating an Outline from Print Sources

Topic: An Introduction to Outlining

Level: This lesson is adaptable for students in grades 3–8.

Estimated Time: 30–45 minutes

Learning Standard

Students will:

- With guidance and support from adults, produce writing in which the development and organization are appropriate to task and purpose. (*CCSS W.3.4*)

Goal

Students will:

- Learn to use outlining to assist them in extracting information from print sources and preparing written reports.

Key Question

How can information be extracted from original print and other media sources, summarized, and reported without plagiarizing those sources?

Behavioral Objectives

- After a demonstration and guided practice in outlining paragraphs from a social studies textbook, each student will outline the main ideas and supporting details from a five-paragraph textbook selection.
- After developing a five-paragraph outline, students will explain the process involved in outlining information from a reading source.

Procedure

Select reading material for this lesson that is appropriate for the grade and reading level of the students. A social studies textbook at the grade level of students will usually be appropriate because it will include information on topics that are investigated for interdisciplinary or multidisciplinary studies. Indented notes indicate the purposes of specific steps in the procedure.

Anticipatory Set

Steps 1–2: *Students are asked to explain the methods they currently use to recall information for their research when using reading materials, and they are introduced to the lesson topic.*

1. Ask the students what they do when they are researching a topic and want to remember information they find in books or other reading materials. *Students are likely to say they copy some of the sentences from the readings into their notebooks.*
2. Explain that the purpose of this lesson is to help them to learn more about how to record such information without copying it and that they will be learning how to outline information they find in a book, an article, or a document on the Internet.

Presentation

Steps 3–5: *The teacher demonstrates outlining for students and invites them to observe and participate in a discussion of the main topic and details in a paragraph used for the demonstration.*

3. Invite the students to watch as you demonstrate a way to outline paragraphs in a reading selection. (Using an LCD or an overhead projector, project a selection that includes three or four paragraphs of content material, preferably a page from the students' social studies textbook. The topic should be one that students are currently investigating.)
4. Direct students' attention to the title and first paragraph of the selection. Have students read the first paragraph silently; then ask one student to read it orally for the class. (Note that although you are demonstrating at this point in the lesson, students should be involved in the thought process as much as possible.)
5. Hold a brief discussion of the content of the paragraph. Ask students what they think is the main point of the paragraph. Phrase the main idea for the students, and demonstrate how to begin the outline by writing the main idea on the chalkboard next to a Roman numeral I.

Steps 6–9: *Demonstration continues. Students are asked to suggest other details and important points in the paragraph as the teacher demonstrates how to include those points in the outline.*

6. Ask students to suggest other important points they recall from the paragraph. Phrase these points, and write each under the main idea, using uppercase letters—*A, B, C,* and so on.

7. Continue demonstrating how to outline each succeeding paragraph in the projected sample, following steps 4 and 5.
8. Ask students to look at the outline and to explain how the outline differs from the text selection. *Students should note that the outline is shorter than the selection, that it includes the most important information, that the wording is different, and that nothing from the text has been copied directly.*
9. If necessary, demonstrate the process with a second projected selection.

Guided Practice

Step 10: *Guided practice begins.*

10. If students appear to understand what has been demonstrated, continue by helping them to apply the skill to a new selection.
    a. Ask the students to read the selection silently.
    b. Ask the students to determine the main idea and other related information for each paragraph in the projected selection.
    c. Guide the students in their wording of the outline.
    d. Continue to guide students as they outline additional projected selections if needed.

Independent Practice

Steps 11–14: *Independent practice begins.*

11. Direct students to a selection in their social studies textbooks. Follow the same procedure outlined in step 10 to guide students through the outlining procedure. Use more than one selection if needed. If students appear to understand the process, continue with step 12.
12. Ask students to individually outline a new five-paragraph selection from their textbooks.
13. Collect the students' outlines after they have had sufficient time to prepare them so that you can assess their success and understanding of the process.
14. After the outlines have been collected, ask the students to explain the process involved in outlining information they locate in reading materials. *Students should explain that the process begins with a careful reading of the selection. Next, each paragraph is analyzed for its main idea and important information related to that idea. Finally, the students should explain that they need to write the outline of these points in their own words and without copying directly from the text.*

Closure

Step 15: *The lesson is brought to closure with a review of the outlining process students have just been taught.*

15. Tell the students they will have further practice with outlining but that the most important practice will be the outlining they need to do when they are researching the topics they are studying.

Assessment Plan

Summary and Evidence

The goal of this skills lesson is to teach students how to develop a summary outline of information presented in readings and other media sources using their own words. The students will need to outline a selection they read in a textbook and also be able to explain the process they used to do so. Steps 12 and 13 of the lesson procedure provide for assessment of the lesson goal.

Materials

- Several three- to five-paragraph selections of content material prepared for overhead or LCD projection
- Copies of the students' social studies textbooks
- An LCD projector and a computer, or an overhead projector with transparencies prepared in advance

Reflections

After teaching this skills lesson the first time, it may be necessary to include additional practice before requiring students to work independently. The plan will be reviewed to determine the need for additional guided practice and other possible modifications to the lesson before using it for another group of students.

Example 2: Understanding Adjectives

Topic: Parts of Speech (Adjectives)

Level: Grade 3 and above

Estimated Time: 30–45 minutes

Learning Standard

Students will:

- Explain the function of nouns, pronouns, verbs, adjectives, and adverbs in general and their functions in particular sentences. (*CCSS LS.3.1a*)

Goals

Students will:

- Know that an adjective describes, modifies, or quantifies a noun or pronoun.
- Know that adjectives are used to clarify a noun or noun phrase.
- Be able to locate adjectives in written materials.

Key Questions

- How is an adjective defined?
- How are adjectives used in our language?

Behavioral Objective

After a demonstration and guided practice in locating adjectives in written selections, each student will write the definition of an adjective, explain how adjectives are used in written materials, and underline at least three of five single (one-word) adjectives in a sample paragraph.

Procedure

Select written materials appropriate for the grade and reading levels of the students in advance, and prepare a practice page having spaces for writing the definition and the use of adjectives as well as a sample paragraph for students that includes five single adjectives. Students must previously have been introduced to *nouns* and *noun phrases*. Indented notes indicate the purposes of specific steps in the procedure.

Anticipatory Set

Step 1: *Students are asked to recall the meaning of a noun or pronoun from their previous lessons on parts of speech.*

1. Ask the students if they can recall the meaning of a noun or pronoun from their previous lesson on the parts of speech. *Students should suggest that they represent persons, places, or things.*

Steps 2–6: *Students are given the purpose of the current lesson along with a brief definition of adjectives. The definition is further clarified for students. (Note that only single adjectives will be used in this introductory lesson.)*

2. Explain that the purpose of this lesson is to help them to learn about adjectives, another part of speech, and that adjectives are used with nouns, noun phrases, and pronouns.
3. Write the noun *house* on the board (or a chart) and ask if anyone can tell more about a house they have seen. *Students will probably use single words, such as white, gray, brown, big, small, and others.*
4. Write several of the words students suggest along with house, such as:

   white house - gray house

   brown house - big house
5. Explain that the words they have suggested are adjectives, and ask students what those words seem to do when they are added to house. *In their own words, students should suggest the idea that the words tell or describe more about what the house is like.*
6. Repeat with several more nouns, such as tree, movie, ice cream, and milk, asking each time for descriptive words to add to those nouns until it appears clear that students understand the idea.

Presentation

Steps 7–9: *The teacher demonstrates locating adjectives in several paragraphs.*

7. Have several sample paragraphs ready to project for use in demonstrating. Each paragraph should include several single adjectives. (LCD or overhead projection should be used for this part of the lesson.)
8. Ask students to look at the first paragraph and to read it silently before asking for a volunteer to read the paragraph orally to the group. After hearing the paragraph, the teacher should demonstrate by (1) underlining each adjective included and (2) circling the nouns, pronouns, or noun phrases each adjective modifies.
9. Repeat the above demonstration with one or more additional paragraphs.

Guided Practice

Steps 10–12: *Guided practice begins as students begin to participate in locating adjectives in new paragraphs.*

10. Project another paragraph. This time guide the students, asking them to suggest the adjectives included in the paragraph. *Correct their responses if necessary.*
11. Next, ask the students to suggest the nouns, pronouns, or noun phrases that each of the adjectives modifies (describes).
12. Repeat with additional paragraphs until it appears clear that most students are able to detect adjectives and the nouns, pronouns, or noun phrases they modify.

Independent Practice

Steps 13–14: *Independent practice begins.*

13. Explain that students will now try to find adjectives on their own in a sample paragraph that will be distributed. Before distributing the papers, provide instructions, asking students to write their names on their papers when they receive them, then read the paragraph silently, locate and underline the adjectives they find in the paragraph, and write their answers in their own words to the two questions about adjectives at the bottom of the page: "What is an adjective?" and "How do we use adjectives?"
14. When students have completed their work, collect their papers to examine later.

Closure

Step 15: *The lesson is brought to closure as students are asked to summarize by defining adjectives and explaining their use.*

15. After the papers have been collected, ask the class to define *adjective*, and ask how adjectives are used. *In their own words, students should include the idea that an adjective is a word that describes a noun, pronoun, or noun phrase and that adjectives help to describe or clarify some features of nouns, pronouns, or noun phrases.*

Follow-Up

Step 16: *The homework paper will provide students with the opportunity for additional independent practice with what they have just learned.*

16. Give students an additional paper to complete for homework. The paper will have two new paragraphs in which they will need to underline the adjectives and circle the nouns, pronouns, or noun phrases in the paragraphs.

(Note: After reviewing students' papers, it may be found necessary to continue teaching this lesson on another day. If so, return to additional guided and independent practice. Should students continue having difficulty locating the adjectives, it may be necessary to further develop the lesson with new demonstration and practice paragraphs.)

Assessment Plan

Summary and Evidence

Sample paragraphs are used in teaching this *five-step lesson.* Students are taught the function of adjectives, and they are required to locate adjectives in several paragraphs, first with the help of the teacher, then independently. Following direct instruction and guided practice, students are required to explain how adjectives are used in written materials. Finally, students are required to locate single adjectives and the nouns, pronouns, or noun phrases modified by the adjectives in sample paragraphs. The behavioral objective, skills goals, and key questions of this lesson can be assessed at step 13 of the lesson procedure. The homework assignment will provide additional evidence of students' individual and independent mastery.

Materials

- Paragraphs that include several single adjectives prepared for overhead or LCD projection
- A worksheet designed to assess the objectives of the lesson with a sample paragraph and two questions
- An LCD projector and a computer, or an overhead projector with transparencies prepared in advance
- A homework paper with two paragraphs that include several adjectives

Reflections

After this lesson has been taught for the first time, notations will be made of any steps in the procedure where students had difficulty understanding or completing the task. For example, there may be a need to include additional sample paragraphs in either the demonstration or guided practice steps of the procedure. After students have completed independent practice, it may be found that they still need further guided practice before continuing the lesson to closure.

Protocol: The Scientific Method

Rick Allen (2005) reminds us that standards developed by the National Research Council in 1996 "calls for K–12 students to both understand and be able to do scientific inquiry" (p. 4). The scientific method is a logical choice when a science lesson involves students in experimentation. In that procedure, students are guided to:

1. Observe a phenomenon.
2. Suggest hypotheses for the phenomenon.
3. Design a method of testing the hypotheses.
4. Use the designed method to experiment.
5. Observe the results.
6. Draw conclusions relative to their hypotheses.

The lesson plan that follows is an example of a lesson in which the procedure follows the scientific method of investigation. It is a lesson that provides students with an opportunity to gain insight in the important understanding that variables in the interactive forces between energy and matter affect changes in motion. In this lesson, students will learn the scientific principle of the pendulum, that the length of a pendulum is the only variable that can affect its swing rate.

Sample Lesson Plan Following the Scientific Method of Investigation

Topic: The Pendulum

Level: Grade 3 or 4

Estimated Time: 20–30 minutes

Learning Standards

- Conduct short research projects following the scientific method of investigation to build knowledge about a topic. *(CCSS W.3.7)*
- Understand that energy and matter interact through forces that result in changes in motion. *(New York State Learning Standard in Mathematics, Science, and Technology 4.5)*

Goals

Students will:

- Understand that it is only the length of a pendulum that affects its swing rate.

- Gain experience in solving problems in physical science by following the scientific method of investigation.
- Develop a positive attitude about failure when investigating in science.

Key Question

How can the swing rate of a pendulum be changed?

Behavioral Objective

After experimentation with a pendulum, students will prepare written statements explaining that it is only the length of a pendulum that affects its swing rate.

Procedure

Set up a simple pendulum before the lesson following the directions in the materials section below. Indented notes indicate the purposes of specific steps in the procedure.

Observation and Introduction

Steps 1–2: *Students observe the model pendulum and recall objects they know that swing and are introduced to the topic of the new unit.*

1. Swing the model pendulum, and ask the students if this reminds them of anything they have seen before. Students may be reminded of swings on the playground and clocks that they have seen. Some students may suggest that it is a "pendulum." However, because other students may not be familiar with the word *pendulum*, you may need to clarify its meaning.
2. While the pendulum is swinging, tell the students: "Today, we are beginning a new unit in which we will be involved in completing several investigations. The first will be a study involving a pendulum."

Steps 3–4: *Students learn how to count pendulum swings and determine the basal swing rate of the pendulum.*

3. Ask the students if they can think of a way to determine how fast the pendulum is swinging. *Timing and counting will probably be suggested.*
4. Because the students will not know how to count pendulum swings to determine the swing rate, demonstrate how to count the swings—one swing for each back-and-forth movement. Decide on how long to time the pendulum swings. Have one student keep time while others count silently; then, record the basal swing rate on the board.

Hypothesizing and Predicting

Steps 5–6: *Students are invited to hypothesize, to suggest ways they think will make the swing rate of the pendulum increase, and their suggestions are listed.*

5. Say, "I wonder if there is a way to make the pendulum swing faster." List the students' suggestions—their hypotheses—on the board under the basal swing rate. *The students may suggest pushing it harder, starting it from a higher position, adding or subtracting weights, and perhaps lengthening or shortening the pendulum.*
6. Ask how they can determine if any of their ideas will make the pendulum swing faster. *The students should indicate that they will need to try each suggestion—to experiment.*

Experimenting

Step 7: *Using their own hypotheses, students experiment to determine if any of their ideas will increase the swing rate of the pendulum.*

7. Provide time for experimentation. Ideally, the pendulum should be set up in a corner of the classroom where all students will have an opportunity to experiment during several days. A schedule, either a sign-up sheet or a list of names, should be posted near the pendulum. Students will need to work in pairs to test their hypotheses—one child to time the swings and one to count. The students should record their hypotheses and the results of each test in their notebooks or on a specially designed worksheet. If you decide that the experimentation should be completed as a whole-class activity (for safety or other reasons), some students should be invited to assist with timing and counting. Others should be reminded to observe carefully.

Closure

Steps 8–10: *The key question and behavioral objective of the lesson are checked.*

8. After the experimentation is completed, engage the class in a discussion. Ask students to individually write their answers to, "What will change the swing rate of a pendulum?" *The response should include the idea that only shortening the pendulum will increase its swing rate.*
9. Collect any student records—notebooks or worksheets—of their experimentation. Indicating each of the hypotheses—on the board—that failed to increase the swing rate of the pendulum, ask the following five questions:
   - Can anyone explain why you thought that would work? (This question helps the students to analyze their thinking about each hypothesis.)
   - How do you suppose we could correct a clock with a pendulum that is losing time?
   - If you want your backyard swing to swing faster, what would you have to do to it?
   - Do you think there is any other way to make a pendulum swing faster?
   - What will we have to do to make the pendulum swing more slowly?
10. The questions raised at step 9 require students to apply their new information about pendulums to authentic situations.

Other Procedures

Procedures suitable for demonstrations, applications, and practice sessions can involve combinations of the preceding protocols. For example, a lesson might begin with a directed listening activity, having students listen to a short selection or book. The listening activity may lead to the preparation of a K-W-L chart to introduce some research the students will be undertaking. Follow-up activities might make use of additional protocols.

Summary

This chapter has reviewed principles of learning and development that are important for planning lessons as well as interdisciplinary and multidisciplinary units. Bloom's Taxonomy, a six-level classification system, and questioning techniques have been outlined and illustrated with examples.

An overview of lesson planning has included explanations of planning formats. The format of a lesson plan involves the learning standards, goals (knowledge, understandings, skills, and dispositions), key questions, behavioral objectives, procedure, assessment plan, and reflection sections. Critical elements in the procedure of a lesson plan have also been listed and explained. Several useful lesson planning protocols have been outlined and illustrated with example lesson plans. Chapter 6 will include basic information on assessment when planning for instruction.

ACTIVITY

Ms. Benson, a sixth-grade teacher, has designed an interdisciplinary unit on an interesting and unusual theme, *Mysteries.* A web design (see Appendix, Exhibit A.6) shows a number of interesting lessons and activities that she plans to include in the study.

Select one of the lessons or activities in the web design and design a complete lesson plan following one of the protocols reviewed in this chapter. Be sure that the protocol followed is appropriate for the type of lesson or activity you select.

Assessment Planning

Authentic and Traditional Strategies

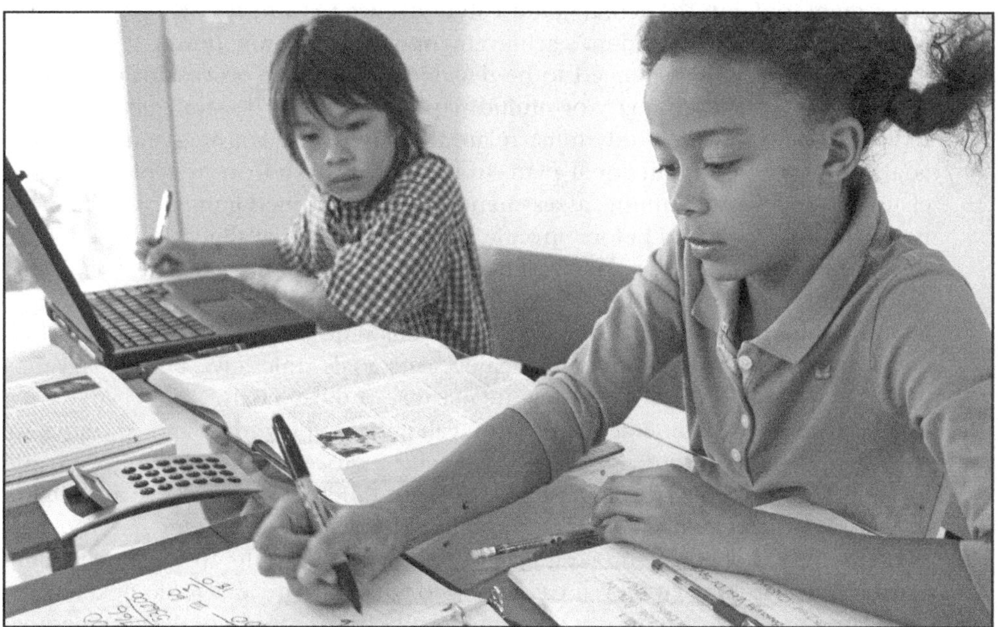

OVERVIEW

This chapter reviews aspects of assessment that are useful for assessing and evaluating lessons, activities, and interdisciplinary and multidisciplinary units, lessons, and activities. The focus of this chapter is on the following questions:

- What is the difference between assessment and evaluation, and how are both useful when planning lessons and interdisciplinary or multidisciplinary instructional units?
- What are authentic assessment techniques and their place in interdisciplinary instruction?
- How are rubrics designed for interdisciplinary instruction?
- How can examinations be useful in the overall evaluation process in interdisciplinary instruction?
- How can teachers prepare valid and reliable test items?

Assessment and Instruction

Assessment of unit and lesson objectives and the evaluation of student achievement are as important in the interdisciplinary instructional approach as with other teaching methods. Although they are sometimes thought to be synonymous, Arends (2015) clarifies the differences between *assessment* and *evaluation.* Assessment includes all the information we gather through various techniques, while evaluation indicates "making judgments, assigning value, or deciding on worth" (p. 211). For example, an examination can be used as an assessment tool, but the actual grade a student earns as a result of taking it results in an evaluation of the student's achievement on that examination.

Assessment strategies need to be decided early in the process of planning a lesson or an interdisciplinary or multidisciplinary study. The strategies and techniques included in the study must relate directly to the learning standards and goals of a specific instructional plan. In chapters 3 and 4 on unit planning and chapter 5 on lesson planning, assessments were determined immediately after the unit or lesson goals and before specific procedures were outlined. This sequence follows *backward design,* and it differs from conventional practice by placing assessment decisions second instead of as the final step in the process of designing both units and lessons. The rationale for this sequence is simply that it is difficult to plan ways to help students achieve our goals unless we know what they will have to do in order to demonstrate mastery of those goals.

There are two general assessment categories—*formative* and *summative*. Assessing students' progress *during* the teaching process, while concepts are still forming, is called *formative assessment*. Shepard (2005) links formative assessment to the Vygotskian concepts of *scaffolding* and *zone of proximal development* because "it is a dynamic process in which supportive adults or classmates help learners move from what they already know to what they are able to do next . . ." (p. 66). "Formative assessments can vary significantly, both in terms of the activities that qualify as assessments and the timing of those activities" (ASCD, 2007, p. 3). Techniques that can serve as formative assessment measures with interdisciplinary and multidisciplinary units include reviewing material students have previously studied in the unit, raising questions about what has been taught, giving quizzes, and observing the ways students work on various tasks and in their committee activities. Formative measures are "made up of a sequence of moves that invite a positive, ongoing relationship between teachers and their students" (Duckor, 2014, p. 29).

Other assessment techniques are used at the end of instruction. Typical of those are final examinations and reports of various kinds. Assessments at the conclusion of instruction are referred to as *summative.* Those techniques help to determine the extent to which students have met the intended standards and objectives of their units and provide for the final evaluation.

Even though assessment is primarily our responsibility as teachers, we need to recognize the importance of involving students in the process. Popham (2006) emphasizes the student role when he defines meaningful assessment as assessment *for* learning as opposed to assessment *of* learning. He explains that "the aim . . . is to empower students to monitor their own progress toward clearly understood goals" (p. 82). Knowing their objectives can "give students a performance target to aim for" (Wilcox, 2006, p. 1). Therefore, both teachers and students have an investment in the process. In interdisciplinary and multidisciplinary studies, students are routinely involved in planning their studies; they can also be encouraged to help decide ways the objectives of their studies will be assessed.

The Purposes of Assessment

While both formative and summative assessment techniques determine the extent to which students have achieved the objectives of instruction, the same techniques can help in diagnosing where students have difficulty with some particular material and the extent to which teaching has been effective.

Achievement and Diagnosis. Both summative and formative assessment techniques can be used to check students' achievement levels and to determine the ongoing diagnosis of students' areas of strength and relative weakness. The purpose of all diagnosis is to help improve learning by designing or redesigning instruction to better meet individual students' needs. The interdisciplinary approach typically involves individual conferences with students and committees to determine how well the students are proceeding with their research and projects. Those conferences can yield information about strengths and limitations for both individuals and groups of students, information that will indicate the need for some specific instruction in the future.

Teaching Effectiveness. Assessment can also help us to learn about the effectiveness of our own teaching. We can use the results of both summative and formative assessment techniques for this purpose. We can note what students have gained from their research by monitoring their oral presentations and individual written reports. We can make use of students' examination scores; however, if we do, it will be important to view those results in combination with our knowledge of the students and informal observations of their work before drawing any tentative conclusions about our teaching.

Assessment Techniques: The Need for Variety

Although most educators agree that some form of assessment is needed in order to evaluate student progress and achievement, not all agree on the techniques to use for different purposes. Ellis (2010) urges teachers to become familiar with several approaches to assessment because experience has not proved that one is better than another. Sternberg (1999) also suggests that "different kinds of assessment . . . complement one another. . . . There is no single 'right' kind of assessment" (p. 51). Instead, all assessment strategies need to be appropriate to the grade level, subject matter, development levels, and skills abilities of the students (Dick, Carey, & Carey, 2009; Jacobs, 1997). Perhaps, as Guskey (2003) suggests, those that are "best suited to guide improvements in students . . . are those that teachers administer on a regular basis in their classrooms" (p. 7).

Wiggins and McTighe (2012) define three types of assessment as those that check for "understanding (such as oral questions, observations, dialogues); traditional quizzes, tests, and open-ended prompts; and performance tasks and projects" (p. 152). The interdisciplinary approach makes use of all those techniques. Rubrics can be designed to assess various student products, demonstrations, and oral presentations. Quizzes may be administered during a study, and examinations are usually given at the conclusion of each unit.

Traditionally, examinations and quizzes have been used more than other assessment tools; however, most paper-and-pencil tests are limited to assessing students' verbal and logical–mathematical achievement. To limit assessment to formal and informal tests is inconsistent with the interdisciplinary approach because it fails to recognize the value of student products, such as papers, projects, and performances, in the process. It also ignores the value of including students in the assessment *process* (Wexler-Sherman, Gardner, & Feldman, 1988); it leaves the responsibility for assessment solely on the shoulders of teachers, with students playing a passive role. Larmer (2014) offers suggestions for teachers regarding the involvement of students in their projects. Participation in the assessment process is also clearly essential.

As mentioned in chapter 5, behaviorally-stated instructional objectives have also been used for many years in lesson and activity plans. Behavioral objectives are useful for short-term purposes in lesson planning and for measuring progress in the development of specific skills. Although they help to determine the effectiveness of a lesson, behavioral objectives are only one factor to consider in the overall assessment process. However, if we consider the importance of assessing individual student progress in areas other than linguistic and logical–mathematical, neither examinations nor behavioral objectives are totally adequate. For example, we may believe that interdisciplinary or multidisciplinary unit activities should foster improvement in dispositions that will result in better cooperation and interpersonal skills among our students. To assess progress in these areas, we need to observe students directly. Thus, using a test would not be the logical choice. By the same token, testing is not helpful for determining students' interests and attitudes or feelings about their own work or individual progress. Realistically, examinations rarely invite student participation in the assessment process. However, authentic assessment techniques do include students in the process.

Using Authentic Assessment Techniques

Many teachers collect representative examples of students' work in folders to use when they are preparing reports and conferring with parents. Students, as well as teachers, can be involved in assembling these folders, which represent the work produced by students day-to-day. When students take part in selecting the items to be included, their folders are referred to as *portfolios*. The portfolio can then become a resource for ongoing assessment of each student's progress during the course of a unit study.

Electronic portfolios, or digital portfolios, are becoming increasingly popular, and online "apps" are available that make it easy for teachers and students to keep their work in this format. Henson (2015, p. 75) cites one example:

> OpenSchool ePortfolio, a free app from iTunes, allows teachers to create and assign student projects; take pictures, video, and audio recordings of student work; and upload them right to a student's ePortfolio and use the built-in rubric maker to view Common Core State Standards as well as other standards that are pre-leveled to facilitate authentic assessment.

Many other free ePortfolio apps for both iOS and Android systems are available online.

A portfolio is an *authentic assessment* device that includes examples of students' actual work and surveys of their interests, feelings, and attitudes. It can often indicate growth in areas for which examinations tend to be less effective. Portfolios prepared by students—or cooperatively by students and teachers—can include many kinds of materials that are useful in the overall assessment process. Johnston (1992) suggests that a student portfolio is analogous to an artist's portfolio because the student has the opportunity to include "work that she sees fit to display and talk about to others" (p. 129). The following list indicates some of the more common materials found in student portfolios that are assembled during the course of an interdisciplinary or multidisciplinary study:

- Notes and memos about their individual research, projects, and committee work
- Student journals in which they record their observations and analyses of what they have gained from instruction, projects, and work on committees; what they feel they have understood and not understood
- Teacher journals and observations of individual student progress, needs, and committee participation
- Surveys of students' feelings and attitudes about their interests and participation in their unit studies
- Student self-evaluations of their papers, projects, and committee work
- Records that are kept during individual pupil–teacher conferences that occur during the research phase of a unit
- Formal and informal quizzes, tests, and examinations administered throughout a unit of study
- Audio and video recordings; individual and committee oral reports and recitations

Selecting materials for a portfolio needs to be a thoughtful process. The materials that are included should provide for balance, with examples that represent the learning processes as well as student products. Work samples should include notes students take during the research phase of a unit, drafts of papers or other products in progress as well as those that have been completed (Pappas, Kiefer, & Levstik, 1999). We need to develop criteria for guiding students in the selection of the samples they include. Clear criteria will also help students understand how their materials will be assessed and weighted in the final evaluation process. The roles others will have in the evaluation process, including parents, should be made clear (Borich, 2014). Research on the portfolio technique indicates that portfolios have a positive effect on the improvement of instruction and an impact on the insights that students develop about their academic strengths and weaknesses (O'Neil, 1993).

When students are responsible for maintaining their portfolios or parts of the portfolios they prepare during their unit studies, they can monitor their own development and progress. If students are asked to provide notations on the materials that they include in their unit portfolios, the process becomes even more reflective for them. Shores and Grace (2005) suggest that this encourages students to use important strategies such as "questioning, discussing, guessing, proposing, analyzing, and reflecting" (p. 11).

Thus, unit portfolios can be exceptionally useful, authentic assessment tools for use with interdisciplinary and multidisciplinary studies because they provide concrete evidence to help assess students' mastery of the unit goals. Portfolios also provide a vehicle for reflection and interaction between students and teachers, and they add concrete evidence that can be combined with formal examinations in the overall evaluation process.

Assessing Authentic Products with Rubrics

During the course of an interdisciplinary or multidisciplinary unit, students prepare reports and projects of different kinds, including written and oral reports, art projects, constructions, panel discussions, exhibits, experiments, and so on. Methods of assessing these student products should be as thoughtful and objective as possible. Although subjectivity cannot be eliminated entirely, using clearly defined criteria in the assessment and evaluation processes can help to minimize it. One of the most effective tools for this purpose is using rubrics that clearly define grading criteria.

Rubrics are scoring tools that are prepared before an assignment is given and that can be used to assess and evaluate a completed student product. If the same assignment has been given in the past and samples of the product have been collected, it is useful to study those samples when designing rubrics for similar products. This exercise can help to make delineating the criteria easier and more realistic of what students can be expected to do with the assignment.

Rubrics indicate quality gradations for each criterion they include. Student products—papers, projects, performances, constructions, and so on—are then examined for compliance with the criteria. Having the criteria to apply in advance of the grading process can help to make that process easier and fairer. When designing rubrics, some teachers examine work samples of previous students to help them decide the criteria that will be reasonable for a particular student product.

There is considerable support for involving students in the assessment process, a key element of interdisciplinary instruction. For example, Henson (2015, p. 406) cites a 2014 study by Panadero and Romero that compared two groups of students, one group that used rubrics and the other that did not use any specific self-assessment tool. The results showed that the rubric group used higher-level learning strategies and had higher levels of performance and accuracy. Goodrich (1997) has suggested that use of rubrics may "improve student performance, as well as monitor it, by making teachers' expectations clear and by showing students how to meet these expectations" (p. 14). In an experimental writing program, Porcaro and Johnson (2003) found that requiring students to use rubrics in the form of writing checklists motivated the students to "look critically at their work" as they edited their papers (p. 78). Thus, it is clear that rubrics can assist teachers with the grading process and that, when shared with students in advance, can provide students with clear expectations for their work.

In some schools, sample sets of rubrics are available for teachers to use to assess student products in various disciplines or subject areas. For example, the Chicago Public Schools (2007) provide a *Rubric Bank*. Another valuable source on the Internet is *Kathy Schrock's Guide to Everything* (Schrock, 2015b) which offers a rubric creation tool for teachers to create their own rubrics for many different purposes and that address the Common Core State Standards.

An example of rubric construction is shown in Exhibit 6.1 on the following page. This set of rubrics will be used to assess the reports that a group of students will be writing on endangered animals. Note that the format in the example can be used to design rubrics for other products and grade levels. In the example, the rubrics for evaluating student reports on endangered animals indicate that each report must include a clear introduction, provide information about why the animal is endangered, and include two possible ways to correct the problem that are supported by the student's research findings. The reports will also be examined for organization, clarity, and writing quality. This set of rubrics has three classifications—Excellent (3 points), Satisfactory (2 points), and Needs Improvement (1 point). Each criterion is rated, and the total number of points is used to determine the grade. Either a general level—excellent, satisfactory, fair, needs improvement—can be assigned, or the total can be divided by 15 for a percentage grade. Rubrics are not all prepared in the same way as shown in the example. Some include more than three levels, some are simple checklists indicating whether or not the student has met a specific criteria, and others show the level a student has attained but do not assign points.

Examinations

A unit examination is often administered at the end of an interdisciplinary or multidisciplinary unit. Most examinations are designed to measure verbal and/or logical-mathematical achievement; therefore, these examinations are useful for only a part of the total evaluation process in the interdisciplinary approach. All tests are limited in length for practical purposes, so a single test can provide only a small sample of all the test items that are possible for assessing the same concepts, standards, and objectives.

Common Test Scores

Two scores can be used when grading interdisciplinary or multidisciplinary unit examinations. The *raw* score is the total number of test items a student answers correctly or the total number of points earned on an examination.

The raw score can easily be converted to a more useful score, the *percentage score*. This score is computed by dividing the number of items a student answers

Exhibit 6.1 Example Rubric for Written Reports on an Endangered Animal.

Rubrics for a Report on an Endangered Animal				
	-Rating Scale-			
Criteria	3 Exceptional	2 Satisfactory	1 Needs Improvement	Rating (3–1)
Introduction	The introduction clearly specifies the endangered animal studied and indicates all of the specific information to be included in the report.	The introduction specifies the endangered animal studied and indicates some of the specific information to be included in the report.	The introduction specifies the endangered animal studied but fails to indicate the specific information to be included in the report.	3
Reason for Endangerment	The report provides a clear, well-detailed explanation about why the animal is endangered.	The report provides a minimal explanation about why the animal is endangered.	The reason for the animal's endangerment is not clearly explained.	3
Suggestions for Correcting the Problem	Two clearly presented, well-detailed, logical solutions to the animal's endangerment are offered.	One clearly presented, well-detailed, solution is offered for the animal's endangerment.	The solutions presented are unclear and lacking in detail.	3
Support	The reasons and solutions presented for the endangerment of the animal are exceptionally well supported by the student's research.	The reasons and solutions presented for the endangerment of the animal are adequately supported by the student's research.	The reasons and solutions presented for the endangerment of the animal are not clearly supported by the student's research.	3
Writing	The report is clearly written with no more than one error in grammar and punctuation.	The report is adequately clear with no more than three errors in grammar and punctuation.	The report is not clearly written, or it includes more than three errors in grammar and punctuation.	3
			Total Points:	15/15
			Grade:	100%

correctly by the total number of items on the examination. The student who answers 22 items correctly on a 30-item examination will earn a score of .73, or 73 percent. The percentage score is one of the most frequently used scores because it allows us to compare and note progress on different examinations.

Two other scores are used primarily with standardized tests. *Percentile* scores are computed to express the rank, or placement, of an individual student in a hypothetical group of 100 students; and *grade equivalent* scores express a student's raw score as a grade level equivalent (e.g., a score of 4.6 means the student has achieved the equivalent of a fourth-grade student after six months in that grade).

Validity and Reliability

We need to determine whether students have gained the specific knowledge, skills, and dispositions listed as objectives of an interdisciplinary unit. The informal examinations we prepare for our units can be helpful for assessing the degree to which the students have met some of our objectives, provided all items on the test are prepared carefully to ensure that they are as *valid* and *reliable* as possible.

Validity. "Is the test assessing what we intend it to assess?" This is the main question raised in determining the validity of a test. Test validity depends on several factors. First, all test items—the questions—included on a unit examination must address the standards and objectives for which the test is written. For example, if we write a test to help determine whether students have gained specific concepts from an interdisciplinary or multidisciplinary unit on the Middle East, the test items must address only what students have been given the opportunity to learn during the unit study.

A serious factor influencing the validity of a test is its readability. Written tests involve the need to read with full comprehension. If a test is designed to assess students' conceptual knowledge rather than their ability to read and understand, the readability of the questions on the test must be at a level low enough for the students to read independently. Otherwise, the test will be measuring the students' reading ability. Validity can also be affected by the extent to which students have been prepared with readings and other materials during their unit for the questions they will be asked.

Reliability. Test reliability is also a major concern. We need to ask if the result of the examinations we give are reliable estimates of what students have gained from their unit studies. A test cannot be reliable if it is not valid to begin with; it cannot be reliable if the directions for the test or the questions are unclear. Directions must be clarified in advance and be included on the test paper so that students can refer to them if needed.

Reliability can also be affected by the length of the test and the amount of time allotted for students to complete it. In general, a test will be more reliable if it includes a larger sampling—a greater number of test items. This is accomplished by having enough test items and by allowing students sufficient time to complete these items. For example, except for some essay examinations, a test with only a few test items inadequately samples what students may have gained from their units. Of course, the length of a test must be reasonable for the amount of time allowed to complete it. Teacher-prepared examinations should be designed so that all students can complete them without the pressure of time constraints. Only speed and accuracy tests, which are rarely used in unit testing, need to be restricted with severe time limits.

A relatively simple statistic to use for checking a unit examination is the *split-half correlation*. Computing this statistic involves three easy steps. First, while marking the test results, it is necessary to keep an account of the number of students who have passed each item on the test.

Second, the test is "split in half" between the odd-numbered and even-numbered items. Dividing the test in this way helps to compensate for possible difficulty differences in the levels of questions raised in the first half and second half of an examination. In the following example, the total number for the odd-numbered items is 98, and the total for even numbered items is 102.

The third step is simply to divide the smaller (odd total in this example) by the larger (the even total) to determine the reliability coefficient, a percentage. In the example, the result is about .96, or 96 percent. The percentage indicates an estimate of the extent to which the we can rely on the scores as accurate indicators of the students' mastery of the test content.

During the administration of an examination, two additional factors can affect the results of the examination: guessing and cheating. Although guessing may be thought to be a serious concern, it usually is not. Consider a multiple-choice test with four answer choices. If a student has no idea which of the four choices is correct and guesses wildly, the chance of choosing the right answer is only 25 percent. If 10 questions are on the test, the chance of guessing all answers correctly is a negligible 2.5 percent. Most tests have more than 10 items, and most students try to the best of their ability to determine the correct response to each question. Therefore, guessing does not seriously affect the reliability of most test results. Several precautions will help to minimize the possibility of cheating:

Exhibit 6.2 Sample Test Results for a Group of 25 Students.

Item Number	Number of Students Passing
1	22
2	19
3	21
4	15
5	24
6	17
7	19
8	25
9	12
10	26

- Ensure that the test is given in a business-like atmosphere free from distractions.
- Provide adequate seating with enough space between desks.
- Supervise your own examinations, because students need the security of knowing that their teacher is available to respond to questions.
- Review directions with students before the test begins, and include written directions on the test paper.

- Have students check that they have all pages of the test in the event that a page was missed during collation.
- Use clear, unambiguous language in writing the test items.
- Ensure that the questions are written so that they discriminate accurately between students who know and those who do not know the information required for a correct response.

Writing Valid and Reliable Test Items

The test items that teachers prepare for interdisciplinary and multidisciplinary unit examinations can fall into two general categories:

- *Supply-type items:* Students provide the answers, as in sentence completion, fill-in, short answer, and essay items.
- *Objective-type items:* Students are provided with choices from which to select their responses, as in true–false, multiple-choice, and matching formats.

To ensure greater validity and reliability, we need to be sure that our questions are clear and that each test item addresses the standards and objectives of our units. Following are some suggestions for test-item construction with examples for preparing items in each testing format. Using these simple guidelines can help to ensure a higher degree of validity and reliability on unit examinations.

Short Answer or Fill-In Item Suggestions:

- Maintain uniformity in the length of all blanks on a completion test to avoid suggesting the length of different words. Make all blanks long enough for the longest answer.
- Include only one blank per test item to avoid the possibility that, in addition to testing for its intended objective, the test will be testing for *closure*—the ability to bridge gaps left in a sentence and to expand on the author's message—or for the ability to use context clues during reading.

EXAMPLES

(Poor)

A ______________ is used in a house to help prevent the ______________ of the electrical wiring.

(Better)

The overheating of electrical wiring in a house may be prevented if ______________ are installed.

- Use one blank, even for names with two words, such as *Los Angeles* and *New York*. Two separate lines may suggest the correct answer.
- Construct the test item so that the blank appears either at or near the end of the statement. If the blank appears early in the sentence, we may be testing students' ability to use closure and context clues in addition to our intended unit objectives.

Examples

(Poor)

______________ is Brazil's most important product.

(Better)

Brazil's most important product is ______________.

- Include a key word or phrase that indicates the category to which the answer must belong. For example, if a statement calls for the name of a country, the student will know that unless a country is named, the answer cannot be correct. Indicating the kind of information that must be included in the blank for a fill-in response helps to lessen ambiguity and the possibility of multiple correct answers.

Examples

(Poor)

When did the English first arrive in North America? ______________

(Better)

In what year did the English first arrive in North America? ______________

The first example above is poor because a number of possible correct responses that can be written in the blank. For example, the word "when" can suggest a date, or to some students it may mean that they need to provide an historical period or event. The better example specifies that students must supply a year.

- Avoid copying material directly from sources that students have used for their information. Quoting text material for an informal test not only models plagiarism but also encourages students to memorize the text instead of developing genuine concept comprehension.
- Check all items on a test to determine if one of the questions gives students an answer to another item.
- Always use clear syntax, correct grammar, and accurate punctuation when writing test items.

Essay Item Suggestions:

- Phrase essay questions so that they clearly indicate the task. Be precise about what and how much information is expected in the response.
- When a test includes several essay items, suggest time allotments for each item to help students budget their time.
- In general, do not offer choices on essay examinations. If each essay item addresses an important standard or objective, it is not logical to offer choices. Any item that is not important should not be included on the exam. However, when the purpose of the test is to determine whether students can write a well-developed essay, students may be given a choice of topics.

- Develop grading criteria—or rubrics—before administering the test. Prepare an outline of what is expected for a complete answer to each essay question and decide how to weigh each essay item before beginning the grading process.
- Use a consistent scoring method: rubrics, a rating scale, rubrics combined with a rating scale, or holistic scoring. Teachers who use *holistic* scoring assign a single numerical score, often using a 10-point scale, in assessing the overall quality of a work. Establish a policy for handling other factors in advance, such as any irrelevant information that students include, and the mechanics of spelling, handwriting, punctuation, grammar, and syntax.
- Read all students' responses to one essay question before reading others; that is, read all student responses to the first essay question, then continue to read all responses to the second, and so on. Comparing all responses to the same essay question can help to maintain a more even scoring of the responses, especially when we are using a holistic grading method.

EXAMPLES

(Poor)

Discuss what you have learned about the British Parliament and the United States Congress.

(Better)

Describe two major differences and one similarity between the British Parliament and the United States Congress.

It is obvious that the first question is poor because there is an absence of clear directions for the student. In fact, if a student had not learned anything much, he or she might just say that. The better question clearly asks for two differences and one similarity between the two systems.

True–False Item Suggestions:

- Keep the wording succinct and clear in true–false items.
- Avoid broad statements and words, such as *always, never, all, may, seldom, usually,* and so on.
- Use negatives sparingly at all grade levels. If they are used, always draw attention to them with underlining, italics, or bold type. Completely avoid negatives in examinations for children in the primary grades because very young children have considerable difficulty with reversals in thought.
- Avoid ambiguity in the statement. A true–false item should be unequivocally true or false.
- Keep the items as uniform in length as possible.
- Try to balance the numbers of true and false items. When an overbalance of either exists, students may be led to believe they must have answered some questions incorrectly.

EXAMPLES

(Poor) ________ Birds eat more than mammals.
________ Martha and George Washington had two children.

(Better) ________ Considering body weight, birds eat more than mammals do.
________ Martha and George Washington raised two children.

Multiple-Choice Item Suggestions:

- A multiple-choice test item comprises two parts: a stem and several answer choices. The stem should present enough information so that the answer choices can be relatively short. If students have to read lengthy choices after reading the stem, the questions may actually be testing students' short-term memory. Unless this is the purpose of the test, this memory factor may interfere with the validity of the item.
- Use negatives sparingly, and highlight them if they are used. Avoid negatives in tests for children in the primary grades.
- Avoid determiners, such as *all, some, often, usually,* and so on.
- Use special alternatives such as *all of the above* and *none of the above* sparingly.
- Try to keep the answer choices similar in length to avoid suggesting that any particular answer is the correct one.
- Make sure that all the answer choices are somewhat feasible while ensuring that only one correct answer exists.
- Ensure that all answer choices are grammatically consistent with the stem of the item.

EXAMPLES

(Poor)

An example of:
A. an animal that is a mollusk is a whale.
B. an animal that is a mollusk is a clam.
C. an animal that is a mollusk is a crab.
D. an animal that is a mollusk is a lobster.

(Better)

An example of a mollusk is a:
A. whale.
B. clam.
C. crab.
D. lobster.

The poor example includes needless repetition in the answer choices. The better example corrects this problem.

Matching Items Suggestions:

- Each matching item comprises a set of premises and response choices listed in two columns. The matching set should be relatively short. Requiring students to search through too many choices for an answer may test their short-term memory as well as their knowledge of the material for which the test is intended. This will lower the validity of the test. Try to limit any matching set to seven or fewer premises. Prepare more than one matching set if more items need to be tested.

- The material being tested in a single matching set should be as homogeneous as possible. For example, if the testing is about simple machines, avoid other topics.
- Include as much material in the premises as needed, but keep the length of response choices relatively short to avoid testing short-term memory instead of content.
- Include one or two extra response choices to avoid the certainty that a student who has one answer wrong will have another wrong.

EXAMPLES

(Poor)

Column A	*Column B*
_____ 1. Thermometer	A. An instrument that measures humidity
_____ 2. Barometer	B. An instrument that measures rainfall
_____ 3. Wind vane	C. An instrument that measures wind direction
_____ 4. Rain gauge	D. An instrument that measures air pressure
_____ 5. Hygrometer	E. An instrument that measures temperature

(Better)

Column A	*Column B*
_____ 1. An instrument that measures wind direction	A. Thermometer
_____ 2. An instrument that measures temperature	B. Barometer
_____ 3. An instrument that measures humidity	C. Wind vane
_____ 4. An instrument that measures rainfall	D. Humidifier
_____ 5. An instrument that measures air pressure	E. Hygrometer
	F. Telemeter
	G. Rain gauge

The two columns should be reversed in the poor example above. It is easier to read the definitions and then look down the list of possible answer choices, which are short. Also, additional answer choices are needed. These problems are corrected in the better example.

Summary

This chapter has discussed several authentic assessment techniques, including student portfolios that are used to collect samples of a student's completed work and work-in-progress as well as other items that are useful in assessing the student's progress. The preparation of rubrics for grading students' papers, projects, and performances has been explained and illustrated. Explanations and methods of determining test validity and reliability have been provided. Suggestions for the construction of different types of test items have been included and illustrated with examples.

Activity

Michael DeLaney is an English (literacy) teacher in a middle school. He is a member of a teaching team that designed a multidisciplinary unit on westward expansion in the United States. As a part of their research, students have been studying the history of the Trail of Tears. One of the assessments for the unit is a student essay on this historical event. Mr. D. was responsible for assigning and assessing the essay. He provided students with the following directions during a lesson in which he introduced the assignment:

> Prepare an essay about the Trail of Tears that is written in the first person from the viewpoint of a Cherokee Native American child of your age. Your essay must include three historical facts you have learned about the event.

An essay is not an easy student product to evaluate fairly and evenly. However, the use of rubrics for grading essays can help to make the process one that is more consistent from paper to paper. Using the criteria outlined in the requirements of the essay, prepare a set of rubrics to use for grading the students' essays.

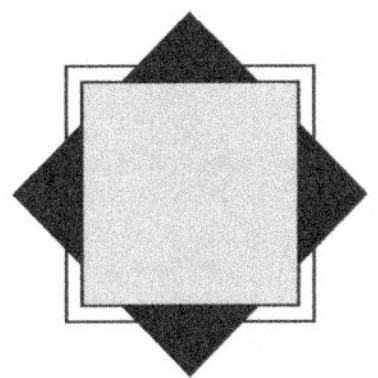

Appendix

Sample Interdisciplinary Unit Plan Web Designs

Web designs for interdisciplinary unit plans may be constructed in a number of different ways. The purpose of the sample webs in this appendix (Exhibits A.1 through A.10) is to show designs that differ stylistically from one another. Because the samples vary in the number of lesson and activity planning ideas included, amount of detail, and overall quality, they are only intended to show alternative ways to construct them.

The essential components are included in all of the web designs. Each includes a central theme and related disciplines to be employed in exploring the theme as well as brief statements or phrases describing the planner's ideas for related lessons and activities. Most of the designs include interconnecting lines that serve to indicate the planner's interdisciplinary thinking about the relationships among the various components.

Each sample represents a graphic design of the learning plan for an interdisciplinary unit. Its design also serves as a succinct reminder of the activities and lessons to be included in the unit when it is taught. Therefore, the diagrams do not give detailed information about learning options, materials, processes, or content that the unit will include. Those details are provided in the *Descriptions of Lessons and Activities* section of the unit plan. Although web designs can include greater detail, doing so often tends to make them overcrowded and difficult to read.

The samples indicate only the general level for which the unit topic is appropriate—primary, intermediate, or middle school. Designs for intermediate and middle school levels can be converted to become multidisciplinary units as described in chapter 4.

Exhibit A.1 Families (Primary).

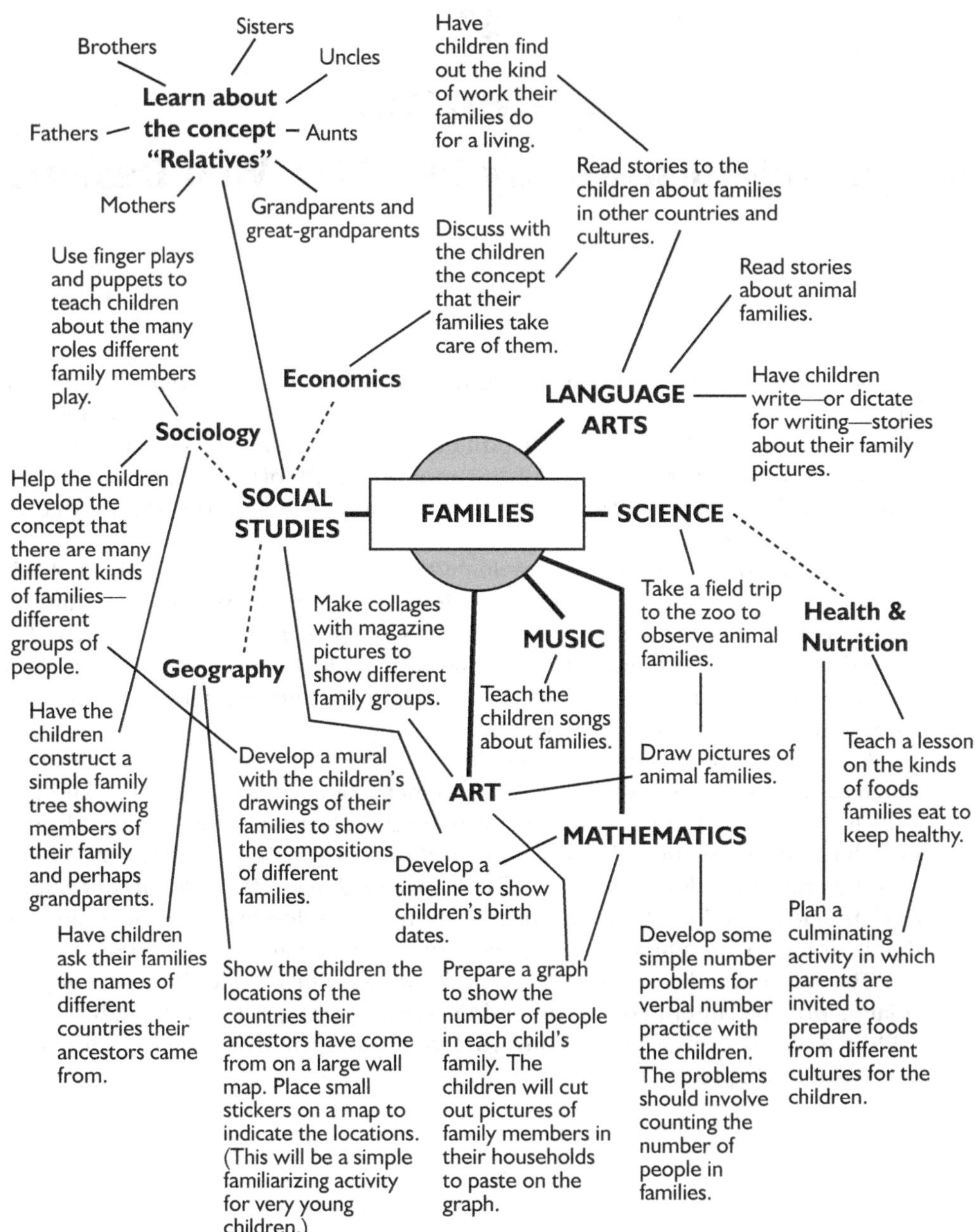

Sisters
Brothers
Uncles
Learn about the concept "Relatives"
Fathers
Aunts
Mothers
Grandparents and great-grandparents
Have children find out the kind of work their families do for a living.
Read stories to the children about families in other countries and cultures.
Discuss with the children the concept that their families take care of them.
Use finger plays and puppets to teach children about the many roles different family members play.
Read stories about animal families.
Economics
LANGUAGE ARTS
Have children write—or dictate for writing—stories about their family pictures.
Sociology
Help the children develop the concept that there are many different kinds of families—different groups of people.
SOCIAL STUDIES
FAMILIES
SCIENCE
Make collages with magazine pictures to show different family groups.
MUSIC
Take a field trip to the zoo to observe animal families.
Health & Nutrition
Geography
Teach the children songs about families.
Have the children construct a simple family tree showing members of their family and perhaps grandparents.
Develop a mural with the children's drawings of their families to show the compositions of different families.
ART
Draw pictures of animal families.
Teach a lesson on the kinds of foods families eat to keep healthy.
MATHEMATICS
Develop a timeline to show children's birth dates.
Have children ask their families the names of different countries their ancestors came from.
Show the children the locations of the countries their ancestors have come from on a large wall map. Place small stickers on a map to indicate the locations. (This will be a simple familiarizing activity for very young children.)
Prepare a graph to show the number of people in each child's family. The children will cut out pictures of family members in their households to paste on the graph.
Develop some simple number problems for verbal number practice with the children. The problems should involve counting the number of people in families.
Plan a culminating activity in which parents are invited to prepare foods from different cultures for the children.

Exhibit A.2 Our Neighborhood (Primary).

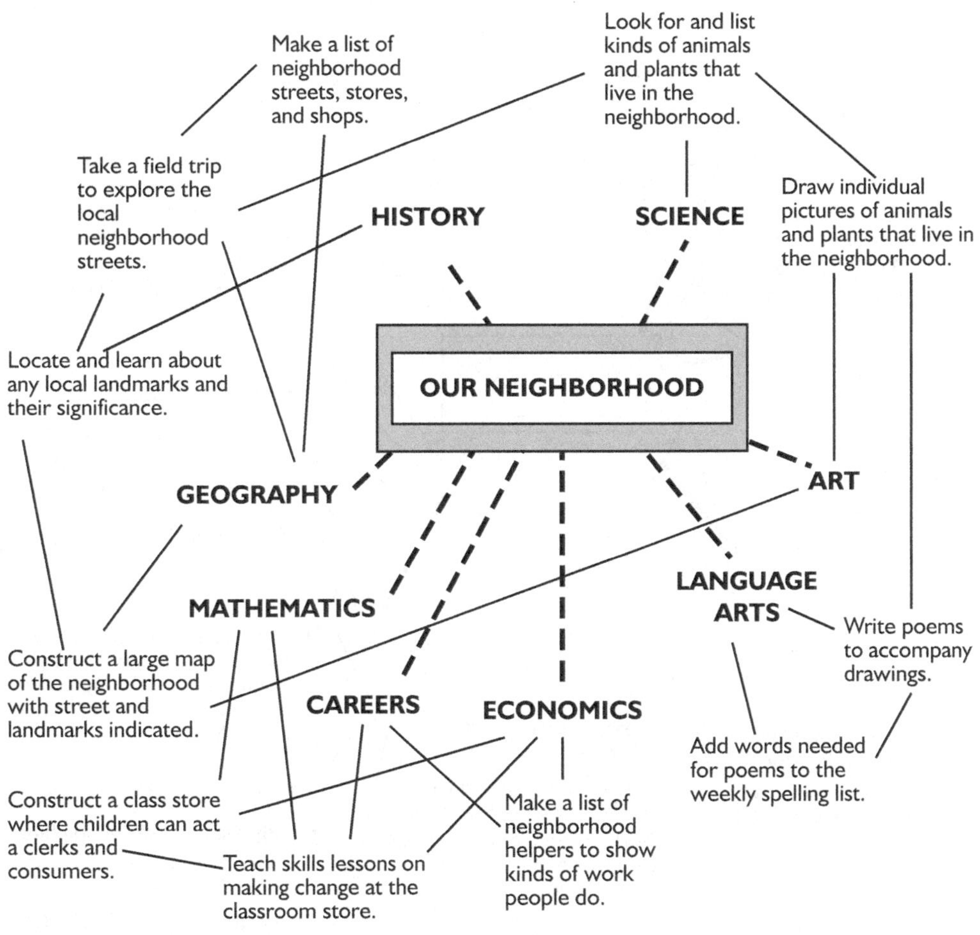

Exhibit A.3 Dolphins (Upper Primary/Intermediate).

DOLPHINS

Mathematics

- Graph the number of dolphins at an early date in history and then at a later date.
- Create paint-by-number activities. (Numbers will be answers to division and multiplication questions.)

Music

- Listen to dolphin sounds and write stories.
- Keep a journal or draw pictures about how the sounds affect people.
- Write songs about dolphins.

History

- Take a trip to the aquarium to learn about the different types of dolphins.
- Watch a video on why dolphins are endangered.

Sociology

- Teach a lesson on how dolphins must stay in schools in order to survive.
- Read a story about a dolphin being separated from its group.

Geography

- Draw maps of where dolphins are located.
- Read a book on how and why dolphins migrate from place to place.

Economics

- Teach a lesson on how some tuna companies have had to change their capturing policies to avoid killing dolphins when fishing for tuna.

Language Arts

- Write poems about dolphins.
- Write creative stories about dolphins.
- Read books about dolphins, and write book reports.
- Write an essay about why dolphins are endangered.

Art

- Create collages of all different types of dolphins.
- Draw pictures of dolphins, and label the body parts.
- Work in cooperative groups to create a bulletin board for the unit.

Science & Technology

- Study the life cycle of dolphins.
- Teach a lesson on the mating habits of dolphins.
- Look at pictures of dolphins, and observe their physical features.
- Introduce the unit by preparing a K-W-L chart on dolphins.

Courtesy of Carla Cardoso, Donna Fuchs, and Evelyn Kaszuba

Exhibit A.4 Birds of America (Upper Primary/Intermediate).

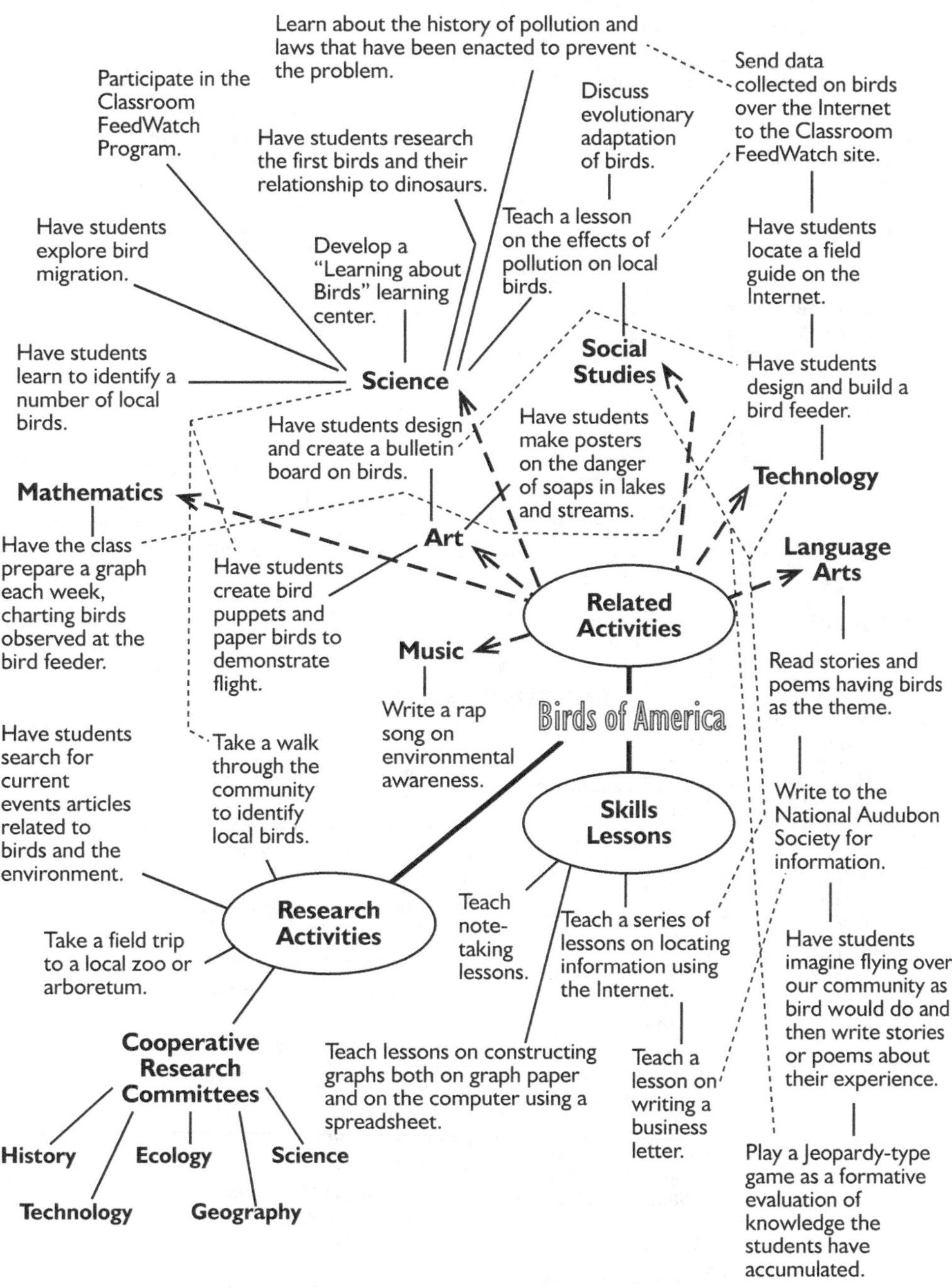

Courtesy of Margaret Kenzie and Sheryl Schuhose

Exhibit A.5 The American Revolution (Intermediate/Middle School).

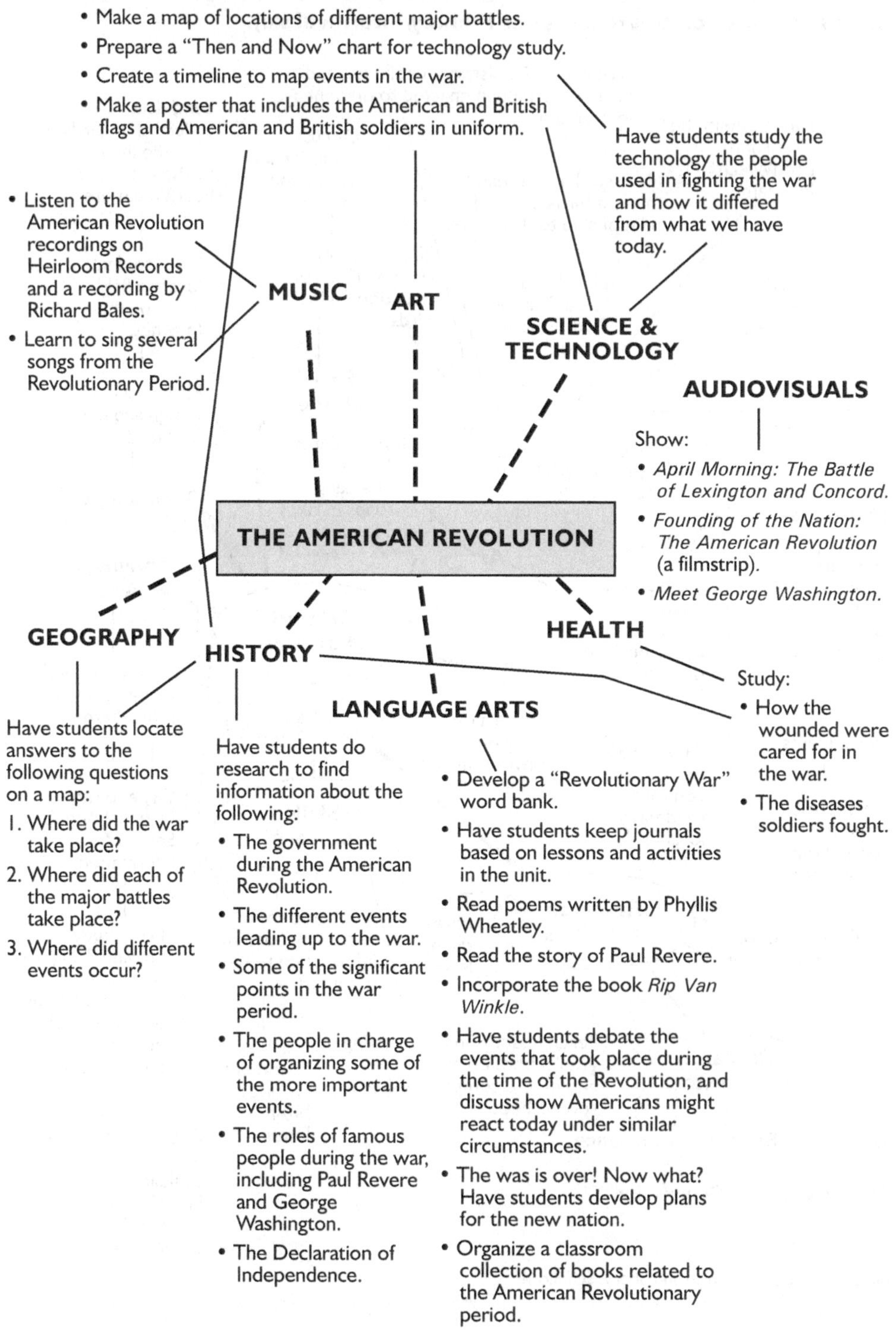

THE AMERICAN REVOLUTION

ART

- Make a map of locations of different major battles.
- Prepare a "Then and Now" chart for technology study.
- Create a timeline to map events in the war.
- Make a poster that includes the American and British flags and American and British soldiers in uniform.

MUSIC

- Listen to the American Revolution recordings on Heirloom Records and a recording by Richard Bales.
- Learn to sing several songs from the Revolutionary Period.

SCIENCE & TECHNOLOGY

Have students study the technology the people used in fighting the war and how it differed from what we have today.

AUDIOVISUALS

Show:

- *April Morning: The Battle of Lexington and Concord.*
- *Founding of the Nation: The American Revolution* (a filmstrip).
- *Meet George Washington.*

GEOGRAPHY

Have students locate answers to the following questions on a map:

1. Where did the war take place?
2. Where did each of the major battles take place?
3. Where did different events occur?

HISTORY

Have students do research to find information about the following:

- The government during the American Revolution.
- The different events leading up to the war.
- Some of the significant points in the war period.
- The people in charge of organizing some of the more important events.
- The roles of famous people during the war, including Paul Revere and George Washington.
- The Declaration of Independence.

LANGUAGE ARTS

- Develop a "Revolutionary War" word bank.
- Have students keep journals based on lessons and activities in the unit.
- Read poems written by Phyllis Wheatley.
- Read the story of Paul Revere.
- Incorporate the book *Rip Van Winkle*.
- Have students debate the events that took place during the time of the Revolution, and discuss how Americans might react today under similar circumstances.
- The was is over! Now what? Have students develop plans for the new nation.
- Organize a classroom collection of books related to the American Revolutionary period.

HEALTH

Study:

- How the wounded were cared for in the war.
- The diseases soldiers fought.

Courtesy of Jennifer Fanno

Exhibit A.6 Mysteries (Middle School).

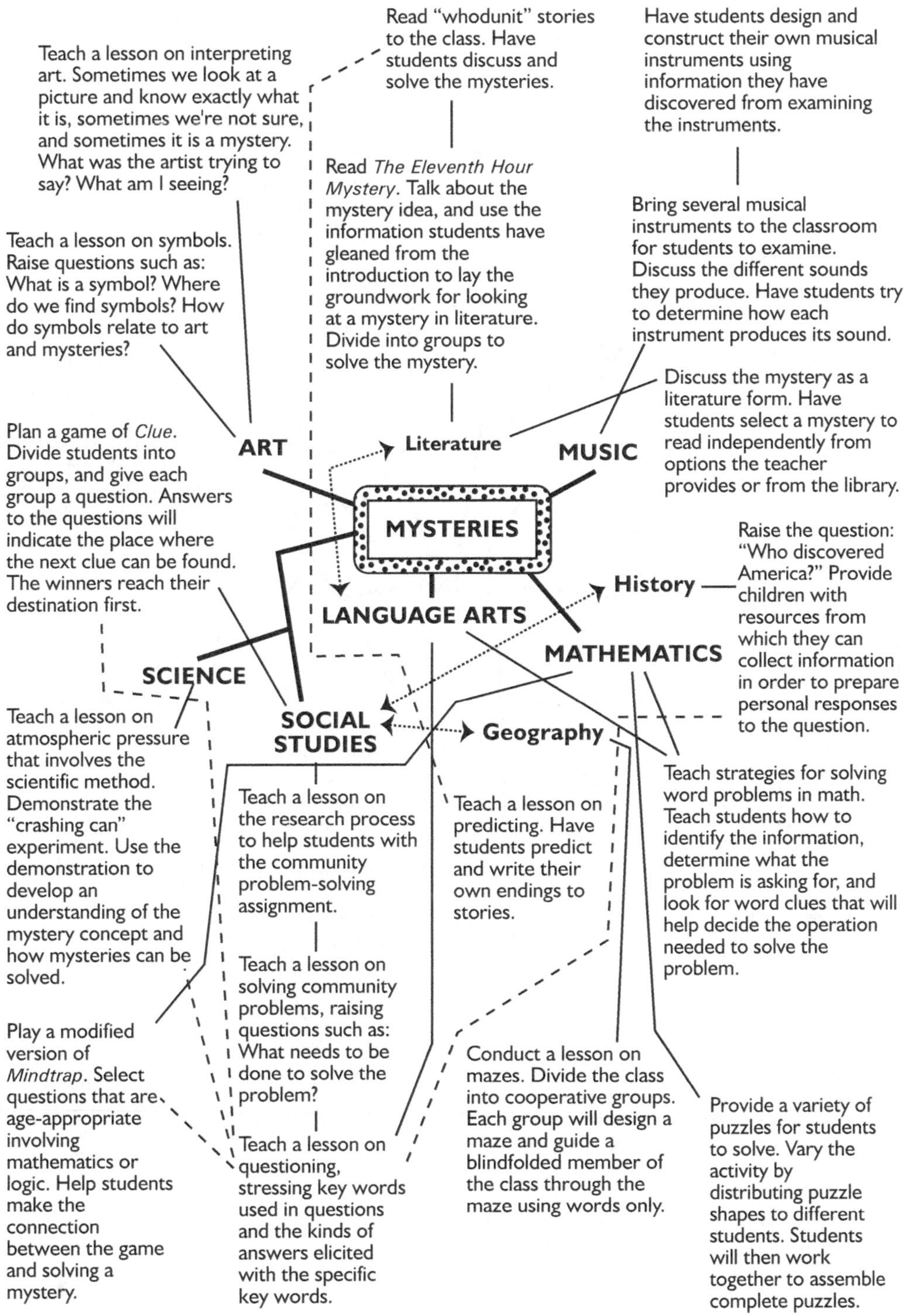

MYSTERIES

ART

Teach a lesson on interpreting art. Sometimes we look at a picture and know exactly what it is, sometimes we're not sure, and sometimes it is a mystery. What was the artist trying to say? What am I seeing?

Teach a lesson on symbols. Raise questions such as: What is a symbol? Where do we find symbols? How do symbols relate to art and mysteries?

Plan a game of *Clue*. Divide students into groups, and give each group a question. Answers to the questions will indicate the place where the next clue can be found. The winners reach their destination first.

LANGUAGE ARTS

Literature

Read "whodunit" stories to the class. Have students discuss and solve the mysteries.

Read *The Eleventh Hour Mystery*. Talk about the mystery idea, and use the information students have gleaned from the introduction to lay the groundwork for looking at a mystery in literature. Divide into groups to solve the mystery.

Discuss the mystery as a literature form. Have students select a mystery to read independently from options the teacher provides or from the library.

Teach a lesson on predicting. Have students predict and write their own endings to stories.

Teach a lesson on questioning, stressing key words used in questions and the kinds of answers elicited with the specific key words.

MUSIC

Have students design and construct their own musical instruments using information they have discovered from examining the instruments.

Bring several musical instruments to the classroom for students to examine. Discuss the different sounds they produce. Have students try to determine how each instrument produces its sound.

SOCIAL STUDIES

History

Raise the question: "Who discovered America?" Provide children with resources from which they can collect information in order to prepare personal responses to the question.

Geography

Teach a lesson on the research process to help students with the community problem-solving assignment.

Teach a lesson on solving community problems, raising questions such as: What needs to be done to solve the problem?

SCIENCE

Teach a lesson on atmospheric pressure that involves the scientific method. Demonstrate the "crashing can" experiment. Use the demonstration to develop an understanding of the mystery concept and how mysteries can be solved.

MATHEMATICS

Teach strategies for solving word problems in math. Teach students how to identify the information, determine what the problem is asking for, and look for word clues that will help decide the operation needed to solve the problem.

Conduct a lesson on mazes. Divide the class into cooperative groups. Each group will design a maze and guide a blindfolded member of the class through the maze using words only.

Provide a variety of puzzles for students to solve. Vary the activity by distributing puzzle shapes to different students. Students will then work together to assemble complete puzzles.

Play a modified version of *Mindtrap*. Select questions that are age-appropriate involving mathematics or logic. Help students make the connection between the game and solving a mystery.

Courtesy of Jane Boyd

Exhibit A.7 China (Intermediate/Middle School).

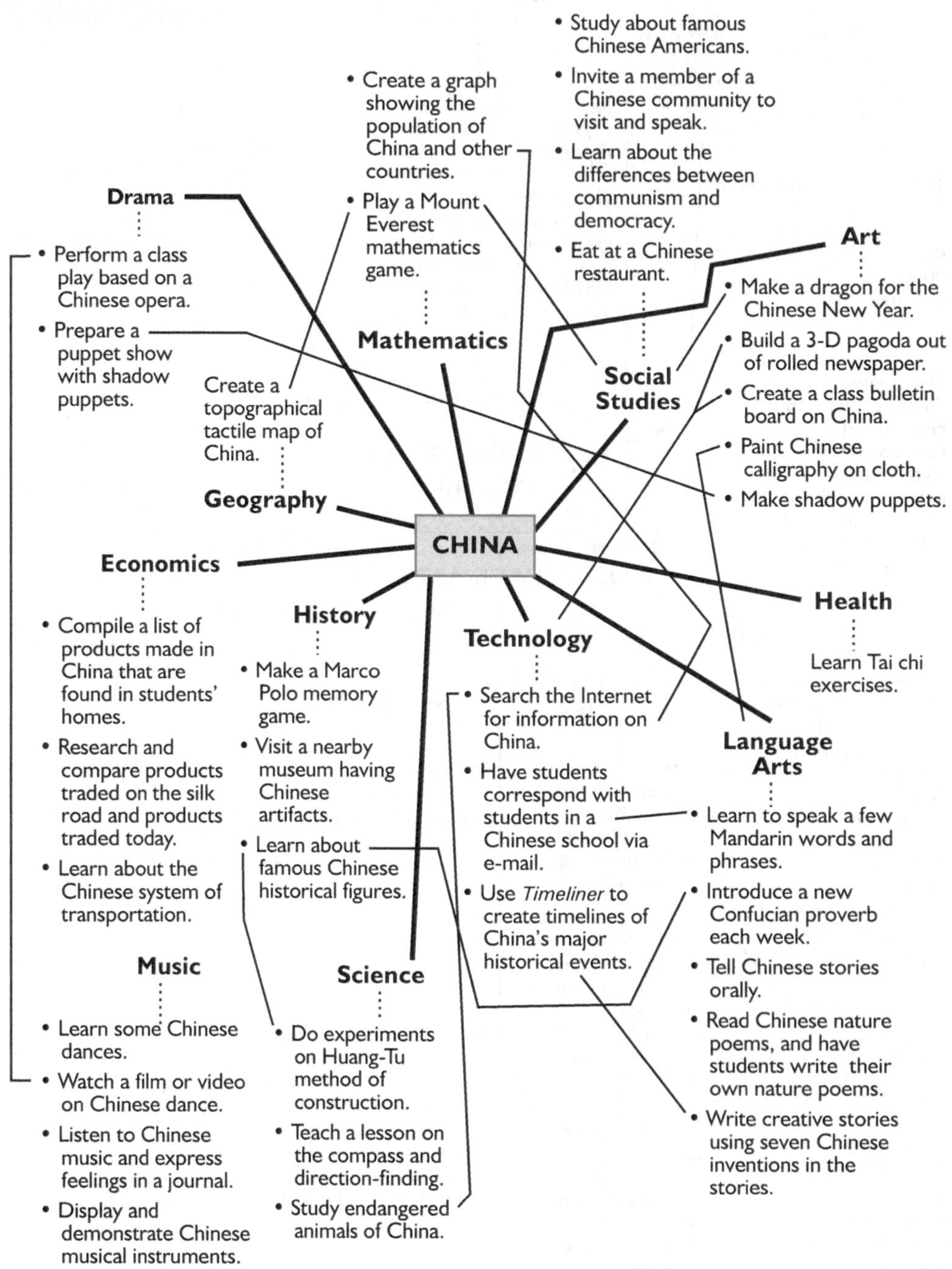

CHINA
Drama
• Perform a class play based on a Chinese opera.
• Prepare a puppet show with shadow puppets.
Mathematics
• Create a graph showing the population of China and other countries.
• Play a Mount Everest mathematics game.
Social Studies
• Study about famous Chinese Americans.
• Invite a member of a Chinese community to visit and speak.
• Learn about the differences between communism and democracy.
• Eat at a Chinese restaurant.
Art
• Make a dragon for the Chinese New Year.
• Build a 3-D pagoda out of rolled newspaper.
• Create a class bulletin board on China.
• Paint Chinese calligraphy on cloth.
• Make shadow puppets.
Geography
Create a topographical tactile map of China.
Economics
• Compile a list of products made in China that are found in students' homes.
• Research and compare products traded on the silk road and products traded today.
• Learn about the Chinese system of transportation.
History
• Make a Marco Polo memory game.
• Visit a nearby museum having Chinese artifacts.
• Learn about famous Chinese historical figures.
Technology
• Search the Internet for information on China.
• Have students correspond with students in a Chinese school via e-mail.
• Use *Timeliner* to create timelines of China's major historical events.
Health
Learn Tai chi exercises.
Language Arts
• Learn to speak a few Mandarin words and phrases.
• Introduce a new Confucian proverb each week.
• Tell Chinese stories orally.
• Read Chinese nature poems, and have students write their own nature poems.
• Write creative stories using seven Chinese inventions in the stories.
Music
• Learn some Chinese dances.
• Watch a film or video on Chinese dance.
• Listen to Chinese music and express feelings in a journal.
• Display and demonstrate Chinese musical instruments.
Science
• Do experiments on Huang-Tu method of construction.
• Teach a lesson on the compass and direction-finding.
• Study endangered animals of China.

Courtesy of Christine Coyle

Exhibit A.8 Rain Forests (Intermediate/Middle School).

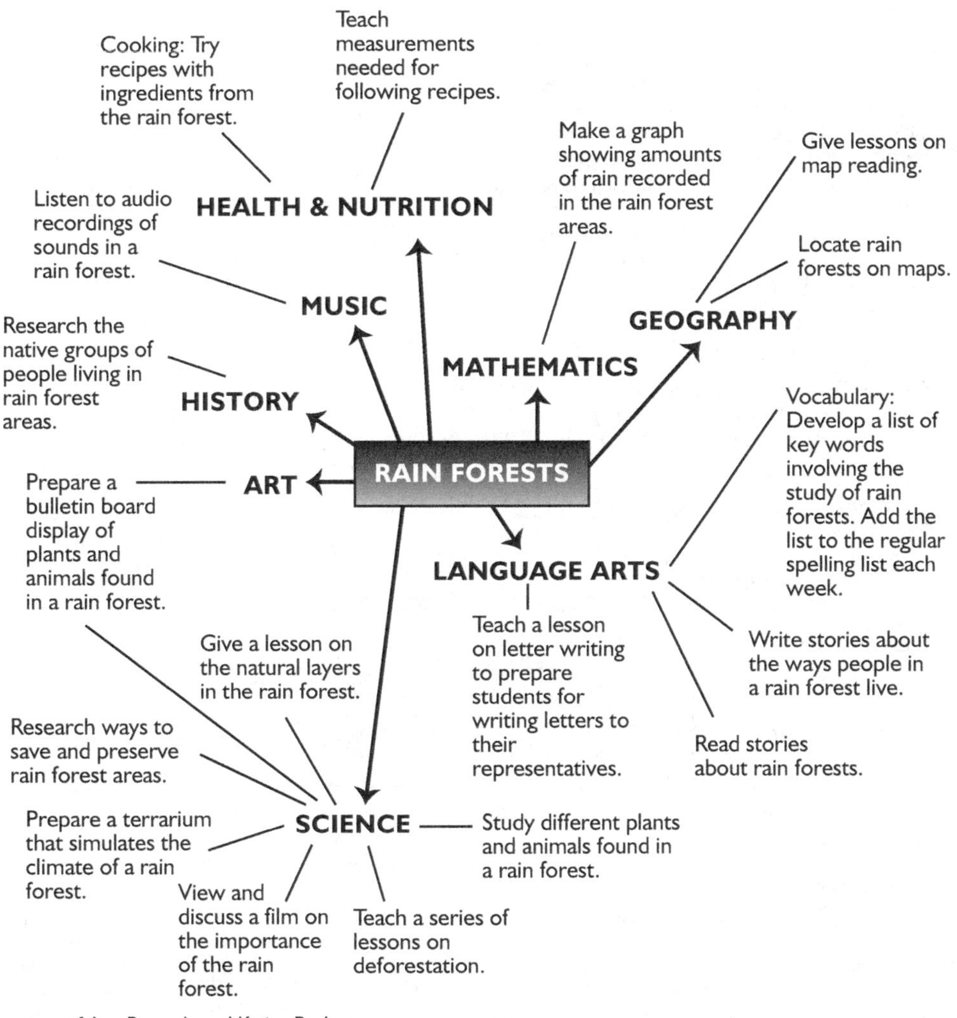

RAIN FORESTS
HEALTH & NUTRITION
Cooking: Try recipes with ingredients from the rain forest.
Teach measurements needed for following recipes.
MUSIC
Listen to audio recordings of sounds in a rain forest.
HISTORY
Research the native groups of people living in rain forest areas.
ART
Prepare a bulletin board display of plants and animals found in a rain forest.
MATHEMATICS
Make a graph showing amounts of rain recorded in the rain forest areas.
GEOGRAPHY
Give lessons on map reading.
Locate rain forests on maps.
LANGUAGE ARTS
Vocabulary: Develop a list of key words involving the study of rain forests. Add the list to the regular spelling list each week.
Write stories about the ways people in a rain forest live.
Read stories about rain forests.
Teach a lesson on letter writing to prepare students for writing letters to their representatives.
SCIENCE
Give a lesson on the natural layers in the rain forest.
Research ways to save and preserve rain forest areas.
Prepare a terrarium that simulates the climate of a rain forest.
View and discuss a film on the importance of the rain forest.
Teach a series of lessons on deforestation.
Study different plants and animals found in a rain forest.

Courtesy of Ann Brancale and Katina Paulsen

Exhibit A.9 The Great Depression (Intermediate/Middle School).

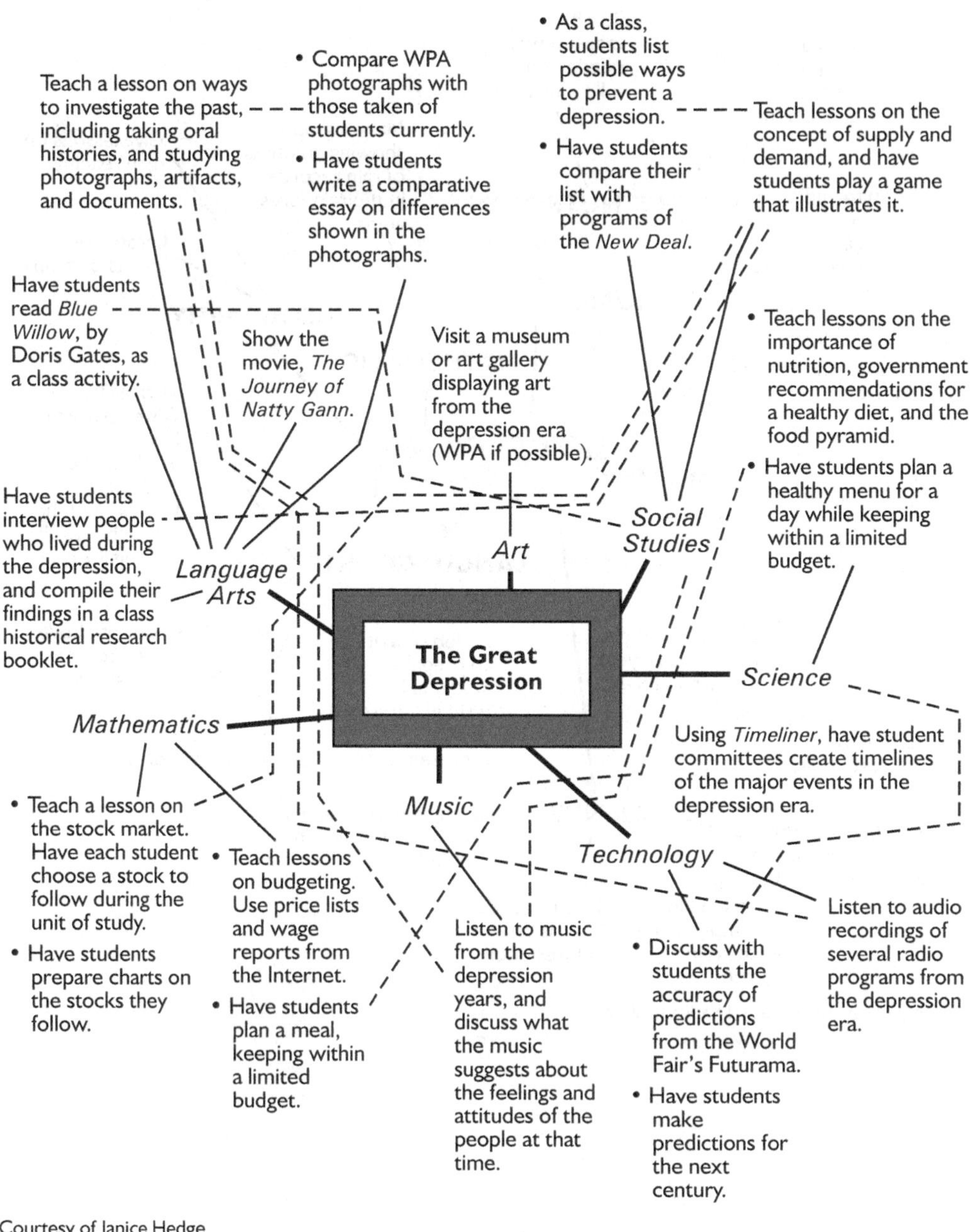

The Great Depression
Language Arts
Teach a lesson on ways to investigate the past, including taking oral histories, and studying photographs, artifacts, and documents.
• Compare WPA photographs with those taken of students currently.
• Have students write a comparative essay on differences shown in the photographs.
Have students read *Blue Willow*, by Doris Gates, as a class activity.
Show the movie, *The Journey of Natty Gann.*
Have students interview people who lived during the depression, and compile their findings in a class historical research booklet.
Art
Visit a museum or art gallery displaying art from the depression era (WPA if possible).
Social Studies
• As a class, students list possible ways to prevent a depression.
• Have students compare their list with programs of the *New Deal.*
Teach lessons on the concept of supply and demand, and have students play a game that illustrates it.
Science
• Teach lessons on the importance of nutrition, government recommendations for a healthy diet, and the food pyramid.
• Have students plan a healthy menu for a day while keeping within a limited budget.
Mathematics
• Teach a lesson on the stock market. Have each student choose a stock to follow during the unit of study.
• Have students prepare charts on the stocks they follow.
• Teach lessons on budgeting. Use price lists and wage reports from the Internet.
• Have students plan a meal, keeping within a limited budget.
Music
Listen to music from the depression years, and discuss what the music suggests about the feelings and attitudes of the people at that time.
Technology
Using *Timeliner*, have student committees create timelines of the major events in the depression era.
• Discuss with students the accuracy of predictions from the World Fair's Futurama.
• Have students make predictions for the next century.
Listen to audio recordings of several radio programs from the depression era.

Courtesy of Janice Hedge

Exhibit A.10 Black History Month (Intermediate/Middle School).

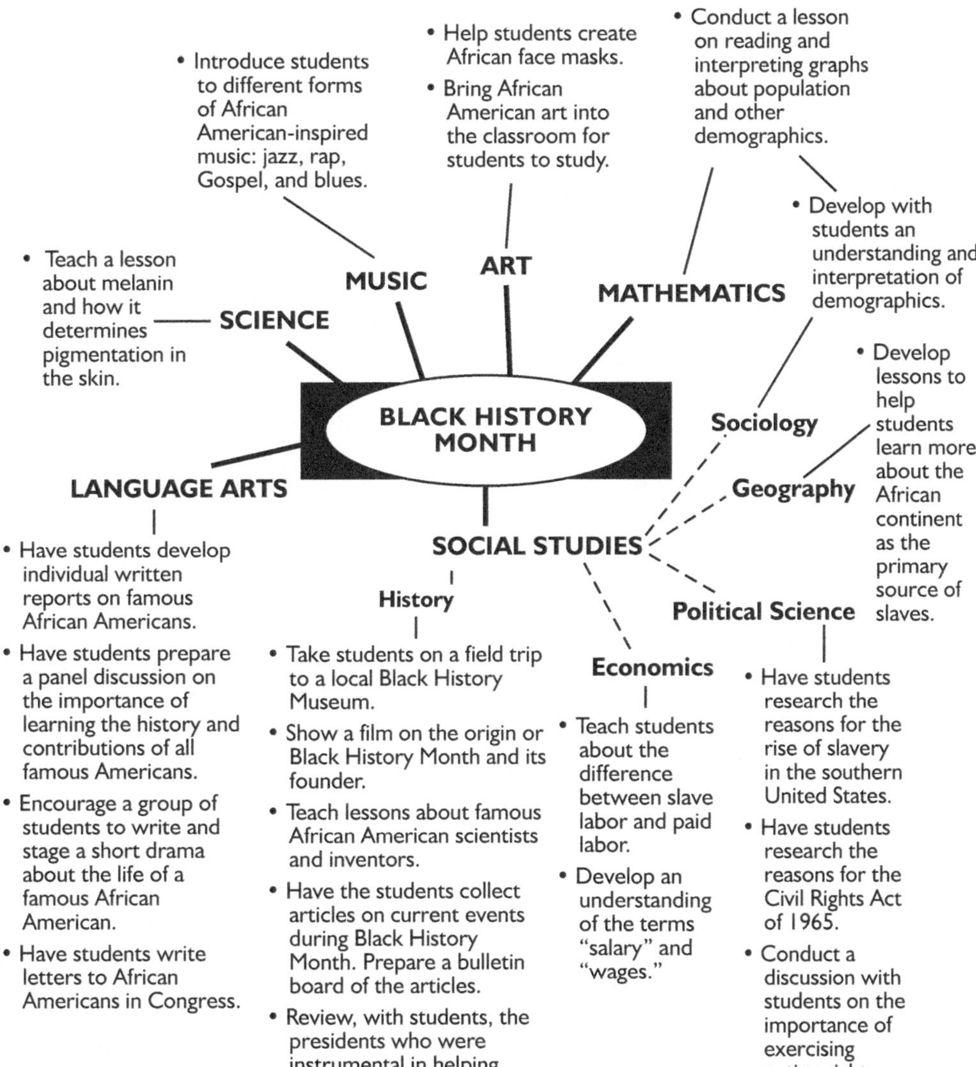

BLACK HISTORY MONTH
MUSIC
• Introduce students to different forms of African American-inspired music: jazz, rap, Gospel, and blues.
ART
• Help students create African face masks.
• Bring African American art into the classroom for students to study.
MATHEMATICS
• Conduct a lesson on reading and interpreting graphs about population and other demographics.
• Develop with students an understanding and interpretation of demographics.
SCIENCE
• Teach a lesson about melanin and how it determines pigmentation in the skin.
LANGUAGE ARTS
• Have students develop individual written reports on famous African Americans.
• Have students prepare a panel discussion on the importance of learning the history and contributions of all famous Americans.
• Encourage a group of students to write and stage a short drama about the life of a famous African American.
• Have students write letters to African Americans in Congress.
SOCIAL STUDIES
Sociology
Geography
• Develop lessons to help students learn more about the African continent as the primary source of slaves.
History
• Take students on a field trip to a local Black History Museum.
• Show a film on the origin or Black History Month and its founder.
• Teach lessons about famous African American scientists and inventors.
• Have the students collect articles on current events during Black History Month. Prepare a bulletin board of the articles.
• Review, with students, the presidents who were instrumental in helping African Americans.
Economics
• Teach students about the difference between slave labor and paid labor.
• Develop an understanding of the terms "salary" and "wages."
Political Science
• Have students research the reasons for the rise of slavery in the southern United States.
• Have students research the reasons for the Civil Rights Act of 1965.
• Conduct a discussion with students on the importance of exercising voting rights.

Courtesy of Dearl Topping

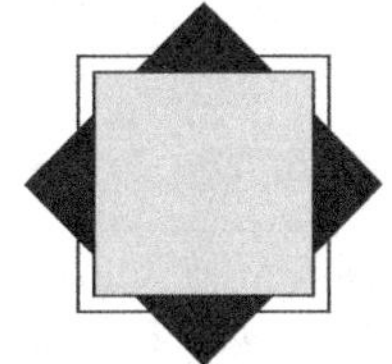

References

Agnes, M. (Ed.). (2008). *Webster's new world college dictionary* (4th ed.). Cleveland, OH: Wiley.

Allen, R. (2005, August). Moving elementary science from afterthought to inquiry. *Education Update 48*(8), 4.

Allis, S. (1999, July 11). The master of unartificial intelligence: Howard Gardner's definition of "smart" still sparks controversy. *The Boston Sunday Globe,* pp. D1–D5.

Arends, R. I. (2015). *Learning to teach* (10th ed.). Boston: McGraw-Hill.

Armstrong, T. (2009). *Multiple intelligences in the classroom* (3rd ed.). Alexandria, VA: ASCD.

ASCD. (2007, Winter) An insider's view: What's behind ASCD's focus on formative assessment. *ASCD Associate News.* Alexandria, VA: Author.

Beane, J. A. (1997). *Curriculum integration: Designing the core of democratic education.* New York: Teachers College Press.

Beane, J. A. (n.d.) The Bean/Brodhagan model of negotiated integrated curriculum. Retrieved from http://coe.winthrop.edu/blackburnb/EDCI%20600/Beane.pdf.

Berk, L. E. (2008). *Infants, children, and adolescents* (6th ed.). Boston: Pearson.

Bloom, B. S. (1956). *Taxonomy of educational goals, by a committee of college and university examiners.* New York: Longmans, Green.

Bolak, K., Bialach, D., & Dunphy, M. (May 2005). Standards-based, thematic units integrate the arts and energize students and teachers. *Middle School Journal, 31*(2), 57–60.

Borich, G. D. (2014). *Effective teaching methods* (8th ed.). Boston: Pearson.

Brandt, R. (1988). On assessment in the arts: A conversation with Howard Gardner. *Educational Leadership, 45*(4), 30–34.

Bronson, P., & Merryman, A. (2013). *Top dog: The science of winning and losing.* New York: Twelve (Hatchette Book Group).

Brooks, J. G., & Brooks, M. G. (1999). *In search of understanding: The case for constructivist classrooms* (rev. ed.). Alexandria, VA: ASCD.

Bruner, J. (1963). *The process of education.* New York: Vintage Books.

Bruner, J. (1990). *Acts of meaning.* Cambridge, MA: Harvard University Press.

Bryk, A. S., & Schneider, B. (2003). Trust in schools: A core resource for school reform. *Educational Leadership, 60*(8), 40–44.

Campbell, L., Campbell, B., & Dickinson, D. (2004). *Teaching and learning through multiple intelligences* (3rd ed.). Boston: Pearson.

Caram, C. A., & Davis, P. B. (2005, Fall). Inviting student engagement with questioning. *Kappa Delta Pi Record, 42*(1), 19–23.

Carolan, J., & Guinn, A. (2007, February). Differentiation: Lessons from master teachers. *Educational Leadership 64*(5), 44–47.

Case, R. (1985). *Intellectual development: Birth to adulthood.* Orlando, FL: Academic Press.

Chance, P. (2008). *The teacher's craft: The 10 essential skills of effective teaching.* Long Grove, IL: Waveland Press.

Channon, G. (1970). *Homework.* New York: Outerbridge & Dienstfrey.

Charbonneau, M. P., & Reider, B. E. (1995). *The integrated elementary classroom: A developmental model of education for the 21st century.* Boston: Pearson.

Chatterton, R. (1968). *The multidisciplinary teaching of class research topics.* Merrick, NY: Merrick School District No. 25.

Checkley, K. (1997). The first seven . . . and the eighth. *Educational Leadership, 55*(1), 8–13.

Checkley, K. (2006, May). Social studies jockeys for position in a narrowing curriculum. *Education Update 48*(5), pp. 1–2, 8.

Chicago Public Schools. (2007). *The rubric bank.* Retrieved from http://intranet.cps.k12.il.us/assessments/Ideas_and_Rubrics/Rubric_Bank/rubric_bank.html

Coffey, H. (n.d.) *Interdisciplinary teaching.* Retrieved from http://www.learnnc.org/lp/pages/5196.

Comer, J. P., & Haynes, N. M. (1991, January). Parent involvement in schools: An ecological approach. *Elementary School Journal, 91*(3), 271–277.

Cooper, J. D., & Kiger, N. D. (2008). *Literacy assessment: Helping teachers plan instruction.* Boston: Houghton Mifflin.

Cooper, J. M. (2006). *Classroom teaching skills* (8th ed.). Boston: Houghton Mifflin.

Cowelti, G. (2006). The side effects of NCLB. *Educational Leadership, 64*(3), 64–68.

Criteria for selection of class research topics. (1966, April 28). *Our 3 C's—Characteristic curricular concepts, 12*(12). (Union Free School District No. 25, Merrick, NY).

Daniels, H., & Zemelman, S. (2004). Out with textbooks, in with learning. *Educational Leadership, 61*(4), 36–40.

Darling-Hammond, L., & Berry, B. (2006). Highly qualified teachers for all. *Educational Leadership, 64*(3), 14–20.

Davis School District. (n.d). Technology resources acceptable use agreement. Retrieved from http://www.davis.k12.ut.us/domain/2416.

Dewey, J. (1916). *Democracy and education.* New York: Free Press.

Dick, W, Carey, L., & Carey, J. O. (2009). *The systematic design of instruction* (7th ed.). Boston: Pearson.

Duckor, B. (2014, March). Formative assessment in seven good moves. *Educational Leadership, 71*(5), 28–32.

DuPlass, J. A. (2008). *Teaching elementary social studies* (2nd ed.). Boston: Houghton Mifflin.

Early elementary resources guide. (1996). Albany, NY: University of the State of New York, State Education Department.

Elder, L., & Paul, R. (2002). *A miniature guide to the art of asking key questions.* Dillon Beach, CA: Foundation for Critical Thinking.

Ellis, A. K. (2010). *Teaching and learning elementary social studies* (9th ed.). Boston: Pearson.

Flavell, J. H. (1985). *Cognitive development* (2nd ed.). Boston: Pearson.

Flowers, N., Mertens, S. B., & Mulhall, P. F. (1999, November). The impact of teaming: Five research-based outcomes. *Middle School Journal, 36*(5), 9–19.

Forman, E. A., Minick, N., & Stone, C. A. (1993). *Contexts for learning.* New York: Oxford University Press.

Fullan, M. (2011). *Change leader: Learning to do what matters most.* San Francisco: Wiley.

Gardner, H. (1983). *Frames of mind: The theory of multiple intelligences.* New York: Basic Books.

Gardner, H. (1991). *The unschooled mind: How children think and how schools should teach.* New York: Basic Books.

Gardner, H. (1993a). *Creating minds.* New York: Basic Books.

Gardner, H. (1993b). *Multiple intelligences: The theory in practice.* New York: Basic Books.

Gardner, H. (1995, January 6). Creating creativity. *The Times Educational Supplement,* No. 4097, p. 15.

Gardner, H. (1999). *Intelligence reframed: Multiple intelligences for the 21st century.* New York: Basic Books.

Goodrich, H. (1997). Understanding rubrics. *Educational Leadership, 54*(4), 14–17.

Guskey, T. R. (2003). How classroom assessments improve learning. *Educational Leadership, 60*(5), 6–11.

Hall, T. (2002). Differentiated instruction. Wakefield, MA: National Center on Accessing the General Curriculum. Retrieved from http://www.cast.org/publications/ncac/ncac_diffinstruc.html

Hancock, L. (2011, September). Why are Finland's schools successful? *Educating Americans for the 21st Century* (Special Report). Retrieved from http://www.smithsonianmag.com/innovation/why-are-finlands-schools-successful-49859555/?no-ist=.

Hardiman, M. M. (2001, November). Connecting brain research with dimensions of learning. *Educational Leadership, 59*(3), 52–55.

Heck, M., & Roose, D. (2005). Dispositions as habits of body, mind, and spirit: Quaker and Native American perspectives. In Smith, R. L., Skarbek, D., & Hurst, J. (Eds.), *The passion of teaching: Dispositions in the schools.* Lanham, MD: Scarecrow Education.

Heilman, A. W., Blair, R. R., & Rupley, W. H. (2002). *Principles and practices of teaching reading.* Boston: Pearson.

Henriquez, M. (Speaker). (1995). Acceptance speech at the academic awards ceremony of the Teacher Education Program at the State University of New York/College at Old Westbury.

Henson, K. T. (2015). *Curriculum Planning: Integrating Multiculturalism, Constructivism, and Education Reform* (5th ed.). Long Grove, IL: Waveland Press.

Hunter, R. (2004). *Madeline Hunter's mastery teaching: Increasing instructional effectiveness in elementary and secondary schools.* Thousand Oaks, CA: Corwin.

Jacobs, H. (Ed.). (1989). *Interdisciplinary curriculum: Design and implementation.* Alexandria, VA: ASCD.

Jacobs, H. H. (1997). *Mapping the big picture: Integrating curriculum & assessment.* Alexandria, VA: ASCD.

Jensen, E. (2001). *Arts with the brain in mind.* Alexandria, VA: ASCD.

Jensen, E. (2005). *Teaching with the brain in mind* (2nd ed.). Alexandria, VA: ASCD.

Johnson, D. D., Rice, M. P., Edgington, W. D., & Williams, P. (2005). For the uninitiated: How to succeed in classroom management. *Kappa Delta Pi Record, 42*(1), 28–32.

Johnston, P. H. (1992). *Constructive evaluation of literate activity.* White Plains, NY: Longman.

Jorgenson, O. (2003). Brain scam? Why educators should be careful about embracing "brain research." *The Educational Forum, 67*(4), 364–369.

Kamii, C. (1973). Pedagogical principles derived from Piaget's theory: Relevance for educational practice. In M. Schwebel & J. Raph (Eds.), *Piaget in the classroom* (pp. 199–215). New York: Basic Books.

Kane, J. (1999). *Education, information, and transformation: Essays on learning and thinking.* Boston: Pearson.

Kellough, R. D., & Kellough, N. G. (2003). *Middle school teaching: A guide to methods and resources* (4th ed.). Boston: Pearson.

Kempton, S. (2014). *Let's find out! Building content knowledge with young children.* Portland, ME: Stenhouse.

Kimpston, R., Williams, H., & Stockton, W. (1992). Ways of knowing and the curriculum. *The Educational Forum, 56*(2), 153–172.

Kohn, A. (2003). Almost there, but not quite. *Educational Leadership, 60*(6), 26–29.

Kohn, A. (2006). *Beyond discipline: From compliance to community* (2nd ed.). Alexandria, VA: ASCD.

Kornhaber, M., Fierros, E., & Veenema, S. (2004). *Multiple intelligences: Best ideas from research and practice.* Boston: Pearson.

Lagemann, E. C., & Shulman, L. S. (1999). *Issues in educational research: Problems and possibilities.* San Francisco: Jossey-Bass.

Larmer, J. (2014, September). Boosting the power of projects. *Educational Leadership, 72*(1), 42–46.

Learning standards for social studies. (1996). Albany: The University of the State of New York/The State Education Department.

Leonard, G. B. (1968). *Education and ecstasy.* New York: Delacorte Press.

Leu, D. J., Zawilinski, L., Forzani, E., & Timbrell, N. (2014). Best practices in teaching the new literacies of online research and comprehension. In Morrow, L. M., & Gambrell, L. B. (Eds.), *Best Practices in Literacy Instruction* (4th ed., pp. 343–364.)

Lillard, P. (1972). *Montessori: A modern approach.* New York: Schocken Books.

Lowery, L. (1998, November). How new science curriculums reflect brain research. *Educational Leadership, 56*(3), 26–30.

Macbeth, D. (2003). Hugh Mehan's learning lessons reconsidered: On the differences between the naturalistic and critical analysis of classroom discourse. *American Educational Research Journal, 40*(1), 239–280.

March, T. (2003 December/2004 January). The learning power of WebQuests. *Educational Leadership 61*(4), 42–47.

Marsh, F. E., & Horns-Marsh, V. (1999). For the record. *Kappa Delta Pi Record, 35*(4), 152.

Mayer, R. E. (2008). *Learning and instruction* (2nd ed.). Boston: Pearson.

Mayhew, K. C., & Edwards, A. C. (2011). *The Dewey school: The laboratory of the University of Chicago School 1896–1903.* Charleston, SC: Nabu Press. (Original work published 1936.)

McKibben, S. (2013, September). Beyond the open-door policy. *Education Update, 55*(9), 1–4, 5.

Miller, E. (1995, January/February). The old model of staff development survives in a world where everything else has changed. *The Harvard Education Letter 11*(1), 1–3.

Minnesota Board of Teaching. (2006, January). *Report to the legislature.* Retrieved from http://children.state.mn.us/mdeprod/groups/Communications/documents/Report/008666.pdf

Montessori, M. (1964). *The Montessori method.* New York: Schocken Books. (Original work published 1912.)

Moore, K. D. (2009). *Effective instructional strategies* (2nd ed.). Thousand Oaks, CA: Sage.

Moran, S., Kornhaber, M., & Gardner, H. (2006). Orchestrating multiple intelligences. *Educational Leadership, 64*(1), 22–27.

Ogle, D. M. (1986). K-W-L: A teaching model that develops active reading of expository text. *The Reading Teacher, 39,* 564–570.

Oliva, P. F. (2013). *Developing the curriculum* (8th ed.). Boston: Pearson.

O'Neil, J. (1993). The promise of portfolios. *Update, 35*(7), 1–5.

Ornstein, A. C., & Lasley, T. J. (2004). *Strategies for effective teaching* (4th ed.). Boson: McGraw-Hill.

Panadero, E., & Romero, M. (2014). To rubric or not to rubric? The effects of self-assessment on self regulation, performance and self-efficacy. *Assessment in Education: Principles, Policy and Practics, 21*(2), 133–148.

Pappas, C. C., Kiefer, B. Z., & Levstik, L. S. (2006). *An integrated language perspective in the elementary school* (4th ed.). Boston: Pearson.

Parker, W. C. (2012). *Social studies in elementary education* (14th ed.). Boston: Pearson.

Pastor, E., & Kerns, E. (1997). A digital snapshot of an early childhood classroom. *Educational Leadership, 55*(3), 42–45.

Phillips, J. L. (1981). *Piaget's theory: A primer.* San Francisco: Freeman.

Piaget, J. (1955). *The language and thought of the child.* New York: Meridian.

Piaget, J. (1966). *Judgment and reasoning in the child.* Totowa, NJ: Littlefield, Adams.

Piaget, J. (1970). *Science of education and the psychology of the child.* (D. Coltman, Trans.). New York: Orion.

Piaget, J. (1973). *To understand is to invent.* New York: Grossman.

Piaget, J. (1974). *Understanding causality.* New York: Norton.

Piaget, J. (1976). *The grasp of consciousness.* Cambridge, MA: Harvard University Press.

Piaget, J., & Inhelder, B. (1969). *The psychology of the child.* New York: Basic Books.

Popham, W. J. (2006). Assessment for learning: An endangered species? *Educational Leadership, 63*(5), 82–83.

Porcaro, J. J., & Johnson, K. G. (2003, Winter). Building a whole-language writing program. *Kappa Delta Pi Record, 39*(2), 74–79.

Post, T. R., Ellis, A. K., Humphreys, A. H., & Buggey, L. J. (1997). *Interdisciplinary approaches to curriculum: Themes for teaching.* Boston: Pearson.

Ravitch, D. (1987, Summer). Tot sociology: Or what happened to history in the grade schools. *American Scholar, 56*(3), 343–354.

Ray, J. A. (2005). Family friendly teachers: Tips for working with diverse families. *Kappa Delta Pi Record, 41*(2), 72–76.

Recesso, A., & Orrill, C. (2008). *Integrating technology into teaching: The technology and learning continuum.* Boston: Houghton Mifflin.

Reese, R. (2014, June). Lesson closure: Stick the landing. *Educational Update, 56*(6), 5.

Reiser, R. A., & Dick, W. (1996). *Instructional planning: A guide for teachers* (2nd ed.). Boston: Pearson.

Renner, M. (2007, Spring). NCLB–A Triage Experience. *Long Island Education Review, 7*(1), 9–14.

Richardson, E. S. (1969). *In the early world: Discovering art through crafts.* New York: Pantheon Books.

Roberts, P. L., & Kellough, R. D. (2008). *A guide for developing interdisciplinary thematic units* (4th ed.). Boston: Pearson.

Ruso, B. (2013, August). *Best practices to invite parent involvement* [Web log post]. Retrieved from http://vingapp.com/best-practices-to-invite-parent-involvement

Ryan, K., Cooper, J. M., & Tauer, S. (2008). *Teaching for student learning: Becoming a teacher.* Boston: Houghton Mifflin.

Santrock, J. W. (2012). *Children* (12th ed.). Boston: McGraw-Hill.

Schrock, K. (2015a). Critical evaluation survey: Elementary school level; middle school level. Retrieved from the *Kathy Schrock's guide to everything* website, http://www.schrockguide.net/critical-evaluation.html

Schrock, K. (2015b). Teacher helpers: Assessment & rubric information. Retrieved from the *Kathy Schrock's guide to everything* website, http://www.schrockguide.net/apps/search?q=Teacher+Helpers:+assessment+&+rubric+information

Shepard, L. A. (2005). Linking formative assessment to scaffolding. *Educational Leadership, 63*(3), 66–70.

Shores, E. F., & Grace, C. (2005). *The portfolio book: A step-by-step guide for teachers.* Boston: Pearson.

Slatin, C., Galizzi, M., Devereaux Melillo, K., & Mawn, B. (2004, January-February). Conducting interdisciplinary research to promote healthy and safe employment in health care: Promises and pitfalls. *Public Health Reports, 119*(1), 60–72.

Smith, M. K. (2002). Howard Gardner, multiple intelligences and education. Retrieved from the *infed.org* website, http://infed.org/mobi/howard-gardner-multiple-intelligences-and-education/

Stauffer, R. G. (1969). *Teaching reading as a thinking process.* New York: Harper & Row.

Stephens, L. S. (1974). *The teacher's guide to open education.* New York: Holt, Rinehart & Winston.

Sternberg, R. J. (1985). *Beyond IQ: A triarchic theory of human intelligence.* New York: Cambridge University Press.

Sternberg, R. J. (1997). *Thinking styles.* New York: Cambridge University Press.

Sternberg, R. J. (1999). Ability and expertise. *American Educator, 23*(1), 10–13ff.

Sternberg, R. J. (2006). Recognizing neglected strengths. *Educational Leadership, 64*(1), 30–35.

Stevenson, C., & Carr, J. F. (Eds.). (1993). *Integrated studies in the middle grades.* New York: Teachers College Press.

Sylwester, R. (1995). *A celebration of neurons: An educator's guide to the human brain.* Alexandria, VA: ASCD.

Tomlinson, C. (2001). *How to differentiate instruction in mixed-ability classrooms* (2nd ed.). Alexandria, VA: ASCD.

Tomlinson, C., & Moon, T. (2013). *Assessment and student success in a differentiated classroom.* Alexandria, VA: ASCD.

Tovani, C. (2005, October). The power of purposeful reading. *Educational Leadership, 63*(2), 48–51.

Udell, C. (2013). *Using cameras as powerful mobile learning tools.* Retrieved from the Float Mobile Learning website: http://floatlearning.com/2013/06/using-cameras-aspowerful-mobile-learning-tools/

U.S. Department of Education. (n.d.) Race to the Top Fund. Retrieved from http://www2.ed.gov/programs/racetothetop/index.html

Vacca, R. T., & Vacca, J. L. (2014). *Content area reading: Literacy and learning across the curriculum* (11th ed.). Boston: Pearson.

Viadero, D. (1995, November 8). Expert testimony. *Education Week, 15*(10), 33–34.

Vygotsky, L. S. (1978). *Mind in society: The development of higher psychological processes.* Cambridge, MA: Harvard University Press.

Vygotsky, L. S. (1986). *Thought and language* (new rev. ed.). Cambridge, MA: MIT Press.

Wakefield, A. P. (1993). Developmentally appropriate practice: "Figuring things out." *The Educational Forum, 57*(2), 134–143.

Wallace, M. L. (1996). *America's deserts: Guide to plants and animals.* Golden, CO: Fulcrum Kids.

Wertsch, J. V. (1985). *Vygotsky and the social formation of the mind.* Cambridge, MA: Harvard University Press.

Westwater, A., & Wolfe, P. (2000, November). The brain-compatible curriculum. *Educational Leadership, 58*(3), 49–53.

Wexler-Sherman, C., Gardner, H., & Feldman, D. H. (1988). A pluralistic view of early assessment: The project spectrum approach. *Theory Into Practice, 27*(1), 77–83.

Wiggins, G. (1993). *Assessing student performance.* San Francisco: Jossey-Bass.

Wiggins, G., & McTighe, J. (2012). *Understanding by design* (2nd ed.). Alexandria, VA: ASCD.

Wilcox, J. (2006, February). Less teaching, more assessing. *Education Update, 48,*(2), 1ff.

Wiliam, D. (2014, March). The right questions, the right way. *Educational Leadership, 71*(5), 16–19.

Wiles, J., & Bondi, J. (2015). *Curriculum development: A guide to practice* (9th ed.). Boston: Pearson.

Williams-Boyd, P. (2003). *Middle grades education: A reference handbook.* Santa Barbara, CA: ABC-CLIO.

Willingham, D. T. (2006, Fall). "Brain-based" learning: More fiction and fact. *American Educator, 30*(3), 27–32ff.

Bibliography

Following are additional recommended classic and contemporary readings on selected topics related to the various discussions in this book.

Assessment Techniques

Darling-Hammond, L., Ancess, J., & Falk, B. (1995). *Authentic assessment in action: Studies of schools and students at work.* New York: Teachers College Press.

Eby, J. W., Herrell, A., & Jordan, M. (2006). *Reflective planning, teaching, and evaluation: K–12* (4th ed.). Boston: Pearson.

Engel, B. S. (1994). Portfolio assessment and the new paradigm: New instruments and new places. *The Educational Forum, 59*(1), 22–27.

Moore, K. D. (2015). *Effective instructional strategies: From theory to practice* (4th ed.). Los Angeles: Sage.

Penta, M. Q. (2002). Student portfolios in a standardized world. *Kappa Delta Pi Record, 38*(2), 77–81.

Popham, W. J. (2008). A misunderstood grail. *Educational Leadership, 66*(1), 82–83.

Popham, W. J. (2009). A process—not a test. *Educational Leadership, 66*(7), 85–86.

Popham, W. J. (2012). *Classroom assessment: What teachers need to know* (7th ed.). Boston: Pearson.

Scriffiny, P. L. (2008). Seven reasons for standards-based grading. *Educational Leadership, 66*(2), 70–74.

Vyzyak, L. (1996). *Student portfolios: a practical guide to evaluation.* Bothell, WA: Wright Group.

Wasserstein, P. (1994, Fall). To do or not to do portfolios: That is the question. *Kappa Delta Pi Record, 31*(1), 12–15.

Change in Education

Ashton-Warner, S. (1963). *Teacher.* New York: Simon & Schuster.

Epstein, J., Sanders, M. G., Simon, B. S., Salinas, K. C., & Van Voorhis, F. L. (2009). *School, family, and community partnerships: Your handbook for action* (3rd ed.). Thousand Oaks, CA: Sage.

Hentoff, N. (1966). *Our children are dying.* New York: Pitman.

Holt, J. (1964). *How children fail.* New York: Delta.

Holt, J. (1967). *How children learn.* New York: Pitman.

Holt, J. (1969). *The underachieving school.* New York: Pitman.

Holt, J. (1989). *Learning all the time.* Reading, MA: Addison-Wesley.

Kohl, H. (1988). *36 children.* New York: New American Library.

Kozol, J. (1990). *The night is dark and I am far from home* (new rev ed.). Boston: Houghton Mifflin.

Pines, M. (1967). *Revolution in learning: The years from birth to six.* New York: Harper & Row.

Postman, N., & Weingartner, C. (1969). *Teaching as a subversive activity.* New York: Delacorte Press.

Reeves, D. B. (2006)). Of hubs, bridges, and networks. *Educational Leadership 63*(8), 32–38.

Richardson, E. S. (1969). *In the early world: Discovering art through crafts.* New York: Pantheon Books.

Silberman, C. E. (1970). *Crisis in the classroom: The remaking of American education.* New York: Random House.

Classroom Management

Arends, R. I. (2015). *Learning to teach* (10th ed.). Boston: McGraw-Hill.

Chance, P. (2008). *The teacher's craft: The 10 essential skills of effective teaching.* Long Grove, IL: Waveland Press.

Charles, C. M. (2014). *Building classroom discipline* (11th ed.). Boston: Pearson.

Charles, C. M., & Senter, G. W. (2012). *Elementary classroom management* (6th ed.). Boston: Pearson.

Edwards, C. H. (2008). *Classroom discipline and management* (5th ed.). Hoboken, NJ: Wiley.

Holt, L. C., & Kysilka, M. (2006). *Instructional patterns: Strategies for maximizing student learning.* Thousand Oaks, CA: Sage.

Moore, K. D. (2015). *Effective instructional strategies: From theory to practice* (4th ed.). Thousand Oaks, CA: Sage.

Ormrod, J. E. (2015). *Essentials of educational psychology* (5th ed.). Boston: Pearson.

Traynor, P. L., & Traynor, E. (2005). *Got discipline? Research-based practices for managing student behavior.* Irvine, CA: EduThinkTank Research Group.

Common Core Standards, Goals, and Instructional Objectives

Arends, R. I. (2015). *Learning to teach* (10th ed.). Boston: McGraw-Hill.

Behavioral verbs for writing objectives in the cognitive, affective and psychomotor domain. Retrieved from http://www.isst-d.org/2007conference/Wordingforobjectives.pdf

Dick, W., Carey, L., & Carey, J. O. (2014). *The systematic design of instruction* (6th ed.). Boston: Pearson.

Gronlund, N. E. (2009). *Gronlund's writing instructional objectives* (8th ed.). Boston: Pearson.

Holt, L. C., & Kysilka, M. (2006). *Instructional patterns: Strategies for maximizing student learning.* Thousand Oaks, CA: Sage.

Mager, R. (1997). *Preparing instructional objectives: A critical tool in the development of effective instruction* (3rd ed.). Atlanta, GA: Center for Effective Performance.

Marchesani, R. J. (2007). *The field guide to teaching: A handbook for new teachers.* Boston: Pearson.

Marzano, R. J., Yanoski, Hoegh, J., Simms, J., Heflebower, T., & Warrick, P. (2013). *Using common core standards to enhance classroom instruction and assessment.* Alexandria, VA: ASCD.

Ormrod, J. E. (2015). *Essentials of educational psychology* (5th ed.). Boston: Pearson.

Palmer, E. (2014). *Teaching the core skills of listening and speaking.* Alexandria, VA: ASCD.

Silver, H., Dewing, R., & Perini, M. J. (2012). *The core six: Essential strategies for achieving excellence with the common core.* Alexandria, VA: ASCD.

Twachtman-Cullen, D. (2011). *The IEP from A to Z: How to create meaningful and measurable objectives* (2nd ed.). San Francisco: Jossey-Bass.

Educational Technology

Allen, S. M., Dutt-Donner, K. M., Eini, R. F., Chuang, H-H., & Thompson, A. (2005/2006, January). Four takes on technology. *Educational Leadership 63*(4), 66–71.

Cennamo, K., & Ross, J. (2013). *Technology integration for meaningful classroom use: A standards-based approach*. Belmont, CA: Wadsworth/Cengage.

Davis, A. P., & McGrail, E. (2009, March). The joy of blogging. *Educational Leadership 66*(6), 74–77.

Lever-Duffy, J. & McDonald, J. B. (2015). *Teaching and learning with technology* (5th ed.). Boston: Pearson.

Newby, T. J., Stepich, D. A., Lehman, J. D., & Russell, J. D. (2006). *Instructional technology for teaching and learning: Designing instruction, integrating computers, and using media* (3rd ed.). Boston: Pearson.

Smaldino, S. E., Lowther, D. L., Russell, J. D., & Mims, C. (2015). *Instructional technology and media for learning* (11th ed.). Boston: Pearson.

Whitehead, B. M., & Jensen, D. (2013). *Planning for technology: A guide for school administrators, technology coordinators, and curriculum leaders*. Thousand Oaks, CA: Corwin.

Five-Step Lesson Plan

The Madeline Hunter model of mastery learning. (n.d.). Retrieved from http://www.csun.edu/sites/default/files/Holle-Lesson-Planning.pdf

Instructional Methodology

Bruner, J. (1960). *The process of education.* New York: Vintage Books.

Dean, C. B., & Hubbell, E. R. (2012). *Classroom instruction that works: Research-based strategies for increasing student achievement* (2nd ed.). Alexandria, VA: ASCD.

Dewey, J. (1933). *How we think.* Boston: Heath.

Dewey, J. (1938). *Experience and education.* London: Collier–Macmillan.

Estes, T. H., Mintz, S. L., & Gunter, M. A. (2010). *Instruction: A models approach* (6th ed.). Boston: Pearson.

Jacob, S. H. (1982a). Piaget and education: Aspects of a theory. *The Educational Forum, 46*(2), 265–282.

Jacob, S. H. (1982b). Piaget and education: Aspects of a theory. *The Educational Forum, 46*(3), 221–238.

Katz, L., & Chard, S. C. (2014). *Engaging children's minds: The project approach* (3rd ed.). Santa Barbara, CA: Praeger.

Wilen, W., Kindsvatter, R., & Ishler, M. (2008). *Dynamics of effective teaching* (6th ed.). Boston: Pearson.

Learning and Diversity

Au, W. (2014). *Rethinking multicultural education.* Milwaukee, WI: Rethinking Schools.

Banks, J. A., & McGee Banks, C. A. (2009). *Multicultural education: Issues and perspectives* (7th ed.). Hoboken, NJ: Wiley.

Battalio, R. (2005, Fall). Setting the stage for a diverse audience. *Kappa Delta Pi Record 42*(1), 24–27.

Chicago: Society for Research in Child Development, University of Chicago Press.

Flavell, J. H., Green, F. L., & Flavell, E. R. (1995). *Young children's knowledge about thinking* (Monographs of the Society for Research in Child Development). Chicago: University of Chicago Press.

Forman, G. E., & Kuschner, D. S. (1977). *The child's construction of knowledge.* Monterey, CA: Brooks/Cole.

Furth, H. G., & Wachs, H. (1974). *Thinking goes to school.* New York: Oxford University Press.

Souto-Manning, M. (2013). *Multicultural teaching in the early childhood classroom: Approaches, strategies and tools, preschool-2nd grade (early childhood education).* New York: Teachers College Press.

Wadsworth, B. J. (2004). *Piaget's theory of cognitive and affective development* (5th ed.). Boston: Pearson.

Learning Centers

Clarke, C. (2012). *Shoe box learning centers: Math: 40 instant centers with reproducible templates and activities that help kids practice important math skills—independently!* Broadway, NY: Scholastic.

Fisk, L., & Lindgren, H. (1974). *Learning centers.* Glen Ridge, NJ: Exceptional Press.

Fredericks, A., & Cheesebrough, D. (1993). *Science for all children: Elementary school methods.* New York: Harper Collins.

Gardner, H. (1985). *The mind's new science: A history of the cognitive revolution.* New York: Basic Books.

Gardner, H., Feldman, D. H., & Krechevsky, M. (Eds.). (1998). *Project Zero frameworks for early childhood education: Vol. 1. Building on children's strengths: The experience of Project Spectrum.* New York: Teachers College Press.

Isbell, R. (2008). *Complete learning center book.* Lewisville, NC: Gryphon House.

Poppe, C. A., & Van Matre, N. A. (1985). *Science learning centers for primary grades.* West Nyack, NY: Center for Applied Research in Education. Gardner, H. (1982). *Art, mind, and brain: A cognitive approach to creativity.* New York: Basic Books.

Rhodes, I. (2012). *Shoe box learning centers: Science: 30 Instant centers with reproducible templates and activities that help kids learn important science skills and concepts—independently!* Broadway, NY: Scholastic.

Learning Styles

Dunn, R. S. (1994). *Teaching young children through their individual learning styles: Practical approaches for grades K–2.* Boston: Pearson.

Dunn, R., & Dunn, K. (1992). *Teaching elementary students through their individual learning styles: Practical approaches for grades 3–6.* Boston: Pearson.

Dunn, R. S., & Dunn, K. (1993). *Teaching secondary students through their individual learning styles: Practical approaches for grades 7–12.* Boston: Pearson.

Piaget, J. (1963). *Judgment and reasoning in the child.* Totowa, NJ: Littlefield, Adams.

Silver, H. F., Strong, R. W., & Perini, M. J. (2000). *So each may learn: Integrating learning styles and multiple intelligences.* Alexandria, VA: ASCD.

Sprenger, M. B. (2008). *Differentiation through learning styles and memory.* Thousand Oaks, CA: Corwin.

Questioning Strategies

Ormrod, J. E. (2015). *Essentials of educational psychology* (5th ed.). Boston: Pearson.

Rubrics

Cooper, J. D., & Kiger, N. D. (2011). *Literacy assessment: Helping teachers plan instruction* (4th ed.). Belmont, CA: Wadsworth.

Freiberg, H. J., & Driscoll, A. (2005). *Universal teaching strategies* (3rd ed.). Boston: Pearson.

Ormrod, J. E. (2015). *Essentials of educational psychology* (5th ed.). Boston: Pearson.

Recesso, A., & Orrill, C. (2008). *Integrating technology into teaching.* Boston: Houghton Mifflin.

Roberts, P. L., & Kellough, R. D. (2008). *A guide for developing interdisciplinary thematic units* (4th ed.). Boston: Pearson.

Test Construction

Arends, R. I. (2015). *Learning to teach* (10th ed.). Boston: McGraw-Hill.

Cooper, J. M. (2011). *Classroom teaching skills* (9th ed.). Belmont, CA: Brookes/Cole.

Dick, W, Carey, L., & Carey, J. O. (2014). *The systematic design of instruction* (6th ed.). Boston: Pearson.

Hoy, A. W. (2008). *Educational psychology* (10th ed.). Boston: Pearson.

Marchesani, R. J. (2007). *The field guide to teaching: A handbook for new teachers.* Boston: Pearson.

Unit Planning

Armstrong, T. (2009). *Multiple intelligences in the classroom* (3rd ed.). Alexandria, VA: ASCD.

Ellis, A. K. (2010). *Teaching and learning elementary social studies* (9th ed.). Boston: Pearson.

Katz, L., & Chard, S. C. (2014). *Engaging children's minds: The project approach* (3rd ed.). Santa Barbara, CA: Praeger.

Kindsvatter, R., Wilen, W., & Ishler, M. (2008). *Dynamics of effective teaching* (6th ed.). Boston: Pearson.

Post, T. R., Ellis, A. K., Humphreys, A. H., & Buggey, L. J. (1997). *Interdisciplinary approaches to curriculum: Themes for teaching.* Boston: Pearson.

Roberts, P. L., & Kellough, R. D. (2008). *A guide for developing interdisciplinary thematic unit* (4th ed.). Boston: Pearson.

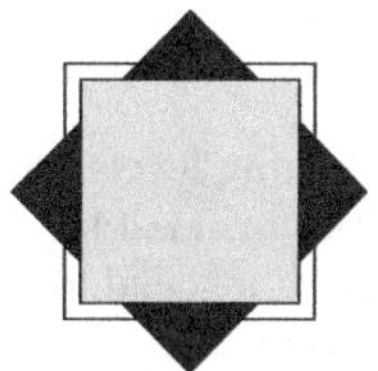

Index